Contemporary Business Law

Margaret E. Vroman

TABLE OF CONTENTS

Chapter 1: Introduction to Law

Introduction to Business Law

As a citizen or business of the United States, it is impossible to avoid contact with our legal system. If you purchase goods or property, you enter into a contract; if you practice a profession or operate a business, there are regulations that must be followed. Every person in the United States of America comes into contact with the legal system in one way or another. As such, a working knowledge of our legal system is essential because it is the mechanism that helps us resolve conflicts, punishes individuals and organizations that violate rules, and protects the public interest. This text provides information on the fundamentals of the U.S. legal system, the basics of its legal process, and an overview of numerous substantive areas of law. Real-life cases are included to demonstrate how this system works, and hypothetical questions are included to challenge students' critical thinking skills and assess their overall comprehension of the subjects covered.

Where Does U.S. Law Come From?

Because America was originally a colony of Great Britain, its legal system is based on the same legal principles used by that country. That means the American legal system is based on Common Law, which is different from the civil law legal system used by most countries of the world.

Common Law

Unlike most of Europe, which was conquered by the Romans and governed by its core legal principles, Great Britain differed from its European neighbors by developing and using what has come to be called the *common law legal system.*

The common law legal system is characterized by case law, which is developed by judges who create specific legal rules from the cases that come before them. They take the rules from one case and apply those rules to other cases with similar facts. The rules may "evolve" as the facts presented to the court in different cases change. This precedent-based process is different from the *civil* law system, which starts with basic legal principles that are codified (made into laws), after which judges apply these laws to individual cases.

Although the United States uses the common law legal system, it also has codes (statutes or laws) that the courts apply. When a case is presented, the court will determine if there is a statute that applies to the facts of the case. If no statute applies, then the court searches for a similar case to see if a rule from that case can be applied. In the common law system, judges have the authority and duty to make legal rules by interpreting the law of earlier cases (precedent) or by creating new and precedent-setting rulings.

Precedent is the common law system's use of rulings rendered in previous legal cases. The body of precedent (legal rules established by previous decisions) is called *common law*. When parties disagree on what the law is, a court will look at past decisions and the precedents they have established and apply them to the facts of the current case. If there is no rule governing a particular situation, a judge may take an existing rule of law and its rationale and use it to create a new rule, which then becomes precedent for the cases that come after it. Under the common law system, if a similar dispute has been resolved in the past, the court is required to follow the reasoning and rule used in that earlier case. This principle is known as *stare decisis*, which is Latin for "let the decision stand."

If, however, the court finds that the current dispute is fundamentally different from all previous cases, it will decide the case as a "matter of first impression." This means the legal issue or question is the first time the court has been presented with it. Once the court makes a ruling on this issue, its decision becomes the rule, or precedent, and all future courts must follow it under the principle of *stare decisis*.

Common law systems are more complicated than civil law systems. The decision of a court interpreting a legal precedent is binding only in its particular jurisdiction, and even within a given jurisdiction some courts have more power than others. A court's jurisdiction is the geographical area over which it has authority. It is also the subject matter over which the court has authority.

Interactions among common law, constitutional law, statutory law, and regulatory law also make understanding the U.S. legal system difficult. However, *stare decisis*, the principle that similar cases should be decided according to similar rules, lies at the heart of all U.S. court decisions.

Sources of Law

There are many different sources of law in the U.S. legal system. Basically, they are (1) the U.S. Constitution, (2) legislation (laws, ordinances, and regulations), (3) precedent [common law], and (4) international law.

The Constitution

Although the U.S. legal system is based on common law, unlike Great Britain it also has a Constitution. The U.S. Constitution is a document adopted by the country's founders and designated as the supreme law of the land. It establishes the principles of government upon which the United States is based. Individual states may also have constitutions, but the U.S. Constitution is superior to all state constitutions and state and federal laws. The Constitution defines three separate branches of government: executive (president), legislative (congress), and judicial (courts). It also divides the country's governing powers between the federal government and the states. It details specific powers that only the federal government has. For example, it states that only the federal government has the right to establish a military. Because of this, there can be no state militias (today referred to as armies).

Legislative

Statutes and ordinances are legislation (laws) passed at the federal, state, and local levels. As long as a state law is not preempted, or contradicted by a federal law, a state is free to pass its own laws in that same area. Regulations are rules passed by administrative agencies that have the effect of laws in the area under which the administrative agency has authority.

Precedent (Common Law)

Common law is based on precedent, in which the facts of the case before the court are compared to those of previous cases having similar facts. The rule of law applied in the earlier case is applied to the current case and perhaps modified a bit to deal with the new situation.

Common law can evolve as technologies and society change, but it also offers a predictable and stable form of law around which commerce can thrive. The criticism of common law is that it may result in judge-made law when judges fail to honor the principle of *stare decisis*. When this happens, it may lead to unpredictable and unfair applications of law.

International Law

International law is the law dealing with the various laws, rules, and customs among the different nations of the world, including their governments, businesses, and organizations.

This includes international treaties, accords, charters, protocols, precedents of the International Court of Justice, and more. There is no international governing authority or enforcement entity, so international law is really a voluntary effort wherein the power of enforcement exists solely because of the parties' commitment to honor their agreement.

Priorities in Law

The U.S. system of government is unique because it has both a federal and state system of laws. In addition to laws passed by the federal government, which everyone in the country must follow, our Constitution recognizes the right of states and local governments to make their own laws. Because of this, U.S. citizens are subject to the laws and rules of several different entities at the federal, state, and local levels.

Naturally, there is a priority in the application of these laws, and if there is a conflict between them, the law issued by the higher governing body is controlling and will be applied. If there is a conflict between the laws, the court will rule that the lesser, conflicting law is invalid. The priority of laws is as follows:

1. The U.S. Constitution

2. Federal statutes

3. State constitutions

4. State laws

5. Local laws (ordinances)

6. Common law (not codified)

7. Administrative (regulatory) law

The Constitution

Because the U.S. Constitution is the "supreme law" of the land, no state may make a law that conflicts with it or with any federal law. Under the Tenth Amendment to the Constitution, any power that is not specifically given to the federal government is reserved to the states. Similarly, powers that are not specifically reserved by states in their constitutions may be exercised by local governments.

When the Constitution or a federal statute gives the federal government sole control over an area, it "preempts" (prevents) the states from passing any law in that area. For example, because the Congress has passed a law giving the federal government control over immigration issues, no state may pass a law that attempts to regulate immigration.

The Constitution also grants Congress the right to make laws that it deems "necessary and proper" to carry out the powers granted to it by the Constitution. This implied power is the rationale used to give Congress the authority to pass many laws.

Federal Laws and Regulations

When a bill is passed by the United States Congress, it becomes a federal law and part of the U.S. Code. The U.S. Code (USC) contains public laws that are applicable to all U.S. citizens in all states. Federal regulations, which must be followed like laws, are adopted by agencies under the Administrative Procedures Act. They are codified in the Code of Federal Regulations (CFR), which is also an important source of federal law. Each agency has its own set of regulations.

State Constitutions

Every state in the United States of America has adopted its own constitution. Just like the federal Constitution, each state constitution provides for the legal and political organization of its governmental entity. However, while the U.S. Constitution prescribes the limits of federal power, state constitutions describe the structure and process of its governmental powers not otherwise delegated to the federal government. Many state constitutions also address specific issues that the state's legislature determined were of sufficient importance to be included in the constitution rather than in a statute. As long as a provision in a state constitution does not contradict the U.S. Constitution, it is enforceable.

State Laws

A state is free to pass any law that does not conflict with the U.S. Constitution or a federal law. A state may also regulate any area that the Constitution or federal law leaves them free to regulate. Sometimes a federal law may regulate part of a subject area without preempting the entire field. If this happens, a state may pass some laws on a subject but not those prohibited by the federal law. In some instances, a federal statute may explicitly state that it is preempting an entire area of law and preventing states from enacting their own, but often it does not. In such instances, it is the courts that must decide whether the area has been preempted or if a state has the authority to pass laws on the subject.

If the court determines a state law is in conflict with a federal law, it will rule that the federal law preempts that of the state. However, if an area is not preempted, there may be both a federal and a state law on the same subject. The federal law will apply when federal courts have jurisdiction over the parties, and the state law will apply when the state has jurisdiction. If preemption is not an issue, a state may pass a law that is more restrictive than a federal law, but it cannot pass a valid law that is broader than a federal law. For example, if a federal law states that no skyscraper may be more than sixty stories tall, no state may enact a valid law that would allow skyscrapers to be seventy stories tall. However, a state may pass a law that says no skyscrapers may be built within its boundaries that are more than fifty stories tall. If, however, the entire subject of skyscraper construction were preempted by federal statute, a state could not legally pass any law concerning the construction of skyscrapers.

Just as the U.S. Constitution specifies certain areas where the federal government preempts state government authority, a state constitution may specify areas where its authority preempts that of local governments.

The U.S. Constitution also leaves the states in charge of certain things. It does this by saying that any authority not given to the federal government may be exercised by the states. Because it doesn't specify what these areas are, the courts are left to interpret what the Constitution's drafters intended. Thus, since each state has its own separate government with its own constitution, each state has the power to make laws covering anything that is not preempted by the U.S. Constitution or federal statutes. Many states have legal codes, just as the federal government has. Codifying laws passed by the legislature was adopted from the civil law system. Thus, our legal system uses both the common law principle of precedent and the civil law method of codifying statutes or laws.

Louisiana is the only state that does not base its legal system on common law. This is because Louisiana was originally settled by the French, who followed the French civil code system of law.

Local Laws (Ordinances)

An ordinance is a law made by a city, county, or other local government. Just as the federal government has left certain law-making authority to the states, the states have left certain law-making authority to local governments. This authority usually entails the power to pass laws governing property and conduct within the local government's geographical boundaries. These laws, called *ordinances*, are valid if they don't conflict with state or federal laws or constitutions. Much of what local government ordinances regulate is the use of land (zoning) and permits for such things as building construction or outdoor activities. These ordinances are subject to judicial interpretation, just like their federal and state counterparts.

Classification of Civil Law and Criminal Law

There are two types of laws that legislatures pass: civil laws and criminal laws.

Civil Law

Civil law regulates the rights and duties of, and between, individuals, groups, and organizations. It encompasses both the substance of laws as well as the process of judicial proceedings involving lawsuits between private parties.

Criminal Law

Criminal law regulates and punishes individuals for conduct that is offensive to society as a whole. It refers to a set of rules and regulations describing behaviors prohibited by the government. It involves the prosecution by the state of wrongful acts considered to be so serious that they are a breach of the government's peace and that cannot be deterred or remedied by lawsuits between private parties. The result of a criminal conviction is often incarceration in jail or prison. Incarceration is not a remedy available in civil cases. Its purpose is not to seek justice or compensation for the individual who has been wronged but to protect all citizens and prevent the wrongdoer from committing any future harmful acts.

Most crimes committed in the United States are prosecuted and punished at the state level. Federal criminal law focuses on areas unique to the federal government, such as failure to pay federal income tax or interstate crimes like drug trafficking and wire fraud.

All states have somewhat similar laws regarding the most serious crimes, although penalties for these crimes may vary from state to state. Both the state and federal government distinguish between two levels of crimes: felonies and misdemeanors. Felonies are the most serious criminal offenses—murder, rape, or robbery. Felony convictions result in longer prison sentences as well as probation, fines, and orders to pay restitution to victims. Misdemeanors are less serious criminal offenses—simple assault, drunk driving, or disturbing the peace—and typically result in less than a year in jail and/or a fine.

Depending on the conduct at issue, it is possible for a person to be charged both civilly and criminally because of a single action. For example, if a person commits an assault and battery against another person, the person may be sued civilly *and* prosecuted criminally. The civil case compensates the injured person (victim) for such things as medical bills, pain and suffering, and lost wages, while the criminal case punishes the perpetrator for conduct that negatively impacts society or the state. The civil case compensates the injured party, and the criminal case deters similar conduct and punishes the perpetrator.

Burden of Proof

More evidence is needed to find the accused at fault in a criminal case than to find the defendant at fault in a civil case. To find someone guilty of a crime (defendants in a civil case are found "liable" rather than "guilty"), the prosecution must demonstrate proof beyond a reasonable doubt that the person committed the crime. Judges and juries cannot convict someone they believe *probably* committed the crime—they must be almost certain. This gives the accused the benefit of any reasonable doubt and makes it less likely that an innocent person will be wrongfully convicted and imprisoned. In a civil case, however, a person or organization must be proven responsible by a preponderance of the evidence, meaning it is more likely than not that the defendant caused the harm or loss. This is a lesser burden of proof since the consequences are not as severe and include only economic loss, not imprisonment or possibly even death.

Cause of Action

Whenever one party sues another in court by filing a lawsuit, it must state a legal cause of action that entitles the party to proceed. It is possible that a party will have more than one cause of action, but without at least one, the judge will dismiss the case.

The *cause of action* is the facts and legal theory upon which a person (the plaintiff) seeks judicial redress or relief against another (the defendant).

It is the cause of action that is stated in the plaintiff's complaint, which is the initial pleading that starts a lawsuit. It is not sufficient merely to state that certain events occurred and that the plaintiff is entitled to compensation because of them. The plaintiff must state a legal theory that entitles the plaintiff to the relief sought and must state facts that support all the elements of the legal theory alleged.

The cause of action is often stated by use of deductive reasoning that begins with a major premise (the applicable rule of law), proceeds to a minor premise (the facts that gave rise to the claim), and ends with a conclusion. For example, in a cause of action for battery, the rule of law is that any intentional, unpermitted act that causes a harmful or offensive touching of another is a battery. This is the major premise and would be stated first. Supporting facts, constituting the minor premise, would appear after the rule of law. Typically, a statement of fact for a case of battery might be, "The plaintiff, while walking through Sam's Grocery Store on the morning of January 2, 2016, was tackled by the defendant, a security guard for the store, who knocked the plaintiff to the floor and held him there by kneeling on his back and holding his arms behind him. These actions caused the plaintiff to suffer injuries to his head, chest, shoulders, neck, and back." The cause of action would conclude with a statement that the defendant is responsible for the plaintiff's injuries and that the plaintiff is entitled to compensation from the defendant for his injuries.

The facts or circumstances of a situation might create more than one cause of action. For example, in the preceding example, the plaintiff might assert claims for assault, battery, intentional infliction of emotional distress, and a violation of civil rights. He might also bring claims for negligent hiring if the security guard had a history of violent behavior that the store failed to discover, or for negligent supervision. When damages are caused by an employee, it is common to sue both the employee and the employer. All these causes of action arise from the same set of facts and circumstances but are supported by different rules of law and constitute separate causes of action and claims for relief.

A cause of action can arise from an act, a failure to perform a legal obligation (failure to act), a breach of duty, or a violation of a legal right. The importance of the act, failure, breach, or violation lies in its legal effect and in how the facts and circumstances, considered as a whole, are governed by applicable law. A set of facts may have no legal effect in one situation, whereas the same or similar facts may have significant legal implications in another situation. For example, tackling a shoplifting suspect who is brandishing a gun is a legitimate action by a security guard and would not support a claim for battery if the suspect were injured as a result. By contrast, tackling a shopper who merely acts in a suspicious manner and whom the security guard thinks may be shoplifting is an inappropriate exercise of the guard's job duties and may well give rise to several causes of action.

Real Life Case—Preemption

California passed a law prohibiting the importation or sale within California of products made from kangaroos. In the case of *Viva! International Voice for Animals v. Adidas Promotional Retail Operations Inc*, 162 P. 3d 569 (2007), Adidas Corporation admitted it was violating this law but argued that the federal government's policies concerning the international management of kangaroo populations preempted California's power to regulate the importation or sale of kangaroos.

The California court rejected Adidas's argument and upheld the California law on the ground that no conflict existed between state and federal policies or law in this area. The court analyzed the federal Endangered Species Act (ESA) and concluded that the law was intended to protect endangered and threatened species from depletion and possible extinction. The court said because kangaroos have at times been listed as threatened species, the ESA did not prevent California from regulating the importation of non-endangered species.

However, Adidas argued that kangaroo regulation is the unique province of federal authorities and that because the U.S. government had been working with Australia to develop effective kangaroo management practices, California could not interfere with or contradict federal policies.

Adidas contended that the federal government made an explicit decision not to ban kangaroo importation into the United States as part of an agreement with Australian national and regional governments. In exchange, Australia promised to regulate excessive kangaroo destruction.

The California court rejected this argument and instead relied on the "joint cooperative state–federal approach to wildlife preservation" it found in a preemption provision contained in the ESA itself. Although a section of the ESA does purport to preempt state laws that permit what the ESA and its implementing regulations expressly prohibit, or prohibit what the ESA and its implementing regulations expressly permit, it also says the ESA "shall not otherwise be construed to void any State law or regulation. . . ." and that "any state law or regulation [concerning] endangered species or threatened species may be more restrictive than the exemptions or permits provided for in [the ESA] but not less restrictive than the prohibitions so defined." [1]

The court reasoned that this provision gives states the power to regulate threatened animals like kangaroos that are not currently listed as endangered.

Even if the California court is right that the ESA does not support preemption, the state court decision might still be reversed because of

---

[1] *Viva! International Voice for Animals v. Adidas Promotional Retail Operations Inc,*

the agreement the United States made with Australia. Because the Constitution gives the federal government (and the president) the power to negotiate with foreign countries and foreign companies, California's law could be declared unconstitutional by the U.S. Supreme Court.

Chapter 2: Court Organization

Introduction

The U.S. court system differs from that used by other countries in a number of ways. Our Constitution recognizes not only the authority of the federal government but also the individual states that make up the United States of America. Because of this dual authority, the United States has both federal and state courts. This parallel system of courts can be a bit confusing, but the Constitution establishes the federal court system as superior to that of the states, and it makes the U.S. Supreme Court the highest court in the country, at the top of the federal court system. The Supreme Court's decisions are final and cannot be appealed or overturned by any other court. Because it is the highest court in the country, its decisions are binding precedent on all courts dealing with any issue of federal law or Constitutional interpretation on which it rules.

Underneath the U.S. Supreme Court are the federal appellate courts, which hear and decide cases from the federal district (trial) courts. There are thirteen judicial circuits, each with its own court of appeals.

Beneath the appellate (circuit) courts are the federal district courts, which are the courts that hear evidence and conduct trials. They are the courts that use juries and make the initial rulings and decisions on a case. It is the decisions from district courts that may be appealed to the circuit court and possibly the U.S. Supreme Court.

Typically, a case starts in a trial court, where evidence and witnesses are presented before a judge or jury, who decides the case. If one of the parties believes the judge in a trial court decision made an error of law, that party may appeal the case to an appellate court. Appellate courts do not hear the evidence all over again but only review the claim that the trial court made a mistake in interpreting or applying the law. The appellate court rules on questions of law, not questions of fact. It does not review the evidence in a case or retry the case, but considers only legal issues. If it determines that the trial court judge made an error in interpreting or applying the law, it may reverse the decision of the trial judge or send the case back to the trial judge to reconsider based on its rulings. If it sends the case back to the trial court judge, the case is *remanded* for action consistent with the appellate court's decision. If the appellate court agrees with the trial court and does not find any errors or mistakes, it will *affirm* the lower court's decision on the case.

The state court systems deal with most of the issues affecting everyday life, such as marriage and divorce, real estate, and criminal law. Federal courts have jurisdiction over such issues as civil rights and bankruptcy. There is some overlap in such areas as environmental law and labor relations and criminal law.

The effect of a court decision depends on the level of the court that issued the decision. All courts and the citizens subject to those courts must follow the decisions rendered by the courts of the jurisdiction in which they reside. The higher the court, the more citizens will be encompassed in its jurisdiction. For example, all citizens and lower courts of a state must follow the rulings of a state's supreme court since it is (typically) the highest appellate court in the state, whereas the decision of a municipal or district court is only binding on that particular city or district since it has no authority over any other court or area.

The Federal Court System

The federal court system comprises the following:

The Supreme Court of the United States	The Supreme Court hears cases appealed from federal circuit courts and from state supreme courts that involve an issue of federal law. The court has discretion to choose which cases it will consider.
U.S. Courts of Appeals (also called Circuit Courts of Appeals)	These appellate courts decide cases appealed from federal district courts in their circuit. There are 12 circuits comprised of groups of states plus one for the District of Columbia for a total of 13 circuit courts.
U.S. District Courts	District courts are trial courts that decide cases involving violations of federal civil and criminal law, treaties, or cases between residents of different states.
Specialized Courts	Courts that hear cases dealing with specific topics and specialized areas of law. Federal bankruptcy court and the patent court are federal court examples of specialized courts.

State Court Systems

Each state establishes its own judicial system, so there are many variations, but most state systems are similar to the Michigan court system, described here:

Type of Court	Function	The Michigan Court System
Court of last resort (usually called the supreme court)	This court decides appeals from lower courts. It has discretion to choose which cases it reviews.	The Michigan Supreme Court is the court of last resort for the state of Michigan.
Intermediate appellate courts	Appellate courts hear appeals from lower (trial) court decisions.	In Michigan, the court of appeals is divided into four districts. The districts contain a total of twenty-four judges who sit on three judge panels.
Trial courts	Trial courts conduct trials at which evidence is heard in both civil and criminal cases.	Each county has a circuit court with specialized divisions by subject, which deal with criminal felony cases and civil cases over $25,000. There is at least one district court in each county that deals with traffic cases, misdemeanor criminal cases, and civil cases involving less than $25,000.
Specialized courts	Courts that hear cases dealing with specific topics and specialized areas of law.	Probate court hears trusts and estate cases as well as child neglect and commitment cases.

Chapter 3: Litigation

Introduction

When parties cannot solve a legal disagreement themselves, they may resort to filing a lawsuit in court where a judge or jury will render a decision on the matter, which the court can enforce. The process of filing a lawsuit to achieve a decision in a civil matter is referred to as *litigation.* Not all disputes are subject to resolution by the courts, however. Courts can only decide cases involving disputes that involve a legal violation, not a dispute where the conduct alleged is merely a moral violation.

Moral disputes involve behavior that may be a violation of religious rules for behavior or a violation of societal norms. Moral and religious rules are used when deciding whether conduct is good or bad, and some moral rules have been codified by governments into laws that are legally enforceable. However, there are other moral rules that people may believe should be legally enforceable but actually are not. For example, Sam tells Sally he has cancer and can't afford his medical treatment. She gives him $100 to help pay for his medical bills. If Sam was lying and Sally finds out he doesn't have cancer or any medical bills, does Sally have a right to take back the $100 she gave him? Most courts would say no. Although Sam's conduct is "wrong," the law does not recognize a legal cause of action on the part of Sally to get back the money she gave him based on his lie. Although lying in this instance may be a violation of a *moral* rule, most states do not recognize a legal violation in this instance, so they will not have what the court recognizes as a valid legal basis for it to hear the case in this and take action in this instance—or many other instances wherein someone has merely told a lie. The law requires that several other circumstances be present in addition to the lie before it can be the basis of litigation and a court ordered remedy.

Laws, which often embody moral rules, are enacted by legislative bodies and are intended to govern the behavior of individuals, businesses, and the government, but they do not regulate every aspect of behavior, nor are they intended to. If a party attempts to have a court decide a case that does not involve a legally recognized right or cause of action, the case will be dismissed—even if it involves the violation of a moral rule.

However, when one party seeks to have a court determine whether another has violated a legal duty owed it, it may exercise its constitutionally guaranteed right to trial by using the litigation process.

Deciding to Go to Trial

Not all instances in which the violation of a legal duty is alleged result in litigation. Before filing a complaint and initiating a lawsuit, a party should examine the amount of money at issue and balance it against the cost of litigation and the probability of success. If the financial benefit that may be received from going to trial is higher than the cost of going to trial, it may make sense to go to trial. However, it is not uncommon for attorney fees, court costs, and expert witness fees to cost more than the amount likely to be awarded by a judge or jury even if the party is successful in court. If that is the situation, it may make more sense to negotiate a settlement, recognizing that neither party is likely to achieve all that they want through the costly litigation process.

For example, if the parties disagree over the amount of compensation one of them is due because of the failure of one party to deliver goods as required under their contract, and the difference in their valuations is substantial, then it might make sense to let a judge decide the dollar amount of damage caused by the contract breach. But if the amount of damages alleged is $10,000, and it will likely cost $20,000 to go through the trial process, the party claiming the $10,000 in damages will end up spending more than what it will gain even if it wins in court.

Therefore, before deciding to go to trial, a party should look at the facts of the case objectively. They should be realistic about how the facts will appear to a neutral observer. Too often, emotion and ego cause a party to engage in fruitless litigation. Setting aside emotions and assessing the following will result in a much more rational decision.

Factors to Consider before Deciding to Litigate

1. What are the financial costs of litigation?

- What are the legal fees and costs?

- What are the costs associated with public relations issues?

- What are the costs resulting from disclosing pending litigation?

- What are the costs of alternatives to litigation?

- What are the costs of not litigating?

2. What public relations issues are involved in the litigation?

- What aspects of the litigation might interest the media?

- What aspects of the litigation might produce strong emotions (either positive or negative) in a jury?

- How might litigation affect company shareholders, competitors, and customers?

3. What legal precedents are relevant to this litigation?

- Are there any legal precedents directly on point that make success in litigation extremely unlikely or extremely likely?

- Are there precedents that might be available, though they do not directly apply to this litigation?

4. What factors affect the possibility of settlement?

- Who is the opposing attorney or law firm?

- How complex are the legal issues?

- Are there other legal proceedings involving the same issue?

- What are the weaknesses of our opponent?

- What are the weaknesses of our position?

5. Are there business policies that are relevant to this litigation?

- If so, will they support our claim or be used against us?

6. What are the chances of getting help from other businesses in this litigation?

Managing Costs

If a business decides that litigation is in its best interest, it must then take steps to manage its litigation costs. To do this, it should consider the following:

1. What will the attorney costs be?

- What is the hourly rate for the lawyer or lawyers involved?

- How much assistance will the lawyer(s) need, and what are the hourly rates for those who will be assisting them?

- What types of expert witnesses will be needed, and how much will it cost to have those experts prepare and testify?

- What types of costs and fees will be involved (e.g., court fees, depositions, trial transcripts, and other discovery costs)?

2. How much money is likely to be recovered if the litigation is successful?

- How much money is at issue in this dispute?

- What is the financial condition of the potential defendant?

- Where is the defendant located—in our state or in another state? (If the defendant is in a different state, costs of litigation and collecting the judgment are likely to be much higher.)

3. What reputation does our company wish to maintain?

- What publicity is this action likely to cause?

- What is the public's perception of the issues likely to be?

4. How will the litigation affect relationships with government agencies and regulators?

- Would settling the case be in the business's best interest in this instance?

- What is our ongoing relationship with this regulator?

- What relationship do we wish to have with the government? How will this action affect that relationship?

- Does this action involve a new regulation? Is the agency likely to use our business's case as a test case?

- Are other businesses involved or likely to be involved in this action? If so, might they help us in the suit?

- What is the nature of the regulatory environment involved in this action? How is the current environment likely to affect our case?

The Trial Process

The Adversary System

Under common law, the trial process is based on an adversarial system in which lawyers act as advocates for the parties they represent before an impartial judge or jury, who attempt to determine the truth of the case. In this system, the lawyers ask questions of witnesses, demand the production of evidence, and present cases based on the evidence gathered. This differs from civil law, which relies on an inquisitor system in which judges, rather than lawyers, ask questions and demand evidence. In countries that operate under the civil law system, lawyers merely present arguments based on the evidence that the judges find.

When a case goes to trial, the judge will instruct the jury on the law and how it is to be applied, for it is the judge's role to interpret the law, legal rules, and any issues of law. Conversely, it is the jury's role to determine questions of fact, such as which witnesses are telling the truth. If there is no jury, a judge will serve in that capacity as well, determining issues of both law and fact. Judge trials are often referred to as "bench trials" because lawyers present the case to the judge while he or she is seated on the bench.

If a party decides to litigate, it can be a lengthy and costly process. Although the steps may vary between the federal and state process, and among states, the following is a typical example:

1. A complaint alleging at least one cause of action is filed against the defendant(s).

2. Defendant answers the complaint by admitting or denying the allegations made.

3. A pretrial conference establishing time frames and dates is conducted.

4. Discovery to obtain information in possession of the opposing party is conducted.

5. Depending on the jurisdiction, mandatory arbitration or mediation may be required.

6. Motions may be heard (at any time).

7. Trial is conducted, and a judgment is rendered.

HYPOTHETICAL CASE

Sam's Produce Company has a contract to supply Sally's Grocery Store with 100 bushels of fresh potatoes every week. The price Sally's is to pay for the 100 bushels of potatoes in the contract is stated as "market rate." Sally's Grocery Store advertises the fact that much of its produce, such as Sam's potatoes, is locally grown. Customers seem to prefer buying locally grown produce. However, as Sam's costs continue to rise, he tells Sally he will begin charging $1.00 a bushel more for his potatoes, starting with the next delivery. Sally tells Sam that is too much. Thinking Sally won't pay the new price for his potatoes, and getting angry, Sam contacts a newly opened grocery store and offers it his potatoes at $0.50 more than Sam's Produce Company is currently getting from Sally's Grocery Store but $0.50 less than he told Sally's his new price would be. The new store agrees to buy 100 bushels a week at that price. Sally then contacts Sam and tells him her store will pay him $0.50 a bushel more for his potatoes but not the $1.00 more he said he wants for them. Sam tells Sally that his produce company will not accept anything less than the $1.00 more per bushel he quoted her. Sally's Grocery Store refuses and then contacts a produce company in a neighboring state and ends up buying potatoes at $0.75 a bushel more than what it had been paying Sam's Produce Company.

Does Sally's Grocery Store have a cause of action against Sam's Produce Company? If so, what is it? If you are advising Sally, what, if anything, would you suggest she do in this situation—and why? What are all the issues you are taking into consideration in making your recommendation?

Chapter 4: Alternate Dispute Resolution: Arbitration and Mediation

Introduction

Two legal procedures not involving litigation are available to businesses to resolve disputes. These alternative processes expedite the resolution of disputes without the expense of litigation. They are referred to as *alternative dispute resolution,* abbreviated as ADR.

Businesses often prefer ADR to formal litigation because with ADR, proprietary information, trade secrets, and other confidential information are not subject to intense scrutiny or disclosure as they may be in litigation. In litigation, the right of access to this information by the public and news media can give competitors the opportunity to misappropriate and use the otherwise confidential information.

There are different types of ADR. Each involves a process whereby the parties involved in the dispute agree to submit their arguments and evidence to a neutral person(s) for the purpose of adjudicating their claims. The evidentiary and procedural rules of ADR are usually much less formal than they are in litigation, and there tends to be more flexibility in scheduling and the selection of the decision makers.

The most commonly used method of ADR is arbitration, in which a neutral third party is selected by the parties to hear the case and render an opinion. This opinion may or may not be binding on the parties, depending on the terms of the arbitration clause or agreement under which they are operating. In most contracts today, it is binding. In addition to arbitration, various forms of mediation, private judging, mini-trials, and moderated settlement conferences are available to companies that are unable to resolve their disputes independently but wish to avoid the expense and time involved in the trial process. These are discussed in greater detail later in the chapter.

Each type of ADR offers certain advantages and disadvantages, which may make one process more appropriate than another for resolving a particular dispute. Therefore, the procedures, costs, and benefits of each ADR method should be carefully reviewed with legal counsel.

Types of ADR

Arbitration

Arbitration may be a voluntary proceeding, such as when the parties to a contract have agreed to it as a means of dispute resolution, or it may be a compulsory, court-ordered procedure that is a prerequisite to actual litigation. Companies that wish to avoid the cost and delay of litigation should consider adding arbitration clauses to any contract.

An arbitration clause should specify that the parties agree to submit any controversy or claim arising from the agreement or contract to binding (or non-binding) arbitration. It should also include the choice of location for the arbitration; the method for selecting the arbitrators who will hear the dispute; any limitations on the award that may be rendered by the arbitrator; which party will be responsible for the costs of the proceeding; whether the loser will pay the winner's attorneys' fees; and any special procedural rules that will govern the arbitration (i.e., those used by the American Arbitration Association).

The following arbitration clause is suggested by the American Arbitration Association (AAA):

Any controversy or claim arising out of or relating to this contract, or the breach thereof, shall be settled by arbitration in accordance with the Commercial Arbitration Rules of the American Arbitration Association, and judgment rendered upon the award rendered by the arbitrator(s) may be entered in any court having jurisdiction thereof.

An important consideration for those drafting contracts is whether the decision of the arbitrator will be binding or non-binding. If the parties agree the award will be binding, then they must be prepared to live with the results.

Most often, the arbitrator selected is an attorney whose expertise may be negotiating rather than adjudicating, and therefore his or her decision often results in "splitting the baby down the middle," rather than a clear award for one party. Also, because no jury is involved, there is a much smaller chance of recovering punitive or exemplary damages, since an attorney arbiter is much less likely to be swayed by emotional appeals.

As long as there is nothing unfair or illegal in the arbitration agreement or process, binding arbitration awards will usually be enforced by the court. However, the opinion rendered in a non-binding arbitration is advisory only. In non-binding arbitration, the parties may either accept the decision or reject it and proceed to litigation. One of the major criticisms of non-binding arbitration is that after the decision is rendered, the losing party often threatens to continue with litigation unless the monetary award is increased. As a result, the party that wins the arbitration is often coerced into paying or accepting less than the award recommended simply to avoid litigation after arbitration.

Sources of Arbitration Rules

There are many sources of arbitration rules. The arbitration agreement itself is the primary source of the rules governing the arbitration process, but if the parties have not drafted specific rules and procedures that will govern the arbitration, the two most commonly used are those created by the American Arbitration Association (AAA) and the International Chamber of Commerce. Both can be obtained free of charge.

Increasing Criticism of Mandatory Arbitration

In recent years, and as a result of several Supreme Court decisions, mandatory arbitration has come under increased criticism. Its use by large corporations to force customers and employees into arbitration to adjudicate almost all types of alleged violations of state and federal laws designed to protect citizens against consumer fraud, unsafe products, employment discrimination, nonpayment of wages, and other forms of corporate wrongdoing has enraged consumers and citizen advocates. In addition, many jurisdictions permit corporations to combine mandatory arbitration with a ban on class actions, thereby preventing consumers or employees from joining together to challenge systemic corporate wrongdoing. Some states, however, have found that the insertion and use of these mandatory arbitration clauses in a manner that prevents consumers from knowingly agreeing to them violates the Constitution's guarantee of a right to trial by jury.

Mediation

Unlike arbitration, mediation is typically agreed to voluntarily by both parties, and its results are not binding. However, it may be a compulsory, court-ordered procedure that is a prerequisite to actual litigation. Either party may still choose to go to trial if they cannot settle their dispute through mediation. In this process, a neutral third party assists the parties in resolving a conflict by using specialized communication and negotiation techniques. All participants are encouraged to actively participate in the process, and the mediator acts a facilitator to help the parties find a solution to their conflict. Mediation can also be evaluative in instances where the mediator analyzes legal issues and makes a recommendation concerning the economic value of a cause of action. Increasingly, courts are requiring parties to participate in mediation in the hope of getting them to settle their case before going to trial.

General Advantages of ADR

Some of the typical benefits a company may gain through ADR, as opposed to litigation, are as follows:

- *Disputes are resolved faster.* The reduction of delays in resolving legal claims was one of the driving forces behind the ADR movement. As the number of court cases continues to increase, the courts cannot expeditiously accommodate them. As a result, many parties find it more economical to obtain a final resolution of their disputes outside the courthouse.

- *There are significant cost savings.* A traditional argument in support of ADR, especially arbitration, is that it is much cheaper than litigation. Although this may be true if the parties wish to avoid the expensive costs of discovery and motions, which often are not permitted in ADR, the parties may not find it all that cost effective if forced to pay the fees of a three-person arbitration panel where the panel members consist of high-priced lawyers or retired judges. Thus, when there is a concern that the cost of discovery might outstrip the value of the case, arbitration may be a better alternative.

- *Relationships are preserved.* ADR allows parties to resolve a dispute without the animosity that often destroys a business or personal relationship during litigation.

- *Confidential information is protected.* Litigation often results in the public disclosure of proprietary information, particularly in commercial disputes. Although one party may seek a protective order restricting the other party's access to its trade secrets, the mere process of obtaining such an order exposes the confidential information to outside scrutiny. ADR procedures allow the parties to resolve disputes while better protecting confidential information.

- *There is greater flexibility.* ADR allows the parties to tailor a dispute resolution process to the unique matter at hand. They can select the mechanism, determine the amount of information that needs to be exchanged, choose their own arbitrator or mediator, and agree on a format for the procedure.

- *The result is more durable.* Resolutions achieved by consensus of the disputants are less likely to be challenged than resolutions imposed by third parties.

- *There can be better, more creative solutions.* By giving litigants early and direct participation, ADR provides a greater opportunity for achieving a resolution based on the parties' real interests. Such agreements often produce a solution that makes more sense for the parties than one imposed by a court.

Situations in Which ADR Is Successful

ADR is mostly likely to be successful under these conditions:

- *An ADR contract clause is in place.* ADR is much more likely to be successful if there is an effective contract clause that provides for the use of ADR in the event of a future dispute.

- *There is a continuing relationship between the parties.* If a continuing relationship is possible (e.g., franchisors and franchisees), the chances of ADR success are increased. In these instances, the parties can then continue making money from each other for the duration of their agreement, rather than ending the relationship and suffering the cost and disruption of litigation.

- *The dispute is complex.* If a case involves highly complex technology, there is a significant chance that a jury and even a judge may become confused. Under these circumstances, ADR may be the best option, particularly if the proceedings are conducted before a neutral person who is an expert in the subject matter of the dispute. Since the parties themselves select the arbitrator, they have the opportunity to choose a well-qualified arbitrator rather than someone randomly appointed by a judge and avoid submitting themselves to the uncertainties of the jury process.

- *Relatively little money is at stake.* If the amount of money in dispute is relatively small, the cost of litigation may approach or even exceed that amount.

- *Confidentiality is an important issue.* In an ADR proceeding, it is easier for the parties to maintain confidentiality, not just of their business information but also of the nature of the case. Sometimes the need for confidentiality is more important than any other consideration in selecting a dispute resolution process.

Situations in Which ADR May Not Be Successful

In some instances, ADR may not have a good chance of success:

- *The opposing party is skeptical and mistrusting.* The opposing party may see the other side's efforts to use ADR after a complaint has been filed as a way of getting an advantage in litigation. If the parties are extremely hostile to one another, they may refuse to agree to otherwise well-qualified arbitrators simply because they were suggested by the opponent.

- *Parties or counsel have nasty attitudes.* When the parties or their counsel are extremely emotional, belligerent, or abusive, they are likely to be more concerned about airing their grievances than they are about resolving their dispute. This will obviously make it more difficult to use non-binding ADR successfully.

- *The case is one of many.* If the case at issue is one of many expected to be filed, it is not likely that the defendant will be motivated to agree to the use of ADR, particularly if it is non-binding. This may be one of those rare instances in which litigation is more cost effective due to the efficiency gained by the consolidation of multiple cases in a class action lawsuit.

- *Delays may benefit one party.* If a delay will benefit one of the parties, then the successful use of ADR will be diminished.

- *There are significant monetary imbalances.* If a significant monetary imbalance exists between parties and the wealthier party thinks it can wear down the other party through traditional litigation, then the wealthier party will likely refuse to agree to ADR.

HYPOTHETICAL CASE

Malcom Manufacturing Company is a growing business that makes and sells tires for off-road vehicles. Dune Buggy Inc. is Malcom's largest customer, with a contract to buy 1,000 tires per month for 24 months. Malcom uses chemicals it buys from China in the manufacturing of its tires. Recently, the news media have reported numerous accidents caused by tires made with these Chinese-supplied chemicals. So far, the tires with the problems have been those made by other manufacturers. Dune Buggy Inc. contacts Malcom Manufacturing and asks if its tires contain any of the Chinese-made chemical. When Malcom answers honestly that it does but that no problems have been reported with its tires, and that it is seeking another source for the chemical, Dune Buggy Inc. responds by saying it will not be accepting any more tires made by Malcom because they might be defective, and it can't risk putting them on its dune buggies. Dune Buggy does, in fact, refuse delivery of the next shipment of Malcom Manufacturing's tires, continues to refuse delivery for the fourteen months that remain on its contract, and does not pay for any more tires. As a result, Malcom Manufacturing is forced to file for bankruptcy.

If you are Malcom Manufacturing, would you prefer to subject your breach of contract claims against Dune Buggy Inc. to mediation, or would you rather litigate them? What are the reasons for your decision? If you are Dune Buggy Inc., would you prefer to resolve Malcom's claim with mediation or through trial? What are the reasons for your decision?

Chapter 5: Business Ethics

Introduction

"If you have integrity, nothing else matters. If you don't have integrity, nothing else matters." Alan K. Simpson, former United States Senator

What are business ethics? Business ethics are the ethical principles and problems that arise in a business environment.

It seems that the media are constantly bringing to light examples of excessive greed and malfeasance in the business community. Often, these situations result in the loss of public money as well as confidence. As a result, the public is demanding more ethical behavior from both public and private businesses. Congress has responded by passing more and more stringent legislation in an effort to make companies behave in socially responsible and ethical ways.

Many corporate Web sites now contain a statement addressing their commitment to non-economic social values in addition to information promoting their products or services. Some corporations have defined their core values in the light of ethical considerations. An example would be paper product companies that emphasize their commitment to maintaining sustainable forests.

Of course, businesses exist to make money. There is nothing wrong or illegal about making a monetary profit from running a business. However, the manner in which some businesses conduct themselves disturbs some people and raises the question of ethical behavior. As we will see, good business ethics often make good business sense.

In a research study conducted by the Institute of Business Ethics (IBE), it was found that companies that display a "clear commitment to ethical conduct" consistently outperform companies that do not display ethical conduct.[2]

Why Are Business Ethics Important?

If a company does not practice business ethics and breaks the law, it usually ends up being fined and sometimes prosecuted criminally. There are many examples of companies that have broken anti-trust, ethical, and environmental laws and received fines of millions of dollars. Yet these companies often continue such behavior because

---

[2] *Building the Business Case for Ethics*, Margolis, Walsh, Krehmeyer, Business Roundtable Institute for Corporate Ethics, 2006.

they believe the revenue gained by these violations outweighs the fines they must pay. Billion-dollar profits make some companies ignore ethics, and they fail to see the other costs that result from their lack of ethics.

Even though a business might make millions of dollars, if the public sees it as exploiting child labor in a foreign country or needlessly destroying the environment during its manufacturing process, customers may shun its products, and profits may suffer. The public's reaction to unethical business practices may prompt the company to adhere to proper business ethics. Many other companies pride themselves on their exemplary business ethics, without requiring the prod of public scorn.

Business ethics involve a lot more than compliance with laws, company policies, and financial regulations. Of course, the problems that result from these violations are the ones that are most likely to result in newspaper headlines when they are violated. Yet it's usually the less conspicuous things that cause businesses problems. Examples of areas in which companies are often ethically challenged include deceptive pricing, promotions, or advertising; selling unsafe or defective products; planned obsolescence; poor service; and high-pressure selling.

Because the ethical practices and social responsibility displayed by company managers is transmitted to employees, it establishes the company's attitude, culture, and ethical philosophy. This makes it extremely important that a company's ethical practices are displayed and enforced by top management.

Can a Business Be Both Ethical and Profitable?

According to the group Ethisphere, it is possible for a company to be both extremely ethical and extremely profitable. In 2017 it listed 3M Co., Allstate, Starbucks, Ford Motor Co., UPS, Xerox and Voya Financial, Inc. as some of the world's most ethical companies. These are also some of the most profitable companies.[3]

A company's environmental policy, the way it treats its employees, and the communities in which it operates are all part of its overall behavior that determines how it is perceived by the public. A company's public perception affects its business relationships and its ability to recruit top talent.

---

[3] http://worldsmostethicalcompanies.ethisphere.com/honorees

When a person or business entity is considering investing in a particular company's stock, there are a number of things they look for. Aside from a company's profit margin, consideration is also given to the qualitative aspects of the company, such as its public image and the products it sells. All of these things are taken into account when deciding whether to invest in the company. Therefore, a company that wants to encourage investment should have a strong sense of business ethics. An essential part of business ethics is a responsibility to the investor, and companies that have a strong reputation for ethical business practices also tend to attract more investment from people who are new to the market.

In the business world, joint ventures are common. A business can be made or broken on just one joint venture, and part of the reason that joint ventures are successful is that they combine the forces of two extremely powerful companies on occasion.

When a company seeks a business partner, it usually looks for one that has a good reputation—both in terms of a track record and in terms of its overall business practices. One of the best ways to get a good reputation is to ensure that the company has a strong reputation for ethical business behavior.

Examples of Business Ethics

Business ethics can be examined from various perspectives. There is the perspective of the employee, the commercial enterprise, and society as a whole. Very often, situations arise in which there is conflict between one or more of the parties, so that serving the interest of one party is a detriment to the other(s). For example, a particular course of action might be good for the employee but bad for the company or society.

There are many facets of business wherein ethics, or a lack thereof, are obvious. Following are examples of actions that raise questions of whether or not the behavior is ethical, to greater or lesser degrees.

Ethics of Production

- Using defective, addictive, and inherently dangerous products and services (e.g., tobacco, alcohol, weapons, chemicals)

- Adversely affecting the environment: pollution, carbon emissions

- Using new technologies: genetically modified food, cell phone radiation

- Testing products on animals

- Using economically disadvantaged groups as test subjects

Ethics of Intellectual Property, Knowledge, and Skills

- Engaging in patent, trademark, and copyright infringement

- Committing industrial espionage

- Raiding employees—the practice of attracting key employees away from a competitor to take unfair advantage of their knowledge or skills

- Employing all the most talented people in a specific field, regardless of need, in order to prevent any competitors employing them

International Commercial Ethics

- Taking advantage of international differences, such as by outsourcing production and services to low-wage countries (e.g., clothing manufacturing and technical assistance service centers)

- Conducting international commerce with pariah states

Corporate Ethics Policies

Many companies have internal policies pertaining to the ethical conduct of employees as part of a comprehensive compliance and ethics program. These policies can be simple, very general policies, or they can be very detailed policies containing specific behavioral requirements. The latter are usually called *corporate ethics codes.*

Corporate ethics codes are generally meant to identify the company's expectations of employees and to offer guidance on how to handle some of the more common ethical problems that might arise in the course of doing business. Companies that have corporate ethics codes believe an ethics code will lead to greater ethical awareness, consistency in ethics application, and the avoidance of ethical disasters. Corporate ethics codes may also provide a defense to the company if it is sued for an ethics violation that is also a violation of law. For example, the company may be able to show that the conduct was that of a rogue employee who violated the company's ethics code and that the code demonstrates that the behavior is not sanctioned by the company or its management.

As part of its ethics policy and to aid interpretation and enforcement of its ethics code, companies may have an ethics officer, called a compliance officer or business conduct officer.

Professional Codes of Ethics

Many professions, such as doctors, lawyers, and accountants, have an ethical code that members are expected to follow. If members violate these ethical codes, they may be required to appear before a professional disciplinary body, and their license may be suspended or revoked if the charges are proven.

Many businesses have their own ethical policies contained in a handbook or a separate *code of conduct*. Not only do these policies establish the company's ethical expectations and put employees on notice, but they also may serve as a defense to civil or criminal charges (e.g., sexual harassment).

HYPOTHETICAL CASE

You work in the finance department of a large company. The company has a code of conduct that states, in part: "Employees are required to keep internal matters and disputes in strict confidence. Anyone caught speaking of internal business matters or disputes with non-employees shall be terminated from employment." A good friend is fired from his job in the company. He tells you he believes he was the victim of discrimination. A few days later you notice a notepad his boss left behind from a meeting. On it is written your friend's name, with a note next to it that says, "Next time, hire a female 22 to 32 years old." You tell your friend what you saw, and he wants you to talk to an Equal Employment Opportunity Commissioner (EEOC) investigator about it. Will you? Why or why not?

Chapter 6: Constitutional Law

Introduction

The U.S. legal system is based on common law, but unlike some common law countries, it also has a Constitution, which stands as the supreme law of the land. The body of law that deals with the interpretation of the U.S. Constitution is known as *constitutional law*.

Often, constitutional law deals with relationships between the states and the federal government, between the states, and among the three branches of government. When these disputes arise, the final decision rests with the U.S. Supreme Court. If Congress passes a law that violates a provision of the Constitution, it is the duty of the Supreme Court to invalidate it through the process of judicial review.

The Constitution

The U.S. Constitution was signed on September 17, 1787, but it wasn't until two years later, in 1789, that the first twelve amendments were added and the document was ratified. The first ten of the Constitution's amendments are known as the Bill of Rights because they contain specific protections on the individual liberties of citizens, and they place restrictions on the powers of the government. The Constitution contains seven articles and 27 amendments.

Article I describes the Congress and the legislative branch of government. It both defines and limits these powers and contains the important Commerce Clause and Necessary and Proper Clause, which are used to allow Congress to enact legislation that implements goals and policies that are not expressly limited.

Article II describes the executive branch of government and the office of president. The Twelfth Amendment has modified it by acknowledging political parties, and the 25th Amendment details presidential succession in the event of death or incapacity. It also states that the president is to receive only one compensation from the federal government.

Article III describes the judicial branch of government and the court system. It states that there shall be one court called the Supreme Court. The article describes the kinds of cases the Supreme Court can take as original jurisdiction. Congress can create lower courts and an appeals process. Congress is given the power to define crimes and provide for punishment. Article III also protects the right to trial by jury in all criminal cases, and defines the crime of treason.

Article IV describes the relations among the states and between each state and the federal government. In addition, it defines the process for admitting new states and border changes between the states. It also requires states to give "full faith and credit" to the public acts, records, and court proceedings of the other states. The "privileges and immunities" clause in this article prohibits state governments from discriminating against citizens of other states in favor of its own resident citizens, *e.g.*, having tougher penalties for residents of Wisconsin who are convicted of crimes within Michigan. It also establishes extradition between the states.

Article V describes the process for amending the Constitution. There are two procedures for adopting a proposed amendment: 1) Congress may do so by two-thirds majority in both the Senate and the House of Representatives, or at a national convention (which shall take place whenever two-thirds of the state legislatures collectively call for one). 2) Three-fourths of the states (presently 38 of 50) approve of the amendment by: a) consent of the state legislatures or b) consent of state ratifying conventions. The ratification method is chosen by Congress for each amendment.

Article VI describes the Constitution, and all federal laws and treaties of the United States, as the supreme law of the land. It requires that all federal and state legislators, officers, and judges take oaths or affirmations to support the Constitution. This means that the states' constitutions and laws should not conflict with the laws of the federal constitution and that, in case of a conflict, state judges are legally bound to honor the federal laws and Constitution over those of any state. Article VI also states "no religious test shall ever be required as a qualification to any office or public trust under the United States."

Article VII describes the process for establishing the new form of government. It provided for ratification of the Constitution by popularly elected ratifying conventions in each state.

Supreme Court Justices

Nine justices serve on the U.S. Supreme Court. Each justice is nominated by the president, confirmed by the Senate, and serves for life (or until the justice retires).

The Senate confirmation process begins with hearings before the Senate Judiciary Committee and ends with a vote of the full Senate. A simple majority vote is required for confirmation.

Under the Constitution, justices who commit "high crimes or misdemeanors" are subject to impeachment and may be removed from office. There is no other mechanism for removing a justice from office.

Judicial Interpretation

The Supreme Court has cases brought to it that require it to interpret the meaning of each clause of the Constitution. For example, the "full faith and credit clause" of the Constitution says that each state must recognize the public acts (laws), records, and judicial proceeding of the other states. It also guarantees that a citizen of one state is entitled to the "privileges and immunities" in every other state. Another example is its ruling that a divorce granted in one state must be recognized as valid in another state and that its child support order must also be enforced.

Interpreting the Constitution is often a difficult task. This is because the Constitution is often very vague, and the meaning of the terms it uses are not well defined. The meaning of some of the words used in the document has changed since the document was written, and certainly its drafters could not have foreseen the huge impact technology would have on our society, laws, and law enforcement.

Jurisprudence and Judicial Philosophy

The jurisprudence of Supreme Court justices greatly influences their ruling on cases. *Jurisprudence* is commonly characterized as the study, knowledge, or science of law. In the United States, jurisprudence usually refers to the philosophy of law. Legal philosophy has many aspects, but the most common seeks to analyze, explain, classify, and criticize entire bodies of law. Legal treatises and law school textbooks represent this type of scholarship. The second type of jurisprudence compares and contrasts law with other fields of knowledge such as economics, religion, and the social sciences. The third type of jurisprudence seeks to reveal the historical, moral, and cultural basis of a specific legal concept. This form of jurisprudence focuses on finding the answer to more abstract questions such as, "What is the purpose of law?"

Not only are there different types of jurisprudence, but there are also different philosophies of jurisprudence. Formalism, or conceptualism, treats law like math or science. Formalists believe that a judge identifies the relevant legal principles, applies them to the facts of a case, and logically deduces a rule that will govern the outcome of the dispute. In contrast, proponents of legal realism believe that most cases present tough questions that judges must resolve by balancing the interests of all the parties and creating a ruling that sides with one party in the dispute. This rule is based in part on the political, economic, and psychological inclinations of the judge. Some legal realists even believe that a judge is able to shape the outcome of the case based on personal biases.

Apart from the realist–formalist difference, there is the classic debate over the appropriate sources of law between positivist and natural law schools of thought. *Positivists* argue that there is no connection between law and morality and that the only sources of law are rules that have been expressly enacted by governments or courts of law. *Naturalists* insist that the rules enacted by government are not the only source of law. They argue that moral philosophy, religion, human reason, and individual conscience are also integral parts of the law.

Sometimes the differences between the schools of jurisprudence are not that easy to distinguish. The legal philosophy of a particular legal scholar or justice may contain a combination of beliefs from more than one school of legal thought.

How Cases Make Their Way to the Supreme Court

Cases make their way to the Supreme Court in one of two ways. Most cases begin in a state court. Usually, they start in a city or county court and then progress until they reach the state's highest court. From there, the case can be appealed directly to the U.S. Supreme Court. Cases involving questions of federal law begin in federal district court and move through the Court of Appeals (circuit court) and then to the U.S. Supreme Court.

Interpreting Constitutional Clauses

Unlike trial courts, the U.S. Supreme Court is not concerned with the guilt or innocence of those accused and convicted of crimes. Its purpose and sole responsibility are to make sure that laws are passed and administered in ways that the U.S. Constitution allows. This means that the Court hears only those cases in which the parties are arguing about constitutional issues. For example, imagine that the Court hears the case of *State v. Defendant* in which Defendant was convicted of downloading pornography in violation of state law. The

U.S. Supreme Court will not consider whether Defendant is guilty or innocent of the crime. Rather, it will consider only whether the law itself conforms to the Constitution or whether the process used to convict Defendant conformed to constitutional requirements. This distinction is important because people often see an injustice that seems to have been done to a defendant and expect an appellate court to give justice to wronged party, but this does not always happen. Often, appellate courts cannot administer justice to individuals because their sole responsibility is to interpret the Constitution and the constitutionality of federal and state laws.

Different Judicial Philosophies

Judges may have a number of different judicial philosophies that can affect the way they view their role as a jurist. Their philosophical perspective may also influence how they interpret precedent and therefore decide the outcome of a case. The major judicial philosophies are discussed in the following paragraphs.

1. **Legislative Intent.** When a law is unclear, the courts try to figure out what Congress intended when it passed the statute. Unfortunately, Congress's intent is not always obvious even

when there is a record of its hearings. The court will examine the record of hearings on the bill, speeches, and debate proceedings, legislative records, committee minutes, fact findings, and reports to try to determine what the drafters of the law intended it to mean and do. Proponents of this philosophy believe it is important to figure out and try to accomplish what the original drafters of the legislation sought to accomplish.

2. **Originalism.** Proponents of this set of theories look to be consistent with the "original intent" meant by the law makers when they drafted or ratified a statute or the Constitution. They believe that the law should be interpreted in conformity with what the texts would have been understood to mean at the time they were drafted. Opponents point out that the original intent of the framers of the Constitution was to perpetuate practices that are currently abhorrent to us, such as slavery and the denial of women's right to vote, so they argue this is not necessarily a good practice to follow.

3. **Textualism.** Proponents of this philosophy look to the meaning of the words of a text in the context of the problem it was supposed to remedy. They avoid non-textual sources such as legislative intent. Textualist judges distrust legislative intent as an interpretive

practice because they think the legislature is too large and cannot have a collective intent.

4. **Strict Constructionism.** Believers in strict constructionism limit judicial interpretation to the meaning of the actual words or phrases of the law and avoid examining legislative intent.

5. **Judicial Activism.** Those who practice judicial activism are known to strike down acts of the legislature or executive as unconstitutional. Therefore, all Supreme Court justices are judicial activists. If, however, judicial activism is seen to trespass on the executive or legislative area or powers, then the judges are accused of overstepping their authority or "social engineering."

6. **Judicial Restraint.** This philosophy involves exercising deference to the Constitution and legislature and close adherence to judicial precedent. Most judges value stability and predictability and go to great lengths to defer to the framers of the Constitution, but practitioners of judicial restraint are especially loath to expand the rule of law beyond its existing borders.

7. **The "Living Constitution."** Proponents of "Living Constitution" theories believe that the Constitution is organic and must be read in

a broad and liberal manner so as to adapt to changing times. This theory mandates that Constitutional language be read contemporaneously rather than historically. Although they believe it is important to keep constitutional law stable by limiting interpretation that strays from precedent, they believe that at times it is necessary based on the evolution of society. They believe that originalism promotes antiquated ideas about racism and gender equality that modern society should find offensive.

9. **Judicial Pragmatism.** This is a libertarian theory of interpreting the Constitution as a dynamic document, which must evolve with societal norms. Under this view, for example, the Constitutional requirement of "equal rights" should be read in the light of current standards of equality and not those of decades or centuries ago when the words meant something different. Practitioners of this philosophy believe that the original intent or meaning of the founders is subordinate to currently prevailing views of justice. According to Judge Richard Posner, a libertarian pragmatist who supports this view, we should find it "reassuring to think that the courts stand between us and legislative tyranny even if a particular

form of tyranny was not foreseen and expressly forbidden by the framers of the Constitution."

Individual Constitutional Clauses

The Due Process Clause

The *due process clause* of the Fourteenth Amendment has been interpreted by the Supreme Court as affording citizens protection from interference by the state with almost all of the rights listed in the first eight amendments. The Fourteenth Amendment also guarantees the equal protection of the laws. This Constitutional amendment requires that the laws of a state treat the person in one circumstance the same as they do others in similar conditions. For example, when the Fourteenth Amendment of the Constitution promises "life, liberty," and "equal protection of the laws" to "any person," it is referring to acts that the government must *refrain* from doing, not to any positive duty the government has *to* act. A violation of the due process clause would occur, for example, if a state prohibited an individual from entering into an employment contract because he or she was a member of a particular race—for example, "Only white males may be employed by the United States government." The only time the government has a positive duty to act is when it has already wrongfully deprived a person of liberty.

Privileges and Immunities Clause

The Privileges and Immunities Clause ensures that all people can travel freely throughout the states, without being treated in a discriminatory manner.

The Commerce Clause

The commerce clause of the Constitution gives Congress the authority to create regulatory agencies that, for example, set railroad rates, regulate the quality of foods and drugs, and subject more and more of the economy and business to governmental oversight.

Specifically, the commerce clause states that Congress "has the power to regulate commerce with foreign nations, and among the several states, and with the Indian tribes."

The Supreme Court's interpretation of the commerce clause has changed over time. How the Constitution's drafters understood the word *commerce* is a subject of disagreement among scholars. In the late nineteenth century, the Supreme Court employed a narrow definition of the commerce clause, pointing to the Tenth Amendment of the Constitution, which reserves power to the states that are not delegated to the federal government. Because of its narrow interpretation, it ruled that activities such as manufacturing were not part of interstate commerce, finding instead that they were purely local activities. As local activities, only the states were allowed to regulate them. The Court struck down several congressional attempts to regulate labor practices, wages, and industrial conditions because of this narrow interpretation. But in the late 1930s, in the midst of the Great Depression, the Supreme Court began to change its interpretation of the Commerce Clause. By 1940, after President Franklin Roosevelt had appointed several new justices, the Court's position evolved to the point at which it concluded that anything that affects interstate commerce falls within Congress's commerce power. This interpretation, combined with the power granted under the Constitution's "necessary and proper" clause, has been used to justify all sorts of government regulation of business. Major civil rights laws outlawing discrimination in hiring, for example, have been enacted under the commerce power.

The Contract Clause

The Contract Clause prohibits states from passing any law that retroactively impairs contract rights or interferes with existing contracts. The Contract Clause applies only to state legislation, not federal legislation or court decisions.

The Full Faith and Credit Clause

The Full Faith and Credit Clause requires that state and federal courts are required to respect judgments made by courts in other states as well as judgments made in foreign countries. Thus, persons who are married in Michigan and move to Florida are recognized as being legally married in the state of Florida. Also, a judgment obtained in a court in Ohio may be enforced in a court in Colorado.

Necessary and Proper Clause

The Constitution also grants Congress the right to make laws that it deems "necessary and proper" to carry out its enumerated powers. This means whenever the Constitution specifically gives the government a power, such as to form an army, it also has whatever powers are necessary to actually create and operate that army, such as creating a military draft, taxing citizens to pay for the army, contracting with companies to provide supplies and equipment to the army, and so on. This implied power gives Congress wide leeway in lawmaking.

Preemption

Under the U.S. Constitution's supremacy clause, if state laws conflict with federal objectives, then the federal programs trump and "preempt" the conflicting state provisions. In some instances, federal law will preempt an entire field. When the Constitution or federal statute gives the federal government sole control over an area, it *preempts* the states from passing any law in that area. For example, if the federal government were to enact a law that says, "No state shall pass any law that regulates or attempts to regulate the discharge of chemicals into public waterways," and a state passed a law that said its coal plants could discharge effluents into state rivers, its law would be declared void and unenforceable because the federal law preempted it.

If the federal government passes a law that regulates a field that the U.S. Constitution says is reserved to the states, then the U.S. Supreme Court may declare the federal law unconstitutional. For example, Article V of the Constitution gives the states the power "to require

Congress to convene a constitutional convention for the purpose of proposing amendments to or revising the terms of the Constitution," so if Congress attempted to pass a law saying the Senate could convene a constitutional convention for this purpose, it would be struck down as an unconstitutional attempt to preempt state authority.

Civil Liberties

The Constitution and its amendments also guarantee to the people certain civil liberties, such as the right to be free of government interference in the practice of religion and speech, and civil rights, such as the right to be treated as a free and equal citizen of the country. These liberties and rights are spelled out in the Bill of Rights, which contains the first ten amendments to the Constitution. Additional civil liberties, such as the requirement that the government obtain a warrant based on probable cause before searching a person's property, are also part of the Bill of Rights. In addition to the Constitution, which protects people from actions that the government may take that infringes their stated civil rights or liberties, there are now several federal, and many state, statutes that protect these rights from action taken by private parties and businesses.

Checks and Balances

By dividing and limiting various governmental powers, the Constitution creates a system known as checks and balances. If one branch threatens to become too powerful, other branches may act to block or thwart it. For example, if the president steps beyond his powers, Congress can refuse to provide funds, or the courts can rule the president's actions unconstitutional. An example occurred when President Nixon attempted to claim executive privilege to keep Congress from examining audiotapes it had subpoenaed, which were in his possession.

HYPOTHETICAL CASE

Jamal works as an assistant principal at the local public junior high school. He learns there is an opening for the public high school principal, so he applies since he has been doing many of those same job duties for years, and it would be a logical advancement in his career. He applies for the position and is given an interview. Several weeks later, he learns he did not get the job and that a teacher from another high school was hired. Afterward, one of the teachers from his school casually says to him "Gee, Jamal, I'm sorry you didn't get the principal's job, but you know it's hard for them to promote somebody to principal around here who is a Muslim." Jamal is, indeed, Muslim but never thought that was a problem. When he asks the teacher how he knows that was a factor in him not getting the job, the teacher says, "Everybody knows you're Muslim, and as soon as he heard you applied for the job, Bob (Jamal's boss) said you should become a Christian if you ever expect to get promoted to principal since no school around here is going to have a Muslim as principal." The teacher goes on to say that his wife works at the high school, and she heard the secretary there say she wouldn't work for a boss named

Jamal. Now Jamal is contemplating what, if any, legal action he can take after learning this information.

Can Jamal pursue any legal cause of action? Why or why not? If you think he can, what cause(s) of action will he allege?

Chapter 7: Administrative Law

Introduction

What is administrative law? Administrative law is a branch of public law, often referred to as *regulatory law.* As a body of law, administrative law deals with the decision making of administrative tribunals, boards, or commissions of government agencies. These administrative agencies are part of a national regulatory scheme that deals with international trade, manufacturing, taxation, the environment, and transportation. Administrative law consists of laws and legal principles governing the administration and regulation of both federal and state government agencies. Such agencies are delegated power by Congress (or in the case of a state agency, the state legislature) to act as agents for the executive branch of government. Most often, administrative agencies are organized under the executive branch of government and are created to protect a public interest rather than to vindicate private rights. Administrative law deals with both the substance and procedural rules created by administrative agencies.

Administrative agencies are created by the legislative branch of government (by statute), but their directors are typically appointed by the executive branch. They are created to perform specific duties for the public good or to deal with a specific problem. Examples of administrative agencies are the Environmental Protection Agency (which was established to protect environmental resources) and those governing taxation, immigration, and the regulation of public utilities. Taxation disputes are the most commonly contested administrative decisions. Most government agencies have the authority to make rules, enforce those rules, and contain a procedure to adjudicate the legality of its actions and decisions.

How Administrative Law Works

Administrative agencies are created by Congress through the passage of enabling legislation that details the purpose, name, and specific powers of the agency. It is the agency's Enabling Act that defines its specific purpose, powers, and the rulemaking procedure it is to follow. Agency powers typically include the power to investigate, adjudicate, legislate, and enforce laws within their specific areas of delegated expertise. Agencies have the power to "legislate" by enacting regulations through rule making. These ruled are contained and codified in the Code of Federal Regulations (CFR) and are treated like laws within the area over which the agency has jurisdiction.

The authority of all administrative agencies comes from statutes and are classified as either independent or executive. The head of an executive agency is appointed by the president, if it is a federal agency, or the governor, if it is a state agency. Independent agencies are governed by a board of commissioners. Often, it is the chief executive who appoints the commissioners with the advice and consent of the senate at the federal level. Examples of some independent agencies are the Federal Trade Commission (FTC) and the Securities and Exchange Commission (SEC). Another difference between the two types of agencies is their regulatory authority. Commissions, or independent agencies, often have more narrow authority over multiple areas of a particular industry such as focusing on licensing and rate making, while executive agencies tend to have responsibility for making rules covering a broad area of activities and industries.

Each agency is responsible for a particular body of substantive law, such as taxation or professional licensing, but certain procedural principles apply to all agencies. If an agency does not have its own procedural rule, it will follow those established in the Administrative Procedures Act.

The Administrative Procedure Act

The Administrative Procedures Act states that *rulemaking* is "an agency process for formulating, amending, or repealing a rule." A *rule,* in turn, is "the whole or a part of an agency statement of general or particular applicability and future effect designed to implement, interpret, or prescribe law or policy." *Adjudication* is "an agency process for the formulation of an order," and an *order* is "the whole or part of a final disposition...of an agency in a matter other than rule making but including licensing."

Rulemaking

Under the APA are specific guidelines for agencies to follow in enacting rules. Typically, a rule is proposed, and the public is given an opportunity to comment on it before it is adopted. These rules, or regulations, dictate the dos and don'ts for individuals and businesses subject to the jurisdiction of a particular agency. They may cover such things as reporting information and the filing of documentation to mandating safety equipment and disposing properly of hazardous waste. The two most common types of rules agencies enact are informal and formal rules. A third type, known as the hybrid rule, is less common. An agency's enabling statute establishes which type of rulemaking procedure it must follow. The APA does contain an exemption from rulemaking that allows an agency to decide whether public participation will be allowed. Exemptions include situations involving military or foreign affairs or agency management and personnel. Exemptions are also allowed for proceedings related to public property, loan, grants, benefits, or contracts of an agency. The reason for this is that it has been determined that military and foreign affairs often require secrecy and speed, which are incompatible with the public notice and hearings requirements of rulemaking.

Court cases have held that agencies do not have the power to enact a regulation if the regulation is an unconstitutional delegation of power or the statute that created it explicitly denies it such authority. Regulations will also be struck down if Congress has enacted a separate regulatory scheme for the agency or if the regulation does not serve the "public convenience, interest, or necessity." Also, if the regulation is outside the agency's statutory purpose, the court may declare it is invalid.

Judicial Review of Administrative Agencies

Judicial review is the power of the courts to nullify the acts of the executive and/or the legislative branches of government when it finds them to have violated the law. Judicial review is an example of the "separation of powers" doctrine, whereby the judicial branch reviews the actions of the other two branches of government. Courts have the power to decide all relevant questions of law, interpret constitutional and statutory provisions, and determine the meaning or applicability of an agency's action and regulations. Generally, however, courts will not review an administrative decision until the agency itself has completed its own review and rendered a final decision on it. Before a court will hear a case that comes from an administrative agency, it determines if the case is "ripe" and ready for its review. If a final decision on the case has not been rendered by the administrative agency by a tribunal or other adjudicative body, it will not hear the case.

The adjudicative function in the administrative process is used to resolve disputes between the agency and those affected by its decisions. This process may rely on hearings conducted before administrative law judges or a panel of judges or on an official's review of written records. The final decision of an agency's adjudicative body may be appealed to a court.

An administrative law judge (ALJ) is the official who presides over the adjudicative process, typically referred to as an *administrative hearing*, which is like a trial. Unlike a trial, however, administrative hearings do not use juries. Instead, the administrative law judge acts as both judge and jury, and the hearing procedure at some may not be as formal as that used in court trials. That may be because there are a lot of administrative hearings where it is not uncommon for persons to represent themselves without an attorney. Other agency cases can be very complex and demanding, so it is not uncommon for attorneys and law firms to develop an expertise in handling cases concerning one particular agency.

When courts do review the decision of an administrative agency, they usually give wide discretion to the agency and are reluctant to overturn its decision. They tend to believe the administrative agency is a specialist in the subject it governs and will reverse an agency's decision only if one the following is true:

- The evidence seriously contradicts the agency's conclusion.

- Ex parte contact has tainted the agency's decision.

- Relevant and contradictory points of view were not considered by the agency.

- A significant change in the agency's policy was not fully explained.

Although it is possible to appeal an administrative law case to the court system for judicial review, this is seldom done. One reason is that the court system's judges readily acknowledge that they are not experts in the regulations and rules of the agency before them, and therefore they most always defer to the administrative law judge in any case in which interpretation of a rule is an issue. Another reason administrative law based cases often fail to progress in the court system is that they are filed there prematurely. The court system requires that before an administrative law case cause of action can be filed in court, the plaintiff must have "exhausted" all their administrative law remedies first. That means they must have pursued their administrative law case, and all administrative law appeals, and have gotten a "final disposition" of their administrative law case. It is this "final disposition" of the administrative law case that can and is properly appealed to a court with jurisdiction.

When reviewing an administrative agency's actions, the courts examine the authority given the agency by the statute that created it, known as the *enabling act*. Congress often specifies the terms of judicial review on the merits in the enabling act. Typically, an enabling act will allow the court to reverse an administrative tribunal's decision if it determines that the decision is not support by substantial evidence or is arbitrary and capricious. This is a difficult burden to meet, however, since the courts will usually uphold an agency's decision as long as it can find a rational basis to do so.

In addition to judicial review of an agency's actions, there are other ways the exercise of its powers may be reviewed. Congress may always revisit its enabling act and amend it, or it may even rescind it altogether and eliminate the agency completely. There are also political factors that may limit the power of an agency since the executive branch appoints the head of many agencies and the head of an agency often decides the priorities and policies the agency will pursue. In many instances, the appointment of an agency director by the chief executive may be subject to the approval of the Senate, so that too may require the political process. Even the ability of the public and media to obtain information from the agency and make it known can impact the ability of an agency to take action. The Freedom of Information Act (FOIA) allows members of the public to ask for, and receive, information from public agencies that is not subject to one of the statute's defined exceptions. Common FOIA requests concern statistics, information about funding and budgets, and interpretations of agency policies.

Concerns and Criticisms of Public Agencies

Although agencies are tasked with looking out for the public's interest, they have increasingly come under criticism as being a "captive" of the industries they are supposed to be regulating. One reason for this is the close working relationship that necessarily develops between the employees of the agencies (the regulators) and the employees of the businesses they regulate. Over time, these parties tend to develop a more friendship-based relationship that makes it more difficult for the regulators to write citations for violations or impose fines against those they now consider to be their friends. Also, it is not uncommon for people who have spent many years working for an agency to leave it and then go to work for one of the companies they used to regulate, interacting there with their former employees and, in their new capacity, representing the party being regulated. Obviously, this situation can lead to concerns of bias and an unwillingness to enforce regulations, but others counter that the people with the best expertise are those who know it from the inside and are thus the best hires.

HYPOTHETICAL CASE

You work for Sam's Manufacturing Company, which makes speedboats. The Environmental Protection Agency (EPA) has charged the company with polluting a lake near its manufacturing plant and test facility. The complaint filed by the EPA alleges that the company has discharged large amounts of gasoline into the lake during its constant testing of boat engines. According to the EPA, the company's engine-testing process violates an EPA regulation, which limits the acceptable amount of gasoline that can be discharged into lakes and streams. A hearing was conducted before the EPA, and the company's attorney presented evidence that it tested 60 boats per month in the lake for ten minutes each. The company argued that this produced less pollution than the boats used by the boats owned and operated by people who live on the lake. The administrative law judge ruled against the company. Afterward, you learn that the administrative law judge has a sister who lives on the lake and has complained about all the noise caused by Sam's product testing.

If the company appeals the EPA's decision, what will your arguments be in support of the company? What will they be in support of the EPA's decision?

Chapter 8: Intentional Torts

Introduction

What is a tort? A *tort* is a wrong that is considered a violation of a duty imposed by civil law, causing injury to a person or property. There are three types of torts: intentional torts, negligence torts, and strict liability torts. Most tort law is passed at the state level, although there are some federal laws aimed at punishing tortious conduct.

Intentional Torts

Intentional torts are caused by a deliberate (intentional) act, and the result is foreseeable. For example, if a person picks up a baseball bat and swings it at another person, the act is intentional, and it is foreseeable that it will injure the other person. The act of intentionally touching another person without permission and with the intent to cause injury is a battery. Other examples of intentional torts are defamation, fraud, and intentional infliction of emotional distress.

To be responsible for the commission of an intentional tort, a person must have intended the consequences of an act, or the person must believe the consequences of it are substantially certain to result.

Furthermore, if the intent to injure someone is shown, it doesn't matter that the intended victim was not the one actually injured. The intent to commit a tort can be transferred between victims. Thus, if Kristen throws a rock intending to hit William, but he ducks and the rock hits Susie, who was standing behind William, Kristen can be charged with battery against Susie even though she didn't intend to injure Susie. The element of intent that must be proven is not the intent to harm a specific person, but rather the intent to engage in a specific act, which ultimately results in harm to another. There are intentional torts based on physical injuries to people and property, and there are also intentional torts based on purely economic injury.

Intentional Business Torts

In the business setting, an intentional business tort is an action a party undertakes with the desire to interfere with another's business relationship or business expectancy, and the action is substantially certain to result in such interference (i.e., it is foreseeable). For any tort to be actionable in court, the interference must result in some form of damage or injury.

Examples of intentional business torts:

- Defamation

- Fraudulent misrepresentation

- Unfair competition

- Interference with a business relationship (contract or expectancy)

Defamation

In business, a company's reputation is very important. Most companies work very hard to build up a good reputation and protect it, so they seek to avoid negative publicity and disparaging comments. In the past, false statements about an individual or business that were designed to make them look bad and intended to hurt them were printed in newspapers or perhaps made by someone on television or the radio. Today, however, the Internet makes it extremely easy for anyone to say anything anonymously, true or untrue, about any person or business they don't like. When a false statement is made about a business in this form, or on social media, it can be instantly re-transmitted to thousands of people who don't bother to fact check it, and the result can have devastating consequences on a business's reputation and bottom line. Sometimes, competitors purposely spread false information about rivals in an effort to damage them and enhance their own positions. If the injured business can identify the perpetrator and prove all of the elements of the intentional tort of defamation, which modern technology can often assist them in doing, the damages awarded can be significant.

To be successful in proving defamation, a party must check the statute in the jurisdiction in which the case arose, but typically, statutes require proving the following elements:

- The defendant knowingly made a false statement intending to cause defendant harm.

- The defendant communicated the false statement to a third party.

- The statement caused injury/harm.

Defamation may be in either of two forms: *libel,* which is defamation in a written form, or *slander,* which is defamation in a verbal form.

Corporations have protectable business reputations based on their corporate competence, integrity, and solvency. For example, the Home Shopping Network (HSN) claimed in public statements that it suffered millions of dollars in losses because GTE provided it with defective telephone equipment and services. HSN sued GTE because of this allegation, and GTE responded with a counterclaim for defamation. GTE claimed HSN's public statements about the telephone equipment and services it provided were false. The jury agreed with GTE's position and awarded the company $100 million in damages. In another case, *Brown & Williamson Tobacco Corp. v. Jacobson* (1987), Brown & Williamson sued a television anchorman who stated that Brown & Williamson had adopted an advertising strategy deliberately designed to induce minors to begin smoking cigarettes.

Reporting erroneous and damaging credit information about a company can also result in a defamation lawsuit. When Dun & Bradstreet falsely reported that Greenmoss Builders, Inc. had filed for bankruptcy, it was forced to respond to a defamation lawsuit. In recent years, companies appear to be more willing to pursue claims for harm to their reputations instead of simply tolerating false statements about them as part of doing business.

Defenses to Defamation

Several defenses may be used to successfully defend against a defamation claim:

- The information is true.

- The information is opinion.

- The information is satire.

- No reasonable person would believe it.

Defamation Against Public Officials and Celebrities

Public officials and public personalities have less protection from defamation claims. This is because the law assumes that a person who seeks public office or fame must accept a certain amount of "gossip" or talk about them as a natural consequence of their fame. As a result, for a claim of defamation to be successful against a public figure, the public figure must show the additional element of actual malice, meaning the statement was made knowing it was false or with reckless disregard for the truth.

Fraudulent Misrepresentation

Fraud consists of injuring another party by deliberately deceiving them. For example, if a business submits materially misleading financial statements to a bank in an effort to obtain a loan and the bank, relying on the statements, lends money to the business, the bank will have a fraud claim against the business if it later defaults on the loan.

A fraud claim may result not only from an affirmative statement that is untrue but also from the failure to disclose a material fact if a defendant owed a duty to tell the truth and disclose information. For example, if a financial advisor represents both a buyer and seller of real property, he or she may be liable for fraud if the advisor knows that the property contains toxic chemicals and fails to tell the buyer. In that instance, they are breaching their duty to represent the buyer by failing to tell them important (material) information they know the buyer would need and want to know before making the decision to buy the property.

There are typically six elements of fraudulent misrepresentation:

1. ***The statement is false.*** This means the defendant makes a false representation or false statement.

2. ***The false statement (misrepresentation) is material to the transaction.*** This means it is an essential part of the transaction at hand. For example, if you are selling a car and you lie about it having only been driven in state, it may be a

fraudulent misrepresentation, but it is not material to the transaction. If, however, you lie about how many miles the car has been driven, or the condition of the engine, then that would be a false statement that is material to the transaction because it will make a difference as to whether or not a reasonable person will decide to go through with the transaction.

3. ***The misrepresentation is made with knowledge that it is false, or with reckless disregard as to whether or not it is true.*** This means that a party either knows the information is a lie or has no reason to believe the statement they are making is true. For example, if you are selling an old painting you found in the attic and you tell prospective purchasers it was painted by a famous painter in an effort to get them to buy it, it is possible that it is true, but it is extremely unlikely to be true. The fact that you don't care whether the statement is true or not, and in fact realize it is probably false, supports the argument that it was made with knowledge that it was false or with disregard for the truth.

4. ***The misrepresentation is made with the intention of inducing the other party to act or to refrain from acting.***

This occurs when a party intentionally tries, with a lie, to affect the behavior of the other party in a transaction, such as falsely telling a prospective purchaser the car was previously owned by Elvis Presley or that the painting was made by someone famous.

5. ***The other party has to rely on the lie.*** A party must rely on the misrepresentation in order to have a viable cause of action. For example, a buyer cannot sue the seller for lying about Elvis Presley being the former owner of the car if he doesn't buy the car or if he buys the car for an unrelated reason.

6. ***The lie must cause the other party to suffer damages.*** This means the plaintiff must suffer actual harm by the transaction. For example, a seller lies and says the painting was done by Monet and is worth a million dollars, though he knows this is not true. It turns out the painting was actually painted by a different famous painter, Van Gogh, and is worth a million dollars. The buyer still has suffered no economic injury as a result of the misrepresentation.

Unfair Competition

The law of unfair competition comprises all torts that cause an economic injury to a business through deceptive or wrongful business practices. Unfair competition consists of two broad categories. First, the term *unfair competition* includes those torts that are meant to confuse consumers concerning the source of a product. An example of this practice would be the labeling of an inferior product so that it looks like a much more expensive or higher quality competitor. The other category, *unfair trade practices,* comprises all other forms of unfair competition.

What constitutes an "unfair" act or practice varies with the context of the business, the action being examined, and the facts of each case. The most familiar example of unfair competition is *trademark infringement.* Another common form of unfair competition is *misappropriation.* Misappropriation involves the unauthorized use of intangible assets that are not protected by trademark or copyright laws. Other practices that are included in unfair competition include false advertising, "bait and switch" selling tactics, unauthorized substitution of one brand of goods for another, theft of trade secrets, breach of a restrictive covenant, use of confidential information by former employees to solicit customers, and false representation of products or services.

The law of unfair competition is mainly governed by state law. However, in the areas of trademarks, copyrights, and false advertising, federal law usually applies.

Part of the Federal Trade Commission's (FTC) responsibility is to protect consumers from deceptive trade practices. The FTC indirectly protects competitors because some deceptive trade practices, such as bait-and-switch tactics that injure consumers, also injure competing businesses. Some states have enacted their own laws dealing with specific types of unfair competition. Remember, if there is a conflict between federal and state law, the state law will be preempted.

Remedies for unfair competition may include getting the party at fault to pay monetary damages for their false representations, refunding any revenue lost as a result of the unfair business practice, a cessation of the unfair acts, or the payment of a large fine along with other government-sanctioned penalties.

Intentional Interference with a Business Contract or Relationship

The tort of interference with contractual relations permits a plaintiff to recover damages based on a claim that the defendant interfered with the plaintiff's contractual or other business relations. To be successful, the lack of justification in procuring the breach of contract or interference in the relationship requires a plaintiff to prove that the defendant's interference with the contract was improper. If a defendant's interference with a business relationship or contract is justified, then such interference is not actionable. Only improper interference is actionable.

Elements of intentional interference with a business contract are as follows:

- There is a contract or other economic relationship between the plaintiff and some third party with the possibility of future economic benefit to the plaintiff.

- The defendant knew of the contract or relationship.

- The defendant perpetrated intentional acts with the intent to disrupt the relationship.

- The defendant's actions actually disrupt the relationship.

- The plaintiff suffers damages proximately caused by the acts of the defendant.

There is an important limitation to the use of this tort as a remedy for the disruption of contractual relationships. It can only be asserted against a third party. Courts typically base this on the underlying policy of protecting the expectations of contracting parties from interference by outsiders who have no legitimate social or economic interest in the contractual relationship. Therefore, it limits the tort of interference with a contract to those who are not a party to the contract.

There is a threshold causation requirement to establish the tort of intentional interference with prospective economic advantage. What is required is proof that it is reasonably probable that the lost economic advantage would have been realized *but for* the defendant's interference.

In determining whether a defendant's interference in a business relationship is improper, courts may consider seven things:

1. The nature of the defendant's conduct
2. The defendant's motive

3. The interests of the plaintiff with which the defendant's conduct interferes

4. The interests sought to be advanced by the defendant

5. The social interests in protecting the freedom of action of the defendant and the contractual interests of the plaintiff

6. The proximity or remoteness of the defendant's conduct to the interference

7. The relations between the parties

Trespass to Realty (Trespass to Real Property)

Trespass to realty occurs when a party/defendant intentionally enters upon the land of another without permission. Although most people think of trespass as the traditional walking onto someone else's property without permission, parties may be sued for trespass whenever:

- They enter upon someone else's property without permission.

- They cause an object to be placed upon the land of another without the land owner's permission. (This can be anything from building a cabin to planting crops on someone else's property.)

- They stay on the land of another without permission after the landowner tells them to leave.

- They refuse to remove something from the land of another that they placed there after the landowner has instructed them to remove it.

HYPOTHETICAL CASE

You start a new company that produces automobiles that run on natural gas. The company does much better than expected and takes a large market share away from traditional auto companies. However, when you go to pick up your largest order ever for natural gas widgets used in the manufacture of your automobiles, the supplier tells you it can't (or won't) sell them to you. Your investigation reveals that Montezuma Motors has paid the supplier $3 million for its promise not to supply you with natural gas widgets.

Can you sue Montezuma Motors for intentional interference with a business relationship? Why or why not, and what must you prove to be successful?

HYPOTHETICAL CASE

You start a new company that produces a Web browser that directly competes with Microsoft's Internet Explorer. Several trade magazines tout the superiority of your browser, and sales really go up. However, just when things are taking off and you think you can pay off your business loan, sales plummet. You're at a loss to figure out why, until a customer asks why your company owns a subsidiary that hunts baby seals and clubs them to death to sell the fur to Japanese clothiers. When you get done uttering your expletives, you ask where the customer got such an outrageous idea. The customer says it was posted on a website for software developers by someone who claimed to work for your company. You take a look and verify that such a posting exists. Of course, you submit a posting that refutes the lie, but sales don't come back up.

What, if any, legal cause of action do you have? What can you do if your corporate "detectives" trace the false posting to an employee of Microsoft?

Chapter 9: Negligence

Introduction

What is negligence? Legally actionable *negligence* is doing something that a reasonably prudent person would not do, or the failure to do something that a reasonably prudent person would do under like circumstances. In negligence cases, the perpetrator doesn't intend the consequences of his act to harm anyone, but they do. Not every action that results in injury to a person results in a cause of action for negligence, however; only those actions that violate a duty of care that the law recognizes is owed someone will result in a viable lawsuit.

The negligence concept is centered on the principle that every individual should exercise a minimum degree of care so as not to cause harm to others. To determine negligence, the court looks at whether a person of ordinary prudence, in the same situation and possessing the same knowledge, would have anticipated (foreseen) that someone might be injured by his or her action (or inaction). If a person can foresee that their actions could result in harm to someone, then they should refrain from doing them since often the legal system will conclude so too.

Elements of Negligence

In most jurisdictions, to prove a negligence case a plaintiff must demonstrate five elements:

1. The defendant owed the plaintiff a duty of care.

2. The defendant breached that duty.

3. The defendant's conduct caused the plaintiff injury.

4. The injury/harm was foreseeable if the defendant breached the duty.

5. The plaintiff suffered an injury or was harmed.

Duty of Care

In some instances, a statute may specify a duty that is owed to a person in a particular situation. However, if no law imposes a *duty of care,* a defendant may be found to have breached this legal duty of care by failing to behave the way a "reasonable" person would behave in similar circumstances. A *reasonable person* is a person in the same occupation, situation, or circumstance as that of the defendant or person being examined.

In addition, a successful plaintiff must demonstrate that the defendant's failure to uphold his duty is the reason he or she suffered injury. There must be a factual connection between the action (or inaction) of the defendant and the injury suffered by the plaintiff. Finally, the type of harm caused must be foreseeable.

Generally, if the defendant can foresee injury to a particular person, then he has a duty of care to prevent it.

Here are two examples of a breached duty of care resulting in a negligence claim:

- A shopping mall owner fails to properly fix a faulty automatic entrance/exit door to the mall. A customer with their hands full of packages is injured when the door closes too quickly on them as they are walking through it. The mall owner may be found negligent for breaching a legal duty of care it owed its customers to ensure that they could safely enter and exit the mall through its automatic doors.

- A doctor breaches her duty to provide competent medical treatment by replacing the wrong knee of a patient who came to her for knee replacement surgery, thus causing an additional operation and loss of mobility.

Reasonable Person

When determining whether a duty has been breached, the law employs the hypothetical reasonable person. This reasonable person is used to determine if the defendant acted responsibly or negligently under the circumstances. A person acts negligently if he or she departs from the conduct expected of a reasonably prudent person acting under similar circumstances, with the same educational level, intelligence, age, and experience. The hypothetical reasonable person provides an objective by which the conduct of others is judged. In law, the reasonable person is not an average person or a typical person but a composite of the community's judgment as to how the typical community member should behave in situations that pose a threat of harm to the public. Even though a majority of people in the community may behave in a certain way, that behavior does not establish the standard of conduct of the reasonable person. For example, a majority of people in a community might run red lights, but running red lights still falls below the community's standards of safe conduct.

Causation

After establishing that the defendant owed the plaintiff a duty of care, and that the defendant breached that duty of care, the third element of negligence that must be proved is that it was the breach of the duty owed that is the cause of the plaintiff's injury. This isn't always easy as oftentimes it may appear that there are several ways to explain how the plaintiff received their injuries—but they will only succeed in their negligence case against the defendant if they can prove that it was the defendant's breach of duty that caused their injury. If the defendant is successful in convincing the jury (or judge if it is a judge trial) that some other action or failure is responsible for the plaintiff's injury, then the defendant will not be held liable. When determining causation, the law looks at two different types:

1. Cause-in-fact

2. Proximate (or legal) cause

Cause-in-Fact: The "But-For" Test

Cause-in-fact is determined by the *"but-for"* test. This test asks: But for the defendant's action, would the result have happened? For example, but for defendant's conduct in running the red light, would the collision have happened? Another example: But for the defendant's failure to look behind him when swinging the bat, he would not have hit the plaintiff in the face with the bat.

Proximate Cause

Proximate cause is different from cause-in-fact because it is not a direct cause-and-effect situation. Proximate cause is an event far enough removed, but sufficiently related, to be recognized as a cause of the injury. It is the initial act that sets off a natural and continuous sequence of events that produces injury. It is a natural chain of events leading to the injury.

For example, if a person is driving a car and swerves to avoid hitting a dog in the street and hits a tree, and the tree snaps and falls on a person walking on the sidewalk, did the driver of the car commit an act of negligence that injured the person walking? If the driver swerved and hit the person walking, that would be a cause-in-fact situation because the driver was the direct cause of the person's injuries. But here, the driver didn't directly cause the person's injuries; he hit the tree and the tree snapped and fell on the person, and it was the tree that caused their injuries. So, is it fair to hold the driver responsible? In situations like this, the jury will have to examine the duty of care the driver owed the pedestrian, whether he breached that duty, and whether the breach caused the pedestrian's injuries. They will be asked to apply the reasonable person standard and determine if the defendant should have foreseen that a failure to control his car in such a situation could result in an injury such as this.

However, if you roll a ball down the hill, then a stranger picks it up and throws it through a window, the window breaks, and the broken glass cuts a person who was sitting next to the window, are you the proximate cause of the person's injured arm?

Most courts would conclude that you are not. The reason is that there was an intervening act, that of the stranger picking up the ball and throwing it through the window, which is the proximate cause of the injury. Your act of rolling the ball down the hill would not, if left alone, have resulted in any injury. It did not set off a continuous sequence of *natural* events. Nor is it "but for you rolling the ball down the hill" that is controlling. In this situation, it is "but for the stranger picking up the ball and throwing it through the window" that is the reason for the person's injury.

Therefore, if an intervening act interrupts the natural chain of events and causes an accident and injury, the person who set the initial events in motion will not be found negligent; the person who intervened and caused the injury will.

In some jurisdictions, it may be sufficient for the plaintiff to show that the defendant's breach of duty made the risk of injury more probable. An example of this would be if a mechanic failed to inspect a vehicle's tires as required, then the worn tires caused the car to skid during rain, and it crossed the centerline and hit another car. The mechanic's failure to inspect the tires as required greatly increased the risk of this foreseeable accident.

Damages

In all negligence claims, a plaintiff must show they have suffered some harm or injury. Otherwise, there is no reason for the court to award them any compensation. *Compensatory damages* are designed to do just that, compensate a party for the injuries they have suffered as a result of the defendant's actions or inaction. In negligence cases, the injury suffered must be actual, not merely speculative. That means a negligence case claiming, "I would have been a professional skater if you hadn't broken my ankle," will not be successful in recovering money for the lost income the plaintiff *might* have made as a professional skater. However, if a person *is* a professional skater and can prove how much money he or she makes in that capacity, they may be successful in recovering their lost income.

Damages in negligence cases are usually compensatory. This may include compensation for loss of income, reimbursement for costs incurred because of the negligent act, or medical expenses. Some states also allow *punitive damages*, which are rare but can be awarded in addition to compensatory damages. These are awarded when a defendant's conduct is especially egregious and the jury wants to send a message to the defendant that it, and other similar parties (usually businesses), should cease the type of conduct that resulted in the lawsuit. Thus, punitive damage awards are usually very large since their purpose is to serve as a deterrent to others who might otherwise be tempted to engage in the same type of behavior (e.g., manufacturing of dangerous products).

Res Ipsa Loquitur

In most instances, the plaintiff has the burden of proving all of the elements of negligence. However, there is a legal doctrine that alleviates this necessity. That is the doctrine of *res ipsa loquitur*. In Latin, the phrase *res ipsa loquitur* means "the thing speaks for itself." This is used in situations in which it is argued that the situation makes it clear that the injury couldn't have occurred without negligence. "The circumstances speak for themselves—and the thing they speak is negligence." The wonderful thing about using this doctrine, from a plaintiff's point of view, is that once employed, it shifts the burden of proof, which typically falls on the plaintiff, to the defendant.

In most states, to prove res ipsa loquitur, a plaintiff must demonstrate:

1. The event or situation is the kind of thing that does not ordinarily happen without negligence.
2. The plaintiff had no part in causing the injury, and no third parties are to blame for the injury.
3. The defendant had a duty to the plaintiff that was violated, and this situation falls into conduct that violates that duty.

If these three elements can be proven, then proof of negligence through causation is not required, and *the defendant must prove that they were not negligent* in order to avoid liability.

Defenses to Negligence

As with all causes of action, the law recognizes certain defenses that will exculpate the defendant. In negligence cases, there are three main defenses:

1. Assumption of the risk

2. Contributory negligence

3. Comparative negligence

Assumption of the Risk

Assumption of the risk is where a person voluntarily engages in an activity that involves an obvious risk of injury. Some activities in which an individual is assumed to have accepted a risk of injury are skiing, hang gliding, and horseback riding.

Contributory Negligence

If plaintiffs, through their own negligence, contributed to cause the injury they suffered as a result of defendant's negligence, the court may preclude any recovery from the defendant. For example, if a pedestrian crosses a road at a place other than a designated crosswalk, isn't paying attention, and is hit by a driver who is also driving carelessly, the pedestrian has contributed to her own injury.

At common law, contributory negligence was an absolute defense to a negligence claim. If a defendant successfully raised the contributory negligence defense, he or she would be able to avoid any liability for negligence. This often led to an injustice, wherein the negligence of a plaintiff or claimant was slight in comparison with that of the defendant. As a result, most jurisdictions in the United States have modified this doctrine, either by court decision or by legislation, and have changed the name to comparative negligence.

Comparative Negligence

Comparative negligence was developed as a fairer way of dealing with the situation of plaintiffs contributing to their own injuries than the "all or nothing" position of contributory negligence. In comparative negligence, rather than awarding no damages at all to a plaintiff, the jury reduces the compensation awarded by a percentage that reflects the degree to which the plaintiff's negligence contributed to the damages. For example, if the jury determines that the plaintiff is 30 percent at fault for the injuries received because she failed to cross the street at the crosswalk, the plaintiff's recovery will be reduced by that amount, and she will recover for the 70 percent of the injuries attributable to the careless driver.

Minors

A minor (person 17 years of age or younger) is not held to the same standard of care as an adult. A minor is required to exercise the degree of care that ordinarily is exercised by minors of like maturity, intelligence, and capacity under similar circumstances.

Strict Liability

Strict Liability occurs when the law imposes liability without the requirement of proving fault. In these instances, a local, state, or federal statute holds an individual or entity liable without fault if three conditions can be proven:

1. The activity involves a serious risk of harm to people or property

2. The activity is so inherently dangerous that it cannot ever be safely undertaken, and

3. The activity is not usually performed in the immediate community.

Examples of such activities may include the use of explosives or keeping wild and dangerous animals in urban areas. Legislative bodies may, and do, make other offenses strict liability to avoid having to prove fault even when they do not necessarily involve a dangerous activity. Examples of these are parking citations, statutory rape, and drunk driving.

Strict Liability for Animals

Traditionally, strict liability has been applied for damages caused by animals. Because animals are not governed by a conscience and can cause a great deal of harm if not restrained, those who keep animals have a duty to restrain them. In most jurisdictions, the general rule is that keepers of all animals, including domesticated animals, are strictly liable for the damage caused when their animals trespass on the property of another. Owners of dogs and cats, however, are not liable for their pets' trespasses unless the owners have been negligent or unless strict liability is imposed by statute or ordinance.

For purposes of liability for harm other than trespass, the law distinguishes between domesticated and wild animals. The keeper of domesticated animals, which include dogs, cats, cattle, sheep, and horses, is strictly liable for the harm they cause only if the keeper had actual knowledge that the animal had the particular trait or propensity that caused the harm. The trait must be a potentially harmful one, such as biting, and the harm must correspond to the knowledge. In the case of dogs, however, some jurisdictions have enacted statutes that impose absolute or strict liability for dog bites without requiring prior knowledge of the dog's viciousness.

Keepers of species that are normally considered wild in that region are strictly liable for the harm caused by these animals if they escape, regardless of whether the animal is known to be dangerous. Because such animals are known to revert to their natural tendencies, they are considered wild no matter how well trained or domesticated they are.

HYPOTHETICAL CASE

Sarah Storekeeper runs a boutique business selling handmade soaps and candles. She often makes the products at a work area in the store so her customers can watch. This was a very good way of attracting people into the store. One day, a woman and her five-year-old child were watching Sarah make candles, and the woman and Sarah became engaged in a discussion about the difference in candle-making techniques. Neither one of them noticed as the woman's five-year-old son grabbed the container of melted wax, tipping it over, and spilling its contents on his face and neck.

The child's mother filed a lawsuit on behalf of her son, claiming Sarah's negligence resulted in $100,000 of medical bills and permanent scarring and disfigurement to her child.

What are the arguments on behalf of the mother that support the claim of negligence against Sarah? What arguments may Sarah raise in her defense?

Chapter 10: Product Liability

Introduction

What is product liability? *Product liability* is the law that holds manufacturers, distributors, wholesalers, suppliers, retailers, and others who make products available to the public responsible for the injuries those products cause.

The claims most commonly made when a consumer product fails to work properly resulting in product liability cases are based on negligence, strict liability, breach of warranty, and consumer protection statutory claims. Most product liability cases are tried at the state level, and the elements necessary to prove them vary from state to state. There are three types of defects that might cause injury and give rise to legal liability:

- Design defect

- Manufacturing defect

- Failure to warn (marketing defect)

These claims may succeed even when products are used incorrectly by the consumer, as long as the misuse, and therefore injury, was foreseeable by the manufacturer. Under any theory of liability, a plaintiff in a product liability case must prove that the product that caused his or her injury was defective and that the defect made the product unreasonably dangerous.

Design Defects

Design defects are present in a product from the beginning, even before it is manufactured. It occurs because something in the design of the product is inherently unsafe. A design defect is some flaw in the intentional design of a product that makes it unreasonably dangerous. Thus, a design defect exists in a product from its inception. For example, a vehicle that is designed with only three wheels might be considered defectively designed because it tips over too easily. Design defect claims often require a showing of negligence; however, strict liability may be imposed for an unreasonably dangerous design if the plaintiff can present evidence that there was a cost-effective alternative design that would have prevented the risk of injury. In some cases, if a product was so unreasonably dangerous that it never should have been manufactured, the availability of a safer design might not be necessary to hold the designer liable.

Manufacturing Defects

Manufacturing defects are those that occur during a product's manufacture or assembly. A product has a manufacturing defect when the product does not conform to the designer's or manufacturer's own specifications. Manufacturing defect cases are often the easiest to prove because the manufacturer's own design or marketing standards can be used to show that the product was defective. Still, proving how or why the flaw or defect occurred can be difficult, so the law applies two different doctrines in product liability cases to help plaintiffs recover, even if they cannot prove a manufacturer was negligent.

The first doctrine, described in chapter 9 and known as *res ipsa loquitur,* shifts the burden of proof in some product liability cases to the defendant. *Res ipsa loquitur,* meaning in Latin "the thing speaks for itself," stands for the proposition that the product defect would not exist unless someone was negligent. When the doctrine is successfully invoked, the plaintiff is not required to prove how the defendant was negligent; rather, the burden shifts to the defendant, who is required to prove that it was *not* negligent.

The second rule that helps plaintiffs in product liability cases is that of strict liability. If strict liability applies, the plaintiff does not need to prove that a manufacturer was negligent but only that the product was defective. By eliminating the issue of manufacturer fault, the concept of no-fault, or "strict," liability allows plaintiffs to recover where they otherwise might not. A manufacturer may be found liable in strict liability cases even when the defendant's misuse of the product caused the injury if it can be demonstrated that a reasonable person would or should have foreseen that the product could have been misused in such a way.

Marketing Defects

Finally, marketing defects are flaws in the way a product is marketed, such as improper labeling, insufficient instructions, or inadequate safety warnings, or the failure to warn consumers of a product's hidden dangers. A negligent or intentional misrepresentation of a product may also give rise to a product liability claim. Manufacturers are expected to warn of any foreseeable dangers in using its product, even dangers that arise from the foreseeable misuse of its product.

In addition, some state laws allow claims based on the manufacturer's failure to warn of a product's dangers. These claims are based on negligence.

Strict liability cases are not dependent on how careful the plaintiff was in using the product. In product liability cases, a defendant is liable when it is shown that the product is defective. Whether the manufacturer or supplier exercised great care in designing and manufacturing its product is irrelevant. If the plaintiff can demonstrate that there is a defect in the product that caused him/her harm, the company will be liable for it.

The law of product liability is found mainly in common law and in the Uniform Commercial Code (UCC). Article 2 of the UCC deals with the sales of goods, and it has been adopted by most states.

Responsible Parties

For product liability to arise, the product must have been sold in the marketplace. In the past, a contractual relationship, known as *privity of contract,* had to exist between the person injured by a product and the supplier of the product in order for the injured person to be able to sue and recover damages. However, in many states today, that requirement no longer exists, and the injured person does not have to be the purchaser of the product in a product liability case. Any person who foreseeably could have been injured by a defective product can recover for his or her injuries, as long as the product was sold to someone in the marketplace.

Liability for a product defect can rest with any party in the product's chain of distribution, such as the manufacturer, wholesaler, a retail seller of the product, or a party who assembles or installs the product. For strict liability to apply, the sale of a product must be made in the regular course of the defendant's business. Thus, someone who sells a product at a garage sale or who makes and sells items as a hobby probably would not be held liable in a product liability lawsuit.

Strict Liability in Product Liability

Many states have enacted comprehensive product liability statutes. These statutory provisions can vary greatly. The U.S. Department of Commerce has promulgated a Model Uniform Products Liability Act (MUPLA) for voluntary use by the states, and several have adopted it. There is no federal product liability law. Most product liability claims are not based on negligence but, rather, on strict liability. Strict liability is also discussed in Chapter 9.

In product liability cases involving injuries caused by manufactured goods, strict liability statutes have had a major impact on litigation. In 1963, the California Supreme Court became the first court to adopt strict tort liability for defective products. In strict liability cases, the injured plaintiffs must prove the product caused them harm, but they do not have to prove exactly how the manufacturer was negligent. Purchasers of the product, as well as injured bystanders and others with no direct relationship with the product, may sue for damages caused by the product.

Typically, product liability claims are based not on negligence but on strict liability. Under the theory of strict liability, a manufacturer is held liable regardless of whether it acted negligently. Strict liability allows recovery for an injured party who might not be able to prove what a manufacturer did or did not do wrong in the design or manufacture of its product that is the specific cause of the plaintiff's injury. The public policy behind these statutes is that the complexity of today's products makes it all but impossible for an injured party to meet the burden of proof required in a negligence-based cause of action, which would make them show, by a preponderance of the evidence, the specific way the product failed and exactly how the failure caused their injury. In strict liability cases, the statute basically says "a person who buys a toaster has a right to expect the toaster to toast bread and not to electrocute them. If the toaster electrocutes them when they attempt to retrieve toast from the toaster, the product is defective since it is not performing as a reasonable consumer has a right to expect it to perform." Public policy also presumes that a manufacturer with "deep pockets" is in a better position to absorb the cost of compensating injured consumers and that this expense is factored in when setting the price for its products.

In strict liability product liability cases, the inquiry is focused on the product itself rather than on the behavior of the manufacturer (as in negligence cases). Under strict liability, the manufacturer is liable if the product is defective, even if the manufacturer was not negligent in making that product defective. Because strict liability carries a harsh penalty for a manufacturer, which is forced to pay for all injuries caused by its products even if it is not at fault, strict liability is applied only to manufacturing defects (i.e., when a product varies from its intended design) and almost never applied to design and warning defects.

In those rare instances in which a jurisdiction has a strict liability product defect case, an injured party must prove that the product was defective, that the defect proximately caused the injury, and that the defect rendered the product unreasonably dangerous. A plaintiff may recover damages even if the seller has exercised all possible care in the preparation and sale of the product.

Product Liability and Breach of Warranty

Warranties are legal promises by a manufacturer or seller concerning a product purchased during a commercial transaction. Unlike negligence claims, which focus on the manufacturer's conduct or strict liability claims, which focus on the condition of the product, warranty claims focus on how these issues relate to a commercial transaction. Warranty claims commonly require privity between the injured party and the manufacturer or seller and are therefore based on contract. Breach of warranty-based product liability claims usually focus on one of three things: (1) breach of an express warranty, (2) breach of an implied warranty of merchantability, or (3) breach of an implied warranty of fitness for a particular purpose. Additionally, claims involving real estate may take the form of an implied warranty of habitability. Express warranty claims focus on express statements by the manufacturer or the seller concerning the product (e.g., "This computer can run three programs at once"). The various implied warranties cover those expectations common to all products unless they are specifically disclaimed by the manufacturer or the seller. Warranties are discussed in greater detail in Chapter 11.

Example

Mike bought a bottle of hair dye from Wally's Drug Store to color his gray hair. As soon as he put the dye on, he received a phone call. Mike talked on the phone for half an hour longer than the instructions said to leave the dye on. By the time he hung up the phone, his head was burning, and when he washed the dye off, it took his skin with it. Mike spent several days in the hospital, followed by years of surgery to repair the damage—and he was permanently bald. Mike hired an attorney to file a product liability lawsuit against the manufacturer of the hair dye. Mike contended that the hair dye company failed to warn consumers about the dangers of leaving the product on for more than the recommended five minutes.

The first consideration for Mike and his attorney is a design flaw. Was there something inherently dangerous about the components of the hair dye product? Product liability starts with the very first component providers, which in this scenario would be the chemicals used. Mike's attorney would have to prove that the chemicals used were inherently dangerous and that the company was aware of this and did nothing to correct it. Product liability lawsuits claiming design defects are notoriously difficult to prove, since many companies spend months or years testing their designs and products before releasing them to the public.

Mike's case might also be considered a manufacturing liability. The chemicals used may have been acceptable, but the dye company's manufacturing process may have used too much of them or combined them in a way that made them toxic. Many product liability lawsuits are based on defects caused by poor manufacturing practices or a lack of quality control. The plaintiff's attorney may have to provide expert testimony on the proper construction of a product and compare it with the defective product that caused the injury or damage. In Mike's case, it would have to prove that the chemicals used in Mike's hair dye were significantly stronger than industry standards. This is how many product liability cases based on manufacturing defects are won.

The third line of reasoning involving product liability is called "failure to warn." Companies have a duty to warn consumers about known hazards and dangers surrounding the normal, or even abnormal, use of their products. Usually, a warning label is placed in a conspicuous area of the product or accompanying literature, which details the known hazards. Some of these warnings may seem obvious, but their presence helps companies defend themselves against product liability claims. In many states, if the plaintiff is found even 1 percent at fault for the accident that caused the harm, the company cannot be held liable.

In Mike's case, his attorney can make the argument that the hair dye company failed to warn consumers that leaving the product on for more than five minutes could result in serious physical injury. Even if Mike's own actions contributed to his injury, some states would allow the argument that the dye company should have included a *"Do not leave on hair more than five minutes"* warning on the bottle.

Common Defenses to Product Liability Claims

A defense often raised in product liability cases is that the plaintiff has not sufficiently identified the supplier of the product that allegedly caused the injury. A plaintiff must be able to connect the product with the party(ies) responsible for manufacturing or supplying it. There is an exception to this rule, known as the *market share liability exception, which applies in cases involving defective medications.* Where a plaintiff cannot identify which of the pharmaceutical companies supplying a particular drug supplied the drug he or she took, each manufacturer will be held liable according to its percentage of sales in the area where the injury occurred.

Another defense a manufacturer might raise is that the plaintiff substantially altered the product after it left the manufacturer's control and that this alteration is what caused the plaintiff's injury.

Finally, if a plaintiff misused the product in an *unforeseeable* way, and it is this misuse of the product that caused their injuries, the defendant may be absolved of any liability.

Unavoidably Unsafe Products

Some products simply cannot be made totally safe without losing their usefulness. For example, a chainsaw that is made completely safe so it could never injure anyone would be useless for its intended purpose. For these products, the law assumes that users and consumers are in the best position to minimize their risk of injury. Thus, while a product might not be deemed unreasonably dangerous, manufacturers and suppliers of unavoidably unsafe products must give proper warnings of the dangers and risks their products pose so that consumers can make informed decisions concerning whether or not to use them.

HYPOTHETICAL CASE

Dr. Wizard is a famous heart surgeon who designed a new heart valve that Pacer Company built and sold. Pacer Co. successfully tested the new valve on more than two hundred male patients, aged 70 and older, before selling the new valve in the medical marketplace. Many heart surgeons used the Wizard heart valve in their elderly patients. Art Athlete contracted a virus that seriously damaged one of his heart valves, and his heart surgeon replaced his heart valve with a Wizard heart valve. Art was an avid runner, and once his doctor told him he was well enough to run again, he began his usual running regime. Six months later, Art ran in the Boston Marathon, but halfway through the race he collapsed and died. An autopsy revealed that the Wizard heart valve had jammed, thus stopping the flow of blood into his heart and causing Art's death.

Art's widow wants to sue Dr. Wizard and Pacer. What will her claims against them be, and what are the facts that support them? What defenses will Dr. Wizard and Pacer Co. raise?

HYPOTHETICAL CASE

Skywalker Mall Inc. builds a skateboarding park as part of its newest and grandest mall complex. The skateboard park is designed by Hudino, one of the premier skateboarders in the country, who comes to the park and christens its opening with a demonstration of his skateboarding skills. During this demonstration, he shows off his newest trick, which is a double backwards flip. The crowd is amazed! Hudino says he was able to pull off this great feat only because of the design of the mall's skateboarding park. He states he constructed it especially so he could get the "air" to do this trick. One of the members of the audience is a 10-year-old boy named Hank, who is an avid skateboarder and fan of Hudino. Two months later, Hank tries to duplicate Hudino's double backflip and crashes. He suffers a broken neck and is paralyzed for life. Hank's parents sue Skywalker Mall Inc. and Hudino, claiming the park's defective design is responsible for their son's terrible injury. What are the arguments for, and against, their lawsuit?

Chapter 11: Warranties

Introduction

What are warranties? A *warranty* is a guarantee that a product or service sold is as factually stated or legally implied by the seller. Warranties are promises that the good(s) purchased will perform as the buyer reasonably expects. In its effort to facilitate business transactions, Article 2 of the Uniform Commercial Code (UCC) recognizes several different warranties. It also allows businesses to disclaim these warranties, but it states how businesses must do so for the disclaimers to be effective.

Express Warranty

Express warranties are affirmative promises about the quality and features of the goods being sold. For example, if a company claims that a digital camera is "waterproof to 50 feet," or that a car gets "40 miles per gallon on the highway," these are express warranties.

Express warranties under the UCC include more than just affirmative statements. A description of the goods being sold or samples shown to the buyer also form an express warranty. If the buyer is shown a floor sample of the kind of television she wants to buy, this sample is an express warranty that the television actually sold to her is the same type and quality as the floor sample she observed.

An express warranty can arise in one of three ways:

1. Oral or written representations

2. A detailed description of the product

3. A sample or model creating the impression that all goods purchased will conform to the sample

Note: If the seller gives an express warranty to a buyer, the seller may not legally include language in the purchase contract that disclaims or counteracts the warranty.

Implied Warranty

The UCC also creates a second kind of warranty, called an *implied warranty*. As the name suggests, an implied warranty is made regardless of whether it is specifically mentioned.

The implied warranties created by the UCC ended the old rule of caveat emptor, which literally meant "let the buyer beware." Implied warranties allow buyers to purchase goods and be confident they meet certain minimum standards.

There are two implied warranties the UCC creates:

1. An implied warranty of "merchantability" of the goods being sold

2. An implied warranty of fitness for a particular purpose.

Implied Warranty of Merchantability

Under the UCC's definition of *merchantability*, goods must be at least of average quality, properly packaged and labeled, and fit for the ordinary purposes they are intended to serve.

For example, a watch would have to be at least of average quality as compared to other watches in the same price range, it must tell time, and it cannot come in a package labeled "Rolex" unless it is, in fact, a Rolex watch.

The application of the implied warranty of merchantability is limited to sellers of "goods of that kind," which refers to the kind of goods the seller usually sells in the marketplace. A seller does not make an implied warranty of merchantability when it sells goods of a kind that it does not normally sell. For example, a store that sells bicycles and bicycle supplies warrants that the bicycles it sells are merchantable (i.e. can be ridden as bicycles) because bicycles are the kind of goods it typically sells. However, if the bicycle store purchases one too many cash registers and sells the one it doesn't need to the store next door, the cash register is not subject to an implied warranty of merchantability because the bicycle store does not normally sell cash registers. But if the bicycle store makes an express warranty regarding the cash register, such as, "This cash register is brand new and will last at least a year," it will be held to that express warranty.

Fitness for a Particular Purpose

The implied warranty of fitness for a particular purpose applies if the seller knows, or has reason to know, that the buyer will be using the goods he is buying for a specific purpose. If the seller knows the purpose for which the goods are to be used, the seller impliedly warrants that the goods being sold are suitable for that specific purpose.

For example, a watch salesperson may sell watches that tell time and are suitable for everyday use and are therefore merchantable. But if the salesperson knows the buyer wants to use the watch for scuba diving, the salesperson also impliedly warrants that the watch sold to the buyer is waterproof and suitable for that purpose.

The rationale behind the implied warranty of fitness for a particular purpose is that buyers typically rely on the seller's knowledge and expertise to help them find the specific product that meets their particular need. A buyer who goes into a hardware store to buy a snowblower relies on the hardware salesperson to find the snowblower that fits his specific requirements. The rationale is that it is unfair to allow a seller to sell something that the salesperson knows will not do the job, telling the buyer later that it is not the seller's fault it did not work for the purpose purchased.

Limited Liability Clause

Most sellers try to limit the scope of the warranties they make to avoid liability for as many potential problems as possible. As a result, they include clauses in their sales agreement that place conditions on the warranties they provide. These warranty-limiting clauses are referred to as *limited liability clauses.*

A limited liability warranty is a warranty with certain conditions and limitations on the parts covered, type of damage covered, and/or time period for which the warranty is good.

Following is an example of a limited liability warranty clause:

Mega Co. warrants that for a period of ninety (90) days from the date of shipment from Mega Co: (i) the media on which the Software is furnished will be free of defects in materials and workmanship under normal use; and (ii) the Software substantially conforms to its published specifications. Except for the foregoing, the Software is provided AS IS. This limited warranty extends only to Customer as the original licensee. Customer's exclusive remedy and the entire liability of Mega Co. and its suppliers under this limited warranty will be, at Mega Co.'s or its service center's option, repair, replacement, or refund of the Software if reported (or, upon request, returned) to the party supplying the Software to Customer. In no event does Mega Co. warrant that the Software is error free or that Customer will be able to operate the Software without problems or interruptions.

Warranty Disclaimers

The UCC allows sellers to disclaim both express and implied warranties on goods they sell, within certain limits. These warranty disclaimers are usually enforced by the courts unless doing so is determined to be unreasonable under the circumstances.

A seller who disclaims a warranty under the UCC must do so according to the terms specified in the UCC. A general statement that there are "no warranties, express or implied" is usually ruled ineffective. How express a disclaimer needs to be depends on the kind of warranty being disclaimed.

An express warranty must be expressly disclaimed. A disclaimer that disclaims the implied warranty of merchantability must specifically mention merchantability in the disclaimer.

If a seller wants to disclaim all implied warranties, the seller should do so by stating that the good is being sold "as is," or by using some other phrase that makes it plain to the buyer there are no implied warranties.

The UCC also requires that all disclaimers of implied warranties be in writing. Hiding a warranty disclaimer in the small print of a lengthy sales contract will likely not be enforced, though, because the UCC also requires that a disclaimer be conspicuous. A section of a contract is conspicuous if it clearly stands out from the rest of the contract and draws the eye of the reader to it. Common ways to make contract provisions conspicuous are to put them in bold type, different colored type, larger type, or in all capital letters. Therefore, all disclaimers of warranties should be in writing, should be conspicuous, and should specifically mention the warranty being disclaimed.

Many states require that a buyer have some meaningful remedy if the goods he or she receives are defective, so they will not enforce a total disclaimer of all warranties. Just as a disclaimer that is too broad will not be enforced, neither will a disclaimer that takes all rights away from the buyer. In addition, most states have consumer protection statutes for the purchase of consumer goods. These statutes often provide the buyer with remedies other than those provided by the UCC and also often provide that a consumer's rights under the statute cannot be abridged by means of a disclaimer.

If, after a reasonable opportunity to inspect, the buyer fails to reject the goods, the buyer will be deemed to have accepted them. The failure to reject goods in a reasonable time constitutes acceptance.

Following is an example of a warranty disclaimer:

DISCLAIMER.

EXCEPT AS SPECIFIED IN THIS WARRANTY, ALL EXPRESS OR IMPLIED CONDITIONS, REPRESENTATIONS, AND WARRANTIES INCLUDING, WITHOUT LIMITATION, ANY

IMPLIED WARRANTY OF MERCHANTABILITY, FITNESS FOR A PARTICULAR PURPOSE, NONINFRINGEMENT, OR ARISING FROM A COURSE OF DEALING, USAGE, OR TRADE PRACTICE, ARE HEREBY EXCLUDED TO THE EXTENT ALLOWED BY APPLICABLE LAW.

IN NO EVENT WILL MEGA CO. OR ITS SUPPLIERS BE LIABLE FOR ANY LOST REVENUE, PROFIT, OR DATA, OR FOR SPECIAL, INDIRECT, CONSEQUENTIAL, INCIDENTAL, OR PUNITIVE DAMAGES HOWEVER CAUSED AND REGARDLESS OF THE THEORY OF LIABILITY ARISING OUT OF THE USE OF OR INABILITY TO USE THE SOFTWARE EVEN IF MEGA OR ITS SUPPLIERS HAVE BEEN ADVISED OF THE POSSIBILITY OF SUCH DAMAGES. In no event shall MEGA CO.'s or its suppliers' liability to Customer, whether in contract, tort (including negligence), or otherwise, exceed the price paid by Customer. The foregoing limitations shall apply even if the above-stated warranty fails of its essential purpose. SOME STATES DO NOT ALLOW LIMITATION OR EXCLUSION OF LIABILITY OR CONSEQUENTIAL OR INCIDENTAL DAMAGES.

Extended Warranties

In retail business, an *extended warranty* refers to a guarantee of the reliability of a product under conditions of ordinary use. It is called an "extended" warranty if it covers defects that arise sometime after the date of sale. If the product malfunctions within a stipulated amount of time after the purchase, the manufacturer or distributor typically provides the customer with a replacement, repair, or refund. Extended warranties do not cover the abuse, malicious destruction, or "acts of God" that damage or destroy the product. Automobile manufacturers often make extended warranties part of the marketing of their product; e.g., "This car has a 60,000-mile powertrain warranty!"

Magnuson-Moss Warranty Act

The *Magnuson-Moss Act* is a federal law that outlines the specific guidelines and requirements that manufacturers and sellers must follow. It requires them to disclose detailed information about their warranties to consumers. The act provides consumers protections and the right to receive compensation for defective products, and it requires manufacturers to provide meaningful warranty coverage.

The act contains the "three strikes" principle, which places a limit on the number of times a manufacturer can try to fix a defect before having to compensate the customer. What the three strikes principle says is that if a customer has returned a product for repair three times within a specified period of time and the seller has failed to repair it, the seller must either replace the product with a new one or refund the purchase price of the product. Quite a few states have used this statute as a model for their own consumer protection laws.

Under the Magnuson-Moss Act, when a consumer buys an item that is broken or missing pieces before it was even taken out of the package, it is a defective product and can be returned to the seller for refund or replacement, regardless of what the seller's "return policy" might state (this is not true for secondhand or "as-is" sales).

Also, if the product fails prematurely, it may be considered defective when it was sold and could then be returned for a refund or replacement. If the seller dishonors the warranty, then the buyer has a breach of contract claim.

Remedies for Breach of Warranty

When the seller has breached a warranty, the law recognizes three remedies:

1. The buyer can return the product and receive a refund of the purchase price.

2. The seller can replace the product with a new one.

3. The seller can have the product repaired.

HYPOTHETICAL CASE

Sam goes to Computer Sales, Inc. and talks to a salesperson about his desire to purchase a new computer that he plans to use in his startup graphics design business. The salesperson talks him into buying a computer that is on sale. When Sam sets it up in his new office, he finds the machine doesn't have enough memory or speed to run the programs required for his business. What warranty, if any, has Computer Sales, Inc. breached in selling the computer to Sam?

Chapter 12: Contracts

Introduction

What is a contract? A *contract* is an exchange of promises between parties that the law will enforce. The basis of every contract is an agreement. In an agreement, one party makes an offer, and the other party accepts it. The party who makes the offer is the offeror and the party to whom the offer is made (and who has the power to accept the offer) is the offeree. To reach an agreement, the parties must have a "meeting of the minds." To have a meeting of the minds, the parties must understand each other and intend to reach an agreement. In addition, something of value must be exchanged between the parties. The thing that is of value, and is bargained for, is the consideration for the contract.

Sources of Contract Law

There are three sources of contract law in the United States:

1. Common law

2. Uniform Commercial Code (UCC). Specifically, Article 2 of the UCC deals with commercial sales contracts.

3. Restatement of contracts

Common law developed the equitable doctrines of express and implied contracts, quasi-contracts, promissory estoppel, and unjust enrichment. These doctrines are used to ensure a fair resolution to claims even when all the elements necessary to make a legal contract are not demonstrated.

The Uniform Commercial Code governs commercial transactions for the sale of goods, negotiable instruments, and secured transactions.

The Restatement of Contracts is a legal treatise written by scholars who are experts in the field of contract law.

The Elements of a Contract

There are three basic components of a contract:

1. The Agreement, which consists of the offer by one party and the acceptance of the other

2. Consideration, the bargained-for exchange between the parties—i.e. something of value that is given or given up, that each party was not otherwise obligated to do

3. Legal capacity to enter into the contract, the legal ability to enter into a binding agreement

The Offer

An offer is an act or statement that proposes definite terms and permits the other party to create a contract by accepting those terms. It is a manifestation of intent to be contractually bound upon acceptance by another party. It is not enough for the offeror (person making the offer) to intend to enter into an agreement. The terms of the offer must be definite. An offer creates in the offeree (person receiving the offer) the power to form a contract by accepting the offer. For example, if your neighbor tells you, "I will pay you $50 if you agree by Thursday to mow my lawn this Saturday," he has given you the authority to create a contract by saying, "I agree," by Thursday.

Termination of Offers

An offer may be terminated any time before it is accepted. If the offer is terminated or revoked, it can no longer be accepted, and no contract can be made. An offer may be terminated in one of five ways:

1. Revocation by the offeror

2. Rejection by the offeree

3. Death or incapacity of the offeror

4. Destruction or subsequent illegality of the subject matter of the contract

5. Lapse of time or the failure of other conditions stated in the offer

Also, if a person makes a counteroffer, it is considered a rejection of the offer and is itself a new offer.

Acceptance

Traditionally, the nature of the contract has dictated whether the offer can be accepted by a return promise or by actual performance of the promised act. To accept an offer, the offeree must say or do something to accept. Acceptance of the offer must be communicated to the offeror for it to be effective. This can be done in person or by phone, e-mail, letter, or fax. The modern and UCC view of acceptance is that an offer invites acceptance *by any means reasonable* under the circumstances, unless it is otherwise indicated by language or circumstances. This rule modifies the old common law rule called the mirror image rule, which held that an offer could only be considered accepted if the acceptance "mirrored" exactly the conditions stated in the offer. For example, Mega Co. offered to purchase 1,000 yellow widgets from Minor Co. for $1 each so long as they could be delivered by June 1. If Minor Co. accepted the offer with the additional statement that the widgets would be brown instead of yellow, the mirror image rule would not consider that to be an acceptance since Minor Co.'s acceptance did not exactly "mirror" the offer made by Mega Co. Even though the change of the color of the widgets is probably not important (material) to the contract, the parties would have to treat the change as a rejection of Mega Co.'s offer. The UCC recognized how these situations would greatly impair business transactions, so it modified the common law rule so that non-material terms could be altered and the offer could be accepted when conducting business transactions.

Acceptance is considered effective as soon as the acceptance is out of the offeree's control. For example, once a person puts an acceptance letter in the mail or hits the "send" button on an e-mail, a contract has been formed.

It should also be noted that silence cannot be used as acceptance to create a contract. For example, there is no contract if your friend leaves you a voicemail message that says, "If I don't hear from you by tomorrow, you agree to bring my car from Detroit to Marquette for $500."

Consideration

A promise must be supported by consideration in order to be enforceable. Without an exchange of mutual obligations, there is no contract. Consideration is a bargained-for performance or return promise, which is given by one party in exchange for the promise given by the other party.

Consideration is that which is bargained for in the contract. It is something of value that is exchanged between the parties. For consideration to exist, there must be a bargained exchange in which each party incurs a legal detriment. A legal detriment exists where the party engages in an act that the party was not previously obligated to perform, or the party refrains from exercising a legal right. The thing bargained for can be a benefit to the promisor or a detriment to the promisee.

Consideration does not have to be furnished by or to the parties themselves, as long as it is part of the bargained exchange. For example, someone might say, "If you shovel my grandmother's driveway, I'll pay you $25." However, if a person were to say, "When you turn 21, I'll buy you a beer," there is no contract. Why not? Because you're going to turn 21 regardless of whether someone buys you a beer. You are not doing anything other than what you will do regardless, so there is no bargained-for exchange. If nothing is exchanged, there is no consideration, and if there is no consideration, there is no contract.

Consideration can be anything someone might bargain for, but for the contract to be legal, the consideration must be legal.

What Makes a Contract Enforceable?

To be enforceable, a contract needs four things:

1. *An agreement.* To have an agreement, one party must make an offer, which the other party accepts.

2. *Consideration.* For there to be consideration, something of value must be exchanged between the parties.

3. *Legal subject matter.* For the contract to be legal, it must be undertaken for a lawful purpose.

4. *Parties with capacity.* For the parties to have the capacity to enter into a contract, they must be adults and of sound mind.

In addition, if a contract does not contain enough information to allow the parties to know what is expected of them, it will fail for indefiniteness.

Mirror Image Rule

The mirror image rule requires that acceptance be made on precisely the same terms as the offer. If any term is changed, it is considered a counteroffer. Today, many jurisdictions follow the UCC rule, which is more flexible.

UCC Rule

The UCC dramatically alters the mirror image rule for the sale of goods between merchants. It states that acceptance is valid even when the offeror inserts additional or different terms in the contract. Under the UCC, merchants are treated differently than consumers. If different terms in a UCC-controlled contract cancel each other out, neither term is considered included in the contract.

Illusory Promises

An *illusory promise* is something that appears to be a promise but really isn't one. Thus, it is an illusion, and is no promise at all. Without a valid promise, there is no consideration, and without consideration, there is no contract. For example, if Sally tells Sam she'll sell him her car for $500 if she can't sell it to anyone else for more and Sam says okay, there is no contract. Why not? Because there is no consideration for the contract. Sam has not given anything to secure the agreement. Sally may or may not offer him the car for $500 in the future, and since Sam gave nothing, there is no consideration.

Also, if one party makes a promise based on something the other party has already done, there is no exchange, and there is no consideration that supports a contract. As far as the law is concerned, past consideration is no consideration at all. An example of this would be a promise like, "Since you sacked the quarterback in last week's game, I'll buy you dinner." There is no consideration in this agreement. Nothing was given or bargained for. The service was already performed before the promise was made. As such, the promise was not made with the intention of inducing any act or forbearance.

Contract Doctrines

In some instances, even though all the elements necessary for a legally enforceable contract are lacking, it would be unfair to allow one party to benefit by taking advantage of the other. As a result, common law courts recognized certain situations in which fairness required the imposition of an equitable remedy. Promissory estoppel and quasi-contract are two legal doctrines that courts recognize when justice requires.

Promissory Estoppel

Promissory estoppel is used when a party thinks it has a contract and can demonstrate both inducement and detrimental reliance. In promissory estoppel cases, the court determines that the only way to avoid injustice is to enforce the promise made, even when there is no real contract. Promissory estoppel allows one party to enforce a promise even though the contract fails because it lacks consideration. For example, if an employer promises an employee it will pay for her health insurance every month if she retires, and then she retires in reliance on the promise but the employer refuses to pay, the court may enforce the agreement under promissory estoppel.

Quasi-contract

Quasi-contract is used when the plaintiff reasonably expected to get paid for the benefit provided and the defendant knew this. If the plaintiff gave some benefit to the defendant and the defendant would be unjustly enriched if he did not pay the plaintiff for the benefit, quasi-contract may be used to compensate the plaintiff. For example, if a lawn-mowing company pulled up to the wrong house and mowed the wrong lawn while the benefiting homeowner sat on the front porch and did nothing to tell the company that it was mowing the wrong lawn, the homeowner might be made to pay for the mowing service. If the homeowner did not know of it, and just came home to a nicely mowed lawn, the homeowner would not have to pay.

Types of Contracts

Contracts can be bilateral, unilateral, express, or implied.

Bilateral Contracts

In a bilateral contract, there is an exchange of one promise for another. The offeror makes an offer, which the offeree may accept only by giving a return promise. For example, if a person says, "I'll sell you my snowmobile for $1,500," there is no contract until someone else says, "I agree to pay you $1,500 for your snowmobile." Bilateral contracts are based on the promise to perform an obligation in the future. The failure to fulfill the promise results in a breach of the contract.

Unilateral Contracts

In a unilateral contract, one party makes a promise that the other party can accept only by doing something. In other words, the offer can be accepted only by complete performance of the promise. For example, a person might say, "If I come home from work on December 30 and you've shoveled the snow from my driveway, I'll pay you $20." If the offeree has shoveled the driveway as required, he has accepted the offer by completing the contract and is entitled to $20. If, however, the offeree failed to perform the act, there would not be a breach of contract since no contract is formed until the offeree renders full performance.

Express Contracts

In an express contract, the parties explicitly state all the important terms of their agreement. For example, "I will paint your garage for $500 by October 30 and you agree to buy the paint and provide all brushes, ladders, solvents, and other supplies necessary for the job."

Implied Contracts

In an implied contract, the words and conduct of the parties indicate they intend an agreement. For example, an employer's practice of paying the cost of gas for his pizza delivery employees may result in an implied employment contract to do so.

HYPOTHETICAL CASE

Sally is an avid art collector who especially prizes contemporary sculpture. She meets an up-and-coming sculptor and asks him if he will make a work for her garden. He tells her he'll make one for her for $10,000. Sally agrees to pay him $10,000 if he can deliver the sculpture to her house in two months. The sculptor agrees. Two months later, the sculptor delivers to Sally a fork, a knife, and a spoon welded to a shovel. He sticks the shovel's handle in the ground and congratulates her on buying one of his finest works. Sally is furious and says she wants her money back. What arguments are there for and against enforcing a contract?

Chapter 12 Appendix: Sample Contracts

The following are two sample contracts—an Independent Consultant Agreement and an Authorized Exclusive Distributor Agreement.

INDEPENDENT CONSULTANT AGREEMENT

Agreement made this _____ day of _____,

20___, by and between _____ ("Consultant")

and _____ (Company) with its principal

place of business located at

_____.

Whereas, Consultant is engaged in the business of providing

consulting services on an independent contractor basis in the area of

_____ and, whereas, the company is in need of

_____ and desires to engage the services of Consultant

to assist in the _____ projects, and the Consultant is

agreeable to provide such services to the Company, now, therefore, in

consideration of the exchange of goods and services described herein

and other good and valuable consideration the receipt and sufficiency

of which the parties hereby acknowledge, it is agreed as follows:

1. Services and General Description

    The Company hereby engages Consultant, and the Consultant

    hereby accepts such an engagement, as an independent

    contractor, to provide services to the Company as a Consultant

    with respect to the Company's _____projects.

2. Term

   Unless extended in an amendment to this agreement, the term of this agreement is for a period beginning _____ and ending

   _____.

3. Compensation

   The Consultant shall be paid the sum of _____ for work performed and approved by the Manager, _____.

   The Consultant will submit an invoice, and the Company in turn will pay with a check for the amount specified above within 30 days of receipt of the invoice.

4. Scope and Place of Services

   The Consultant will provide its services to the Company primarily at the Company's location at

   _____.

5. Assignment and Termination

   This agreement is personal, and the Consultant may not assign or delegate any of the obligation and responsibility hereunder without prior written consent of the Company.

6. Relationships and Parties

   The parties agree and acknowledge that the Consultant is a self-employed professional person and that the relationship created by this agreement is that of a company-independent contractor; not employer-employee.

The Company reserves the right to inspect the progress of the project.

For no purpose whatsoever shall the Consultant be considered an employee or agent of the company nor have any authorization to bind or act on behalf of the Company on any matter. Consultant shall be solely responsible for the payment of all state and federal income, self-employment and other taxes. The Company is not responsible for such taxes and is not withholding any amounts from compensation paid to the Consultant hereunder for taxes or other purposes.

Consultant acknowledges that it shall have no rights to receive any benefits which the Company offers to its employees, including but not limited to Workers Compensation Insurance, unemployment insurance, group health, life, dental, disability, pension, or any other benefits.

7. Miscellaneous

   A)   This agreement may be amended at any time by mutual agreement of the parties, and all such amendments must be in writing and signed by both parties in order to be effective.

B)   If any provision of this agreement shall be unfulfilled or invalid for any reason whatsoever, the remaining provisions shall not be affected thereby and shall continue to be fully effective.

C)   The parties agree to cooperate fully with each other in the implementation of this agreement and the Company agrees that it shall provide the Consultant with such assistance and cooperation as may reasonably be necessary in order to facilitate the performance of its services hereunder.

IN WITNESS THEREOF

Director, Human Resources   Date

Consultant   Date

AUTHORIZED EXCLUSIVE DISTRIBUTOR AGREEMENT

This Agreement is made and entered into as of _____ ("Effective Date") between _____ ("Corporation"), a _____ corporation with its principal place of business at _____, and _____ ("Distributor"), a corporation maintaining its principal place of business at _____.

RECITALS

A. Corporation develops, manufactures, and distributes certain computer hardware products, including the products listed in Exhibit A ("Corporation"). This Agreement pertains only to "Corporation" as listed in Exhibit A and not to any other products developed, manufactured, or distributed by Corporation.

B. Corporation and Distributor desire that Distributor be authorized to act as an independent distributor of Corporation under the terms and conditions set forth below.

NOW, THEREFORE, Corporation and Distributor agree as follows:

1. Appointment as Authorized Corporation Distributor.

(a) Exclusive Appointment. Subject to the terms of this Agreement, Corporation appoints Distributor, and Distributor accepts such appointment, as the independent, exclusive distributor of Corporation in and limited to the territory set forth in Exhibit B (the "territory"). As long as Distributor satisfies all of its obligations under this Agreement, and unless Distributor's exclusive status is terminated pursuant to Section 2(c)(iii) of this Agreement, Corporation will not appoint another distributor of Corporation located in the Territory.

(b) Exclusivity Limitations. Notwithstanding Distributor's exclusive appointment, Corporation reserves the right at any time to offer, license and sell any Corporation, directly or indirectly, with no obligation to pay compensation to Distributor (i) to original equipment manufacturers, wherever located, who may in turn distribute Corporation in the Territory, and (ii) to the customers identified in Exhibit C.

(c) Corporation's Reserved Rights. Corporation reserves the rights from time to time, in its sole discretion and without liability to Distributor, to:

(i) change, add to, or delete from the list of Corporation Products;

(ii) change or terminate the level or type of service or support that Corporation makes available; and

(iii) add to or delete from the Territory by written notice to Distributor at least thirty (30) days prior to the effective date of the change.

(d) Nature of Distribution. Subject to the terms of this Agreement, to the extent that any Corporation Product contains or consists of software, Distributor's appointment only grants to Distributor a non-exclusive, non-transferable license to distribute such Corporation Product in the Territory, and does not transfer any right, title or interest to any such software to Distributor or Distributor's customers. Distributor may not distribute any Corporation containing or consisting of software to any third party unless such third party is subject to an end user software license agreement with Corporation that Corporation will provide to Distributor. Corporation will sell Corporation to Distributor only to the extent such Corporation consist of non-software items on the terms specified herein. Use of the terms "sell," "license," "purchase," "license fees," and "price" will be interpreted in accordance with this Section.

2. Obligations of Distributor.

(a) Promotion Efforts. Distributor will use its best efforts to (i) vigorously promote the distribution of Corporation in the Territory in accordance with the terms and policies of Corporation as announced from time to time; and (ii) satisfy those reasonable criteria and policies with respect to Distributor's obligations under this Agreement communicated in writing to Distributor by Corporation from time to time.

(b) Adaptation For Local Market. Distributor will be responsible for translating, at its expense, all Corporation manuals, packaging, advertising, and promotional materials used in connection with Corporation into the language(s) of the Territory if so instructed by Corporation in writing. Distributor will consult with Corporation as to what changes need to be made to written materials pursuant to this Section 2(b), and will obtain Corporation's prior written consent to each such change to written materials. Distributor hereby assigns to Corporation all of Distributor's right, title and interest in all such translated and modified materials, including but not limited to all related copyrights and moral rights.

(c) Minimum Commitments. Distributor agrees to order and pay for, during each of the periods set forth in Exhibit D, at least the minimum quantities of each Corporation Product indicated in Exhibit D for such periods. Corporation, at its sole discretion, shall have the right to amend Exhibit D upon thirty (30) days prior written notice to Distributor. If Distributor fails to order and pay for such minimum quantities during any period, it will provide Corporation within thirty (30) days of the end of such period with a written report explaining Distributor's failure to meet its minimum quantity, and Corporation will determine in its sole discretion which of the following steps is appropriate: (i) mutual agreement as to revision of future minimum quantities; or (ii) an undertaking by Distributor to effect steps necessary to ensure that it will meet its minimum quantities for the ensuing periods.

(d) Advertising Obligations. Distributor will aggressively advertise Corporation in the Territory in accordance with this Agreement, provided that Distributor will not use advertisements that have not been approved in writing by Corporation before such use. Corporation will set aside advertising funds equal to up to one half percent (0.5%) of Distributor's annual purchases. Using such funds, Corporation shall reimburse Distributor up to the amount in such funds for any expenses actually incurred by Distributor in connection with advertising of the Corporation, provided that such advertising has been approved in advance by Corporation.

(e) Inventory. Distributor will maintain at least one warehouse facility in the Territory, and will maintain an inventory of Corporation and warehousing facilities sufficient to serve adequately the needs of its customers on a timely basis. As a minimum, such inventory shall include not less than the quantity of Corporation necessary to meet Distributor's reasonably anticipated demands for a thirty (30) day period. Corporation will authorize an inventory stock rotation twice (2 times) per year, April 1st and September 1st, the maximum amount to be authorized will be 5% of the previous six (6) months purchases at cost in US$ from Corporation by Distributor. A new stocking order of equal dollar amount must accompany the stock rotation request from the Distributor.

(f) Distributor Personnel. Distributor will train and maintain a sufficient number of capable technical and sales personnel having the knowledge and training necessary to: (i) inform customers properly concerning the features and capabilities of Corporation and, if necessary, competitive products; (ii) service and support Corporation in accordance with Distributor's obligations under this Agreement; and (iii) otherwise carry out the obligations and responsibilities of Distributor under this Agreement.

(g) Technical Expertise. Distributor and its staff will be conversant with the technical language conventional to Corporation and similar computer products in general, and will develop sufficient knowledge of the industry, of Corporation and of products competitive with Corporation Products (including specifications, features and benefits) so as to be able to explain in detail to its customers the differences between Corporation and competitive products.

(h) Training. Distributor will send at least one of its technical and/or sales personnel for training on Corporation and services. The training will be provided free of charge at the Corporation offices shown on page one of this Agreement, the amount of training time will be reasonable and appropriate in Corporation's judgment, all such training will be in English, and Distributor will bear all travel and living expenses for such personnel sent to Corporation for training.

(i) Service and Support. Distributor will provide prompt pre- and post-sales or license service and support for all Corporation located in the Territory. Distributor will provide necessary and useful assistance and consultation on the use of Corporation; timely respond to customers' general questions concerning use of Corporation; and assist customers in the diagnosis and correction of problems encountered in using Corporation's Products.

(j) Meetings and Trade Show Attendance. Distributor will at its expense: (i) attend, and aggressively promote Corporation in, such trade shows, conventions and exhibits as Corporation reasonably requests; (ii) attend any sales meetings held by Corporation to which Corporation invites Distributor with reasonable notice; and (iii) notify Corporation of Distributor's sales meetings and provide Corporation personnel adequate opportunity to provide sales and promotion information regarding Corporation in such meetings.

(k) Distributor Financial Condition. Distributor will maintain and employ in connection with Distributor's business under this Agreement such working capital and net worth as may be required in Corporation's reasonable opinion to enable Distributor to carry out and perform all of Distributor's obligations and responsibilities under this Agreement. From time to time, on reasonable notice by Corporation, Distributor will furnish such financial reports and other financial data as Corporation may reasonably request as necessary to determine Distributor's financial condition.

(l) Corporation Packaging. Except as provided in section 2(b), Distributor will distribute Corporation with all packaging, warranties, disclaimers and license agreements intact as shipped from Corporation, and will instruct its customers as to the terms of such documents applicable to Corporation Products.

(m) No Competing Products. Distributor will not represent or distribute during the term of this Agreement any products which, in Corporation's opinion, compete, directly or indirectly, with Corporation. Exhibit E contains a list of products which, as of the Effective Date, compete with Corporation. Upon thirty (30) days prior written notice to Distributor, Corporation may, at its sole discretion, update or modify the list specified by Exhibit E at any time during the term of this Agreement.

(n) Distributor Covenants. Distributor will: (i) conduct business in a manner that reflects favorably at all times on Corporation and the good name, good will and reputation of Corporation;(ii) avoid deceptive, misleading or unethical practices that are or might be detrimental to Corporation, Corporation or the public; (iii) make no false or misleading representations with regard to Corporation; (iv) not publish or employ, or cooperate in the publication or employment of, any misleading or deceptive advertising material with regard to Corporation; (v) make no representations, warranties or guarantees to customers or to the trade with respect to the specifications, features or capabilities of Corporation Products that are inconsistent with the literature distributed by Corporation; and (vi) not enter into any contract or engage in any practice detrimental to the interests of Corporation. Distributor agrees that: (1) it will not disassemble, decompile, or reverse engineer any Corporation product, (2) it will not copy or otherwise reproduce any Corporation product, in whole or in part, and (3) it will not modify the Corporation product in any manner.

(o) Compliance with Law. Distributor will comply with all applicable international, national, state, regional and local laws and regulations in performing its duties hereunder and in any of its dealings with respect to Corporation.

(p) Compliance with U.S. Export Laws. Distributor acknowledges that all Corporation including documentation and other technical data are subject to export controls imposed by the U.S. Export Administration Act of 1979, as amended (the "Act"), and the regulations promulgated thereunder. Distributor will not export or reexport (directly or indirectly) any Corporation Products or documentation or other technical data therefor without complying with the Act and the regulations thereunder.

(q) Governmental Approval. If any approval with respect to this Agreement, or the notification or registration thereof, will be required at any time during the term of this Agreement, with respect to giving legal effect to this Agreement in the Territory, or with respect to compliance with exchange regulations or other requirements so as to assure the right of remittance abroad of U.S. dollars pursuant to Section 5(e) hereof or otherwise, Distributor will immediately take whatever steps may be necessary in this respect, and any charges incurred in connection therewith will be for the account of Distributor. Distributor will keep Corporation currently informed of its efforts in this connection. Corporation will be under no obligation to ship Corporation product to Distributor hereunder until Distributor has provided Corporation with satisfactory evidence that such approval, notification or registration is not required or that it has been obtained.

(r) Market Conditions. Distributor will advise Corporation promptly concerning any market information that comes to Distributor's attention respecting Corporation product, Corporation's market position or the continued competitiveness of Corporation in the marketplace. Distributor will confer with Corporation from time to time at the request of Corporation on matters relating to market conditions, sales forecasting and product planning relating to Corporation.

(s) Costs and Expenses. Except as expressly provided herein or agreed to in writing by Corporation and Distributor, Distributor will pay all costs and expenses incurred in the performance of Distributor's obligations under this Agreement.

3. Inspections, Records and Reporting.

(a) Reports. Within ten (10) days of the end of each calendar month, Distributor will provide to Corporation a written report showing, for the time periods Corporation reasonably requests, (i) Distributor's point of sale report showing shipments of Corporation product by customer name, address, zip code, Corporation part number, number of units sold, and revenue value, (ii) Distributor's customer backlog report, and (iii) Distributor's current inventory levels of Corporation, in the aggregate and by Corporation Product.

(b) Notification. Distributor will: (i) notify Corporation in writing of any claim or proceeding involving Corporation within ten (10) days after Distributor learns of such claim or proceeding; (ii) report promptly to Corporation all claimed or suspected product defects; and (iii) notify Corporation in writing not more than thirty (30) days after any change in the management of Distributor or any transfer of more than twenty-five percent (25%) of Distributor's voting control or a transfer of substantially all its assets.

(c) Records. Distributor will maintain, for at least two years after termination of this Agreement, its records, contracts and accounts relating to distribution of Corporation, and will permit examination thereof by authorized representatives of Corporation at all reasonable times.

4. Order Procedure.

(a) Corporation Acceptance. All orders for Corporation product by Distributor shall be subject to acceptance in writing by Corporation at its principal place of business and shall not be binding until the earlier of such acceptance or shipment, and, in the case of acceptance by shipment, only as to the portion of the order actually shipped.

(b) Controlling Terms. The terms and conditions of this Agreement and of the applicable Corporation invoice or confirmation will apply to each order accepted or shipped by Corporation hereunder. The provisions of Distributor's form of purchase order or other business forms will not apply to any order notwithstanding Corporation's acknowledgment or acceptance of such order.

(c) Cancellation. Corporation reserves the right to cancel any orders placed by Distributor and accepted by Corporation as set forth above, or to refuse or delay shipment thereof, if Distributor (i) fails to make any payment as provided in this Agreement or under the terms of payment set forth in any invoice or otherwise agreed to by Corporation and Distributor, (ii) fails to meet reasonable credit or financial requirements established by Corporation, including any limitations on allowable credit, or (iii) otherwise fails to comply with the terms and conditions of this Agreement. Corporation also reserves the right to discontinue the manufacture or distribution of any or all Corporation at any time (with at least 30 days written notice to Distributor and to offer to Distributor an End of Life Buy a.k.a. EOL on such terms and conditions as Corporation, in its sole discretion, shall specify in an End of Life Buy Letter), and to cancel any orders outside of the 45-day notice period for such discontinued Corporation without liability of any kind to Distributor or to any other person. No such cancellation, refusal or delay will be deemed a termination (unless Corporation so advises Distributor) or breach of this Agreement by Corporation.

5. Prices, License Fees and Payment.

(a) Prices and License Fees. During the term of this Agreement, Corporation shall inform Distributor as to current prices and license fees to Distributor for Corporation. Corporation may change its prices and license fees to Distributor from time to time upon at least thirty (30) days prior written notice.

(b) Price and License Fees Increase. In the event Corporation increases the price or license fees to Distributor for any Corporation Product, the increase shall apply to: any order received by Corporation after the effective date of the increase; and any order or portion thereof to be shipped after the effective date of the increase regardless of the date the order was received; provided, however, that any order or portion thereof transmitted by Distributor prior to Corporation's announcement of the increase and affected thereby, may be cancelled without penalty by Distributor by written notice to Corporation within ten (10) days of such announcement.

(c) Price and License Fee Decrease. In the event that Corporation decreases the price or license fee to Distributor for any Corporation Product, the decrease shall apply to all units of such product in Distributor's inventory that are still new as of the effective date of the decrease, and that had been shipped to Distributor no more than ninety (90) days prior to such effective date. For each unit of product as to which this section applies, Distributor will receive a credit against the price or license fee of a subsequent unit purchased from Corporation within ninety (90) days of the effective date of the price or license fee decrease.

(d) Taxes, Tariffs, Fees. Corporation's prices and license fees do not include any national, state or local sales, use, value added or other taxes, customs duties, or similar tariffs and fees which Corporation may be required to pay or collect upon the delivery of Corporation or upon collection of the prices and license fees or otherwise. Should any tax or levy be made, Distributor agrees to pay such tax or levy and indemnify Corporation for any claim for such tax or levy demanded. Distributor represents and warrants to Corporation that all Corporation acquired hereunder are for redistribution in the ordinary course of Distributor's business, and Distributor agrees to provide Corporation with appropriate resale certificate numbers and other documentation satisfactory to the applicable taxing authorities to substantiate any claim of exemption from any such taxes or fees. Distributor will pay any withholding taxes required by applicable law. Distributor will supply Corporation with evidence of such payment of withholding tax, in a form acceptable to Corporation to meet the requirements for claiming foreign tax credits on Corporation's federal income tax return.

(e) Payment Terms. All payments shall be made in United States dollars, free of any currency control or other restrictions to Corporation at the address designated by Corporation. Unless otherwise agreed by Corporation in writing, at the time of submission of any order for Corporation hereunder, Distributor will either:

(i) Cash Payment. Pay by certified check or wire transfer to a bank account designated by Corporation the amount of the aggregate prices and license fees of the Corporation ordered (plus any applicable taxes, shipping and other charges); or

(ii) Letter of Credit Payment. Cause to be issued by a bank acceptable to Corporation, and confirmed by a bank designated by Corporation, one or more irrevocable letters of credit to be equal to the aggregate prices and license fees of the Corporation ordered (plus any applicable taxes, shipping and other charges) and to provide for payment at sight upon presentation of Corporation's invoices and receipted shipping documents evidencing delivery of the invoiced Corporation to the carrier or freight forwarder.

(f) Credit Terms. At Corporation's option, shipments may be made on Corporation's credit terms in effect at the time an order is accepted. Corporation reserves the right, upon written notice to Distributor, to declare all sums immediately due and payable in the event of a breach by Distributor of any of its obligations to Corporation, including the failure of Distributor to comply with credit terms. Furthermore, Corporation reserves the right at all times either generally or with respect to any specific order by Distributor to vary, change or limit the amount or duration of credit to be allowed to Distributor. Distributor agrees to pay for Corporation as invoiced.

(g) Interest. Interest shall accrue on any delinquent amounts owed by Distributor for Corporation at the lesser of eighteen percent (15%) per annum or the maximum rate permitted by applicable usury law.

(h) No Setoff. Distributor will not setoff or offset against Corporation's invoices amounts that Distributor claims are due to it. Distributor will bring any claims or causes of action it may have in a separate action and waives any right it may have to offset, setoff or withhold payment for Corporation Products delivered by Corporation. Distributor will notify Corporation in writing of any claims or causes of action it may have. Corporation will respond to any such written documentation within thirty (30) days.

6. Shipment, Risk of Loss and Delivery.

(a) Shipment. All Corporation will be shipped by Corporation Mega-Works Factory (as defined in I.C.C. document 450), Corporation's point of shipment. Shipments will be made to Distributor's identified warehouse facilities or freight forwarder, subject to approval in writing by Corporation in advance of shipment. Corporation will specify its point of shipment, which may change from time to time. Unless specified in Distributor's order, Corporation will select the mode of shipment and the carrier. Distributor will arrange, be responsible for and pay all packing, shipping, freight and insurance charges from Corporation's point of shipment to Distributor.

(b) Title and Risk of Loss. Title (except to the extent Corporation Products contain or consist of software) and all risk of loss of or damage to Corporation will pass to Distributor upon delivery by Corporation to the carrier, freight forwarder or Distributor, whichever first occurs.

(c) Partial Delivery. Unless Distributor clearly advises Corporation to the contrary in writing, Corporation may make partial shipments on account of Distributor's orders, to be separately invoiced and paid for when due. Delay in delivery of any installment shall not relieve Distributor of its obligation to accept the remaining deliveries.

(d) Delivery Schedule; Delays. Corporation will use reasonable efforts to meet Distributor's requested delivery schedules for Corporation Products, but Corporation reserves the right to refuse, cancel or delay shipment to Distributor when Distributor's credit is impaired, when Distributor is delinquent in payments or fails to meet other credit or financial requirements established by Corporation, or when Distributor has failed to perform its obligations under this Agreement. Should orders for Corporation exceed Corporation's available inventory, Corporation will allocate its available inventory and make deliveries on a basis Corporation deems equitable, in its sole discretion, and without liability to Distributor on account of the method of allocation chosen or its implementation. In any event, Corporation will not be liable for any damages, direct, consequential, special or otherwise, to Distributor or to any other person for failure to deliver or for any delay or error in delivery of Corporation for any reason whatsoever.

7. Distributor Determines Its Own Prices and License Fees.

Although Corporation may publish suggested wholesale or retail prices, these are suggestions only and Distributor will be entirely free to determine the actual prices and license fees at which Corporation will be sold or licensed to its customers.

8. Trademarks, Trade Names, Logos, Designations and Copyrights.

(a) Use During Agreement. During the term of this Agreement and subject to the terms and conditions specified herein, Corporation grants to Distributor a nonexclusive, nontransferable, limited license to use, in the Territory, Corporation's trademarks, trade names, logos and designations as set forth on Exhibit F only as necessary for Distributor to fulfill its obligations hereunder. Distributor's use of such trademarks, trade names, logos and designations will be in accordance with Corporation's policies in effect from time to time, including but not limited to trademark usage and cooperative advertising policies. Corporation's current trademark use policy is attached in Exhibit F. Changes to this trademark use policy, that Corporation in its sole discretion will specify, shall be effective upon thirty (30) days' written notice to Distributor. Distributor agrees not to attach any additional trademarks, trade names, logos or designations to any Corporation Product. Distributor further agrees not to use any Corporation trademark, trade name, logo or designation in connection with any non-Corporation Product. Corporation reserves the right to review planned uses of its trademarks, trade names, logos and designations to confirm that they are within the guidelines, prior to usage of such trademarks by Distributor.

(b) Copyright and Trademark Notices. Distributor will include on each Corporation Product that it distributes, and on all containers and storage media therefor, all trademark, copyright and other notices of proprietary rights included by Corporation on such Corporation Product. Distributor agrees not to alter, erase, deface or overprint any such notice on anything provided by Corporation. Distributor also will include the appropriate trademark notices when referring to any Corporation Product in advertising and promotional materials.

(c) Distributor Does Not Acquire Proprietary Rights. Distributor has paid no consideration for the use of Corporation's trademarks, trade names, logos, designations or copyrights, and nothing contained in this Agreement will give Distributor any right, title or interest in any of them. Distributor acknowledges that Corporation owns and retains all trademarks, trade names, logos, designations, copyrights and other proprietary rights in or associated with Corporation, and agrees that it will not at any time during or after this Agreement assert or claim any interest in or do anything that may adversely affect the validity of any trademark, trade name, logo, designation or copyright belonging to or licensed to Corporation (including, without limitation any act or assistance to any act, which may infringe or lead to the infringement of any of Corporation's proprietary rights).

(d) No Continuing Rights. Upon expiration or termination of this Agreement, Distributor will immediately cease all display, advertising and use of all Corporation trademarks, trade names, logos and designations and will not thereafter use, advertise or display any trademark, trade name, logo or designation which is, or any part of which is, similar to or confusing with any trademark, trade name, logo or designation associated with any Corporation Product.

(e) Obligation to Protect. Distributor agrees to use reasonable efforts to protect Corporation's proprietary rights and to cooperate at Distributor's expense in Corporation's efforts to protect its proprietary rights. Distributor agrees to promptly notify Corporation of any known or suspected breach of Corporation's proprietary rights that comes to Distributor's attention.

9. Assignment.
Corporation has entered into this Agreement with Distributor because of Distributor's commitments in this Agreement, and further because of Corporation's confidence in Distributor, which confidence is personal in nature. This Agreement will not be assignable by either party, and Distributor may not delegate its duties hereunder without the prior written consent of Corporation; provided, however, that Corporation may (i) assign this Agreement to a subsidiary or entity controlling, controlled by or under common control with Corporation, or (ii) as part of a corporate restructuring, reorganization, divestiture, merger, acquisition or sale or other transfer of all or substantially all of the assets of Corporation, assign the rights and delegate the obligations of this Agreement without the consent of Distributor. The provisions hereof shall be binding upon and inure to the benefit of the parties, their successors and permitted assigns. Any attempt to assign this Agreement in derogation of this Section 9 will be null and void.

10. Duration and Termination of Agreement.

(a) Term. This Agreement will begin on the Effective Date and will continue until December 31, 20__ unless terminated earlier in accordance with the provisions hereof. Nothing shall be interpreted as requiring either party to renew or extend this Agreement.

(b) Corporation Termination for Cause. Corporation may terminate this Agreement at any time prior to the expiration of its stated term in the event that:

(i) Distributor defaults in any payment due to Corporation and such default continues unremedied for a period of ten (10) days following written notice of such default;

(ii) Distributor fails to perform any other obligation, warranty, duty or responsibility or is in default with respect to any term or condition undertaken by Distributor under this Agreement and such failure or default continues unremedied for a period of twenty (20) days following written notice of such failure or default;

(iii) Distributor is merged, acquired, consolidated, sells all or substantially all of its assets, or implements or suffers any substantial change in management or control; or

(iv) Any bill or regulation granting Distributor extracontractual compensation upon termination or expiration of this Agreement is introduced into or passed by the legislature or other governing body of the Territory.

(c) Termination at Will. Distributor or Corporation may terminate this Agreement at will, at any time during the term of this Agreement, with or without cause, by written notice given to the other party not less than sixty (60) days prior to the effective date of such termination.

(d) Automatic Termination. This Agreement terminates automatically, with no further act or action of either party, if: (1) a receiver or trustee is appointed for Distributor or its property or Distributor is adjudged bankrupt, (2) Distributor makes an assignment for the benefit of its creditors, (3) Distributor becomes the subject of a voluntary petition in bankruptcy or any voluntary proceeding relating to insolvency, receivership, liquidation, or composition for the benefit of creditors, (4) Distributor becomes the subject of an involuntary petition in bankruptcy or any involuntary proceeding relating to insolvency, receivership, liquidation, or composition for the benefit of creditors, if such petition or proceeding is not dismissed within sixty (60) days of filing, or (5) Distributor is liquidated or dissolved.

(e) Orders After Termination Notice. In the event that any notice of termination of this Agreement is given, Corporation will be entitled to reject all or part of any orders received from Distributor after notice but prior to the effective date of termination if availability of Corporation is insufficient at that time to meet the needs of Corporation and its customers fully. Notwithstanding any credit terms made available to Distributor prior to such notice, any Corporation product shipped thereafter shall be paid for by certified or cashier's check prior to shipment.

(f) Effect of Termination or Expiration. Upon termination or expiration of this Agreement:

(i) Corporation, at its option and sole discretion, may reacquire any or all Corporation product then in Distributor's possession at prices and refunded license fees not greater than the prices and license fees paid by Distributor for such Products (or, if the Products are not in unopened factory sealed boxes, eighty percent (80%) of current published price on Standard Distributor Price List. Upon receipt of any Corporation so reacquired from Distributor, Corporation shall issue an appropriate credit to Distributor's account.

(ii) The due dates of all outstanding invoices to Distributor for Corporation automatically will be accelerated so they become due and payable on the effective date of termination, even if longer terms had been provided previously. All orders or portions thereof remaining unshipped as of the effective date of termination shall automatically be cancelled.

(iii) For a period of two (2) years after the date of termination or expiration, Distributor shall make available to Corporation for inspection and copying all books and records of Distributor that pertain to Distributor's performance of and compliance with its obligations, warranties and representations under this Agreement.

       (iv) Distributor shall cease using any Corporation trademark, trade name, trade dress, service mark, service name, logo or designation.

       (g) No Damages for Termination or Expiration. NEITHER CORPORATION NOR DISTRIBUTOR SHALL BE LIABLE TO THE OTHER FOR DAMAGES OF ANY KIND, INCLUDING INCIDENTAL OR CONSEQUENTIAL DAMAGES, ON ACCOUNT OF THE TERMINATION OR EXPIRATION OF THIS AGREEMENT IN ACCORDANCE WITH THIS SECTION 10. DISTRIBUTOR WAIVES ANY RIGHT IT MAY HAVE TO RECEIVE ANY COMPENSATION OR REPARATIONS ON TERMINATION OR EXPIRATION OF THIS AGREEMENT UNDER THE LAW OF THE TERRITORY OR OTHERWISE, OTHER THAN AS EXPRESSLY PROVIDED IN THIS AGREEMENT.

Neither Corporation nor Distributor will be liable to the other on account of termination or expiration of this Agreement for reimbursement or damages for the loss of goodwill, prospective profits or anticipated income, or on account of any expenditures, investments, leases or commitments made by either Corporation or Distributor or for any other reason whatsoever based upon or growing out of such termination or expiration. Distributor acknowledges that (i) Distributor has no expectation and has received no assurances that any investment by Distributor in the promotion of Corporation will be recovered or recouped or that Distributor will obtain any anticipated amount of profits by virtue of this Agreement, and (ii) Distributor will not have or acquire by virtue of this Agreement or otherwise any vested, proprietary or other right in the promotion of Corporation or in "goodwill" created by its efforts hereunder.

THE PARTIES ACKNOWLEDGE THAT THIS SECTION HAS BEEN INCLUDED AS A MATERIAL INDUCEMENT FOR CORPORATIONTO ENTER INTO THIS AGREEMENT AND THAT CORPORATION WOULD HAVE ENTERED INTO THIS AGREEMENT BUT FOR THE LIMITATIONS OF LIABILITY AS SET FORTH HEREIN.

(h) Survival. Corporation's rights and Distributor's obligations to pay Corporation all amounts due hereunder, as well as Distributor's obligations under Sections 3(b), 3(c), 5(d), 5(e), 5(f), 5(g), 5(h), 5(i), 8, 12, 13, 14, 15, 16(c), 16(d), 16(g), 16(h), 16(i) and 16(j) shall survive termination or expiration of this Agreement.

11. Relationship of the Parties.

Distributor's relationship with Corporation during the term of this Agreement will be that of an independent contractor. Nothing in this Agreement will be construed as creating or implying a partnership, joint venture, employment, franchise, agency, or any other form of legal association (other than as expressly set forth herein) between the parties. Distributor will not have, and will not represent that it has, any power, right or authority to bind Corporation, or to assume or create any obligation or responsibility, express or implied, on behalf of Corporation or in Corporation 's name, except as herein expressly provided.

12. Indemnification.

(a) Indemnification of Distributor. Corporation will, at its expense, defend Distributor against and, subject to the limitations set forth herein, pay all costs and damages made in settlement or awarded against Distributor resulting from any claim based on an allegation that a Corporation Product as supplied by Corporation hereunder infringes a U.S. patent or copyright of a third party, provided that Distributor (i) gives Corporation prompt written notice of any such claim, (ii) allows Corporation to direct the defense and settlement of the claims, and (iii) provides Corporation with the information and assistance necessary for the defense and settlement of the claim. If a final injunction is obtained in an action based on any such claim against Distributor's use of a Corporation Product by reason of such infringement, or if in Corporation's opinion such an injunction is likely to be obtained, Corporation may, at its sole option, either (i) obtain for Distributor the right to continue using the Corporation Product, (ii) replace or modify the Corporation Product so that it becomes non-infringing, or (iii) if neither (i) nor (ii) can be reasonably effected by Corporation, credit to Distributor the prices and license fees paid for the Corporation Product during the twelve

(12) months prior to the credit, provided that such Corporation are returned to Corporation in an undamaged condition.

(b) No Combination Claims. Notwithstanding subpart (a) of this Section 12, Corporation shall not be liable to Distributor for any claim arising from or based upon the combination, operation or use of any Corporation Product with equipment, data, programming or materials not supplied by Corporation, or arising from any alteration or modification of Corporation.

(c) Limitation. THE PROVISIONS OF THIS SECTION SET FORTH THE ENTIRE LIABILITY OF CORPORATION AND THE SOLE REMEDIES OF DISTRIBUTOR WITH RESPECT TO INFRINGEMENT AND ALLEGATIONS OF INFRINGEMENT OF INTELLECTUAL PROPERTY RIGHTS OR OTHER PROPRIETARY RIGHTS OF ANY KIND IN CONNECTION WITH THE INSTALLATION, OPERATION, DESIGN, DISTRIBUTION OR USE OF CORPORATION.

(d) Indemnification of Corporation. Distributor agrees to indemnify Corporation (including paying all reasonable attorneys' fees and costs of litigation) against and hold Corporation harmless from, any and all claims by any other party resulting from Distributor's acts (other than the mere marketing of Corporation), omissions or misrepresentations, regardless of the form of action.

13. Limited Warranty; Disclaimer of Warranties.

(a) Limited Warranty. CORPORATION MAKES NO WARRANTIES OR REPRESENTATIONS AS TO PERFORMANCE OF CORPORATION OR AS TO SERVICE TO DISTRIBUTOR OR TO ANY OTHER PERSON, EXCEPT AS SET FORTH IN CORPORATION'S LIMITED WARRANTY ACCOMPANYING DELIVERY OF CORPORATION. CORPORATION RESERVES THE RIGHT TO CHANGE THE WARRANTY AND SERVICE POLICY SET FORTH IN SUCH LIMITED WARRANTY, OR OTHERWISE, AT ANY TIME, WITHOUT FURTHER NOTICE AND WITHOUT LIABILITY TO DISTRIBUTOR OR TO ANY OTHER PERSON.

(b) Disclaimer of Warranties. TO THE EXTENT PERMITTED BY APPLICABLE LAW, ALL IMPLIED WARRANTIES, INCLUDING BUT NOT LIMITED TO IMPLIED WARRANTIES OF MERCHANTABILITY,

FITNESS FOR A PARTICULAR PURPOSE AND NONINFRINGEMENT, ARE HEREBY DISCLAIMED BY CORPORATION.

(c) Distributor Warranty. Distributor will make no warranty, guarantee or representation, whether written or oral, on Corporation's behalf.

14. Limited Liability.

(a) REGARDLESS WHETHER ANY REMEDY SET FORTH HEREIN OR IN CORPORATION'S LIMITED WARRANTY ACCOMPANYING DELIVERY OF CORPORATION FAILS OF ITS ESSENTIAL PURPOSE OR OTHERWISE, CORPORATIONWILL NOT BE LIABLE FOR ANY LOST PROFITS OR FOR ANY DIRECT, INDIRECT, INCIDENTAL, CONSEQUENTIAL, PUNITIVE OR OTHER SPECIAL DAMAGES SUFFERED BY DISTRIBUTOR, ITS CUSTOMERS OR OTHERS ARISING OUT OF OR RELATED TO THIS AGREEMENT OR CORPORATION, FOR ALL CAUSES OF ACTION OF ANY KIND (INCLUDING TORT, CONTRACT, NEGLIGENCE, STRICT LIABILITY AND BREACH OF WARRANTY) EVEN IF CORPORATIONHAS BEEN ADVISED OF THE POSSIBILITY OF SUCH DAMAGES.

(b) EXCEPT FOR LIABILITY FOR PERSONAL INJURY OR PROPERTY DAMAGE ARISING FROM CORPORATION'S GROSS NEGLIGENCE OR WILLFUL MISCONDUCT, IN NO EVENT WILL CORPORATION'S TOTAL CUMULATIVE LIABILITY IN CONNECTION WITH THIS AGREEMENT, FROM ALL CAUSES OF ACTION OF ANY KIND, INCLUDING TORT, CONTRACT, NEGLIGENCE, STRICT LIABILITY AND BREACH OF WARRANTY, EXCEED THE AGGREGATE NET AMOUNT PAID BY DISTRIBUTOR HEREUNDER DURING THE SIX (6) MONTHS PRIOR TO THE DATE SUCH CAUSE OF ACTION AROSE.

(c) Distributor agrees that the limitations of liability and disclaimers of warranty set forth in this Agreement will apply regardless of whether Corporation has tendered delivery of Corporation or Distributor has accepted any Corporation Product. Distributor acknowledges that Corporation has set its prices and license fees and entered into this Agreement in reliance on the disclaimers of liability, the disclaimers of warranty and the limitations of liability set forth in this Agreement and that the same form an essential basis of the bargain between the parties.

15. Proprietary Information.

(a) Obligation. Distributor acknowledges that in the course of performing its obligations under this Agreement, it may obtain information relating to Corporation which is of a confidential and proprietary nature to Corporation ("Proprietary Information"). Such Proprietary Information includes without limitation trade secrets, know-how, formulas, compositions of matter, inventions, techniques, processes, programs, diagrams, schematics, customer and financial information and sales and marketing plans. Distributor will (a) use such Proprietary Information only in connection with fulfilling its obligations under this Agreement, (b) during the term of this Agreement and for a period of seven (7) years thereafter, hold such Proprietary Information in strict confidence and exercise due care with respect to its handling and protection of such Proprietary Information, consistent with its own policies concerning protection of its own proprietary and/or trade secret information and (c) disclose, divulge or publish the same only to such of its employees or representatives as are Qualified Personnel (as defined below) and to no other person or entity, whether for its own benefit or for the benefit of any other person or entity. Distributor further agrees to return all copies of all Proprietary Information in its possession, control or custody immediately upon termination or expiration of this Agreement. As used herein, the term "Qualified Personnel" means such employees and representatives of Distributor who (i) have a need to know or have access to Corporation's Proprietary Information in order for such employees or representatives to carry out the purposes of this Agreement and (ii) have executed nondisclosure agreements binding them not to use or disclose such Proprietary Information except as permitted herein.

(b) Exceptions. The obligations contained in Section 15(a) will not apply to Proprietary Information which (a) is or becomes public knowledge without the fault or action of Distributor, (b) is received by Distributor from a source other than Corporation, which source received the information without violation of any confidentiality restriction, (c) is independently developed by Distributor without violation of any confidentiality restriction or (d) is or becomes available to Distributor on an unrestricted basis from Corporation.

16. General.

(a) Waiver. The waiver by either party of any default by the other shall not waive subsequent defaults of the same or different kind.

(b) Notices. All notices and demands hereunder will be in writing and will be served by personal service, mail or confirmed facsimile transmission at the address of the receiving party set forth in this Agreement (or at such different address as may be designated by such party by written notice to the other party). All notices or demands by mail shall be by certified or registered airmail, return receipt requested, and shall be deemed complete upon receipt.

(c) Attorneys' Fees. In the event any litigation is brought by either party in connection with this Agreement, the prevailing party in such litigation shall be entitled to recover from the other party all the costs, attorneys' fees and other expenses incurred by such prevailing party in the litigation.

(d) Execution of Agreement, Controlling Law, Jurisdiction and Severability. This Agreement will become effective only after it has been signed by Distributor and has been accepted by Corporation at its principal place of business, and its effective date shall be the date on which it is signed by Corporation. It shall be governed by and construed in accordance with the laws of the State of California, excluding the Convention on Contracts for the International Sale of Goods and that body of law known as conflicts of laws. Any suit hereunder will be brought in the federal or state courts in _____ and Distributor hereby submits to the personal jurisdiction thereof. The English-language version of this Agreement controls when interpreting this Agreement. Distributor consents to the enforcement of any judgment rendered in the United States in any action between Distributor and Corporation. Any and all defenses concerning the validity and enforceability of\ the judgment shall be deemed waived unless first raised in a court of competent jurisdiction in the United States.

(e) Severability. In the event that any of the provisions of this Agreement shall be held by a court or other tribunal of competent jurisdiction to be unenforceable, such provision will be enforced to the maximum extent permissible and the remaining portions of this Agreement shall remain in full force and effect.

(f) Force Majeure. Corporation shall not be responsible for any failure to perform due to unforeseen circumstances or to causes beyond Corporation's reasonable control, including but not limited to acts of God, war, riot, embargoes, acts of civil or military authorities, fire, floods, accidents, strikes, failure to obtain export licenses or shortages of transportation, facilities, fuel, energy, labor or materials. In the event of any such delay, Corporation may defer the delivery date of orders for Corporation for a period equal to the time of such delay.

(g) Equitable Relief. Distributor acknowledges that any breach of its obligations under this Agreement with respect to the proprietary rights or confidential information of Corporation will cause Corporation irreparable injury for which there are inadequate remedies at law, and therefore Corporation will be entitled to equitable relief in addition to all other remedies provided by this Agreement or available at law.

(h) Entire Agreement. This Agreement constitutes the complete and exclusive agreement between the parties pertaining to the subject matter hereof, and supersedes in their entirety any and all written or oral agreements previously existing between the parties with respect to such subject matter. Distributor acknowledges that it is not entering into this Agreement on the basis of any representations not expressly contained herein. Any modifications of this Agreement must be in writing and signed by both parties hereto. Any such modification shall be binding upon Corporation only if and when signed by one of its duly authorized officers.

(i) Release of Claims. Any and all claims against Corporation arising under prior agreements, whether oral or in writing, between Corporation and Distributor are waived and released-by Distributor by acceptance of this Agreement.

(j) Choice of Language. The original of this Agreement has been written in English. Distributor waives any right it may have under the law of Distributor's Territory to have this Agreement written in the language of Distributor's Territory.

(k) Due Execution. The party executing this Agreement represents and warrants that he or she has been duly authorized under Distributor's charter documents and applicable law to execute this Agreement on behalf of Distributor.

(l) Counterparts. This Agreement may be executed in counterparts, each of which shall be deemed an original, but all of which together shall constitute one and the same instrument.

(m) Captions. The captions to sections of this Agreement have been inserted for identification and reference purposes only and shall not be used to construe or interpret this Agreement.

IN WITNESS WHEREOF, the parties hereto have executed this Agreement effective on the date specified below.

CORPORATION

Signature:

Printed Name:

Title:

Date:

DISTRIBUTOR

Signature:

Printed Name:

Title:

Date:

EXHIBIT A

CORPORATION PRODUCTS

Any products that appear on the Worldwide Distributor Price List.

Corporation   Distributor

Signature:

-------------------------   ------------------------

EXHIBIT B

TERRITORY

(Example) Taiwan, Hong Kong, China

Corporation   Distributor

Signature:

-------------------------   ------------------------

EXHIBIT C

CORPORATION ACCOUNTS

XXXXXXXXXXXXXXXXXX.

YYYYYYYYYY including but not limited to the following:

   a....
   b....
   c....

Corporation   Distributor

Signature:

-------------------------   ------------------------

EXHIBIT D

MINIMUM QUOTAS

Year 20__
Quotas will be equal to Corporation Distributor Forecast

Corporation   Distributor

Signature:

-------------------------   ------------------------

EXHIBIT E

COMPETING PRODUCTS

Any _____ that is designed, manufactured or
distributed by or on behalf of _____
or any of their subsidiaries or affiliates.

Corporation   Distributor

Signature:

--------------------------   -------------------------

Chapter 13: Contract Legality Issues

Introduction

As discussed earlier, the law requires an offer, acceptance of the offer, and consideration for a contract to exist. But just because there is a contract does not mean the law will enforce it. So, what makes a contract legally enforceable? For a contract to be enforceable, the parties must possess the legal capacity to enter a contract, and the consideration for the contract must be something legal. For example, if the bargained-for exchange is an illegal act, such as murder or the sale of illegal drugs, it is not legal, and the law will not enforce it. In some states, gambling contracts are illegal and will not be enforced.

Public Policy

Sometimes a contract may be determined to be invalid, void, or voidable because it violates public policy. Public policy is the term used to describe our collection of laws, mandates, and regulations established through the political process that is used to pursue the needs of citizens and their values. It is the combination of legal and political process in pursuit of an overall policy that, in combination, forms an overall "public policy."

One example in which public policy traditionally discourages a finding of legally enforceable contracts is a life insurance policy taken out on someone else's life. The obvious reason is that the person taking out the life insurance policy will benefit if the person on whom they have the policy dies. Thus, they would not be likely to assist them if they were in a life-threatening situation. Since public policy wants to encourage citizens to assist each other in staying alive, it says life insurance contracts are not enforceable unless the beneficiary has an interest in the insured staying alive—such as the insured owing the beneficiary money, or the beneficiary being married to the insured.

In addition, public policy has also resulted in professional licensing statutes, which are designed to protect the public from people unlawfully practicing a profession or trade. In many states, if a person is not licensed to practice a profession or trade that requires a license, the law will not enforce a contract entered into by such a person. However, if a license requirement is merely to raise revenue (such as a building permit) and not to regulate the profession, a failure to get the license will not invalidate the contract. For example, if a licensed builder contracts to build you a garage and he does so but fails to pull the necessary building permit, you still have to pay him. However, if an unlicensed builder pulls the necessary permit and builds you a great garage, you do not have to pay him under the contract!

Other contracts that have been determined to be against public policy are those that have induced elected officials to leave office before their term expires or those that would restrain trade. A restraint on trade is any agreement that limits trade, sales, or interstate commerce.

Exculpatory Clauses

There are many situations in which one party attempts to eliminate the possibility of being sued as a result of negligence or wrongdoing by including a clause in a contract that releases them from liability or holds them harmless. Such clauses are referred to as *exculpatory clauses* or *hold harmless clauses*. By agreeing to such a clause, a party is waiving the right to sue for such causes of action.

Exculpatory clauses are often included in contracts in which people agree to waive their right to sue for injuries they suffer as a result of playing on an athletic team or for injuries received while renting equipment. Other examples include waiving the right to sue for damage done to property entrusted to someone else's care, such as not holding a business liable if it loses your computer while it is in their possession for repair, or a provision in a lease wherein the landlord will not be held responsible for damage, injury, or loss that occurs on the property.

Exculpatory clauses are likely to be enforced if all of these conditions apply:

- They are between business parties.

- The clause is limited in scope to negligence causes of action.

- It is prominent.

- The contract language is negotiated and not merely a form contract.

- The context of the waiver is fair and reasonable.

- The waiver does not involve the release of a right to sue for negligence of professional services such as that by a physician, accountant, or lawyer.

Nonenforcement of Exculpatory Clause

Exculpatory clauses are usually not enforced if they eliminate liability for intentional torts. Most jurisdictions consider the elimination of the possibility of being sued for intentionally harming someone to be against public policy and will not enforce such a clause.

Courts have also refused to enforce exculpatory clauses when the bargaining power of one party to the contract is so grossly unequal as to put that party at the mercy of the other's negligence, or when enforcing it would be against public interest.

Unconscionable Contracts

An unconscionable contract will not be enforced. Unconscionable contracts are those in which one party has a huge bargaining advantage over the other and the disadvantaged party has no choice but to accept it, even though no reasonable person would do so. It is a contract that is unusually harsh and often "shocks the conscience." In determining whether a contract is unconscionable, the court will examine the commercial setting and the purpose and effect of the clause or contract. A violation of public policy is also used as a basis for not enforcing contracts that are unconscionable.

Under the UCC, if a court finds a contract, or any part of it, to be unconscionable, it may refuse to enforce it, enforce only part of it, or limit the enforcement of it so that it isn't unconscionable.

Adhesion Contracts

Adhesion contracts are contracts in which one party has a much stronger bargaining position than the other and is in a position to effectively tell the other party to "take it or leave it." These types of contracts often get tougher scrutiny by the courts, yet they are often upheld. When reviewing legal challenges to them, the courts examine whether the disputed term was outside the reasonable expectations of the purchaser and if the parties were contracting on an unequal basis. The reasonable expectation is assessed objectively, looking at the prominence of the term, the purpose of the term, and the circumstances surrounding acceptance of the term or contract. Again, as in other instances, the court may decide to set aside only the section of the contract it finds unacceptable and will enforce all other provisions of the contract.

Fraud or Materiality

A fraudulent statement is one made to induce the other party to enter into the contract while knowing it is false or not knowing it is true. A statement is material if the maker of the statement expects the other party to rely on it in reaching an agreement.

Silent Fraud or Fraud by Omission

An act of fraud does not have to be an affirmative act for it to be the basis of rescinding a contract. Silent fraud occurs when a party fails to disclose a material fact. To establish silent fraud, the plaintiff has the burden of proving each of the following seven elements by clear and convincing evidence:

1. The defendant failed to disclose one or more material facts about the subject matter of the claim. Remember, a material fact is something a reasonable person would want to know or rely on in deciding to enter into the contract.

2. The defendant had actual knowledge of the fact(s).

3. The defendant's failure to disclose the fact(s) caused the plaintiff to have a false impression.

4. When the defendant failed to disclose the fact(s), the defendant knew the failure would create a false impression.

5. When the defendant failed to disclose the fact(s), the defendant intended that plaintiff rely on the resulting false impression.

6. The plaintiff relied on the false impression.

7. The plaintiff was damaged because of the reliance on the false impression.

For example, a used car salesman tells Sally the car she is interested in buying had only one owner and had received regularly scheduled maintenance, but he knowingly fails to tell her it was in the owner's garage that was flooded during a hurricane. Sally believes the car is in good shape and buys it based on his assertions, but soon after, the body begins to rust and the engine needs repair. Sally's mechanic tells her, "This vehicle has obviously been under salt water." Sally may sue to rescind the sales contract if she can demonstrate these seven things:

1. The salesman knew the car had been flooded with salt water.

2. He failed to tell her this information because he knew she would not buy the car if he told her.

3. Because he didn't tell her, she got the false impression the car was in good condition.

4. The salesman knew his failure to tell her would cause her to get a false impression.

5. He intended her to rely on the false impression.

6. She did rely on it.

7. She suffered injury as a result of her justifiable reliance because the car she bought was not worth the money she paid for it and now needs expensive repairs.

Justifiable Reliance

Justifiable reliance occurs when the injured party can show she reasonably relied on a false statement that was material to the contract. Thus, if a party can show (1) a false statement of fact; (2) fraud or materiality; and (3) justifiable reliance, the contract may be rescinded.

When a contract is rescinded, it is as if it never took place since the purpose of the remedy is to put the parties in the position they would have been in if the transaction had never occurred. No rescission is permitted if one party is aware of the risk. For example, if a purchaser buys a painting hoping it was painted by Rembrandt but after taking it to a museum curator learns that it was not, he cannot rescind the contract merely because the painting was not what he hoped. He knew when he bought it that he was taking a risk that the painting was done by someone other than Rembrandt. However, if the purchaser was told the painting was done by Rembrandt, relied on that fact when purchasing it, and then learned it was not painted by the famous artist, then she may seek to rescind the contract, return the painting, and get her money back.

Mistake

What if there is no fraud or intentional act to deceive but merely a mistake? A mistake can be either *bilateral* (made by both parties) or *unilateral* (made by one party). A bilateral mistake occurs when both parties rely on the same factual error. A unilateral mistake occurs when one party enters into the contract under a mistaken assumption. The law says that if a contract is based on an important factual error (mistake), it is voidable by the injured party.

Void Contracts: A void contract, sometimes referred to as *void ab initio* (void from the start), is one that was never legally valid, and nothing can ever be done to make it legally valid. For example, if a person does not have the mental ability to enter into a contract because they have a brain injury that prevents them from understanding the obligations to which they are committing themselves, nothing will ever change that situation. Therefore, any contract they sign is void as they will not wake up one morning and be able to understand and reaffirm the obligations they have undertaken.

Voidable Contracts: A voidable contract is one that *may* be invalidated by a party entering into it under certain circumstances. Voidable contracts may also become enforceable, and a party who could have voided it may be unable to invalidate it, if certain conditions are met. For example, a contract entered into by a minor is voidable by the minor until he or she reaches the age of majority (18), but once the minor turns 18, the contract is no longer voidable since the condition that made it so no longer exists.

To rescind a contract when there is a unilateral mistake, a party must prove it entered into the contract because of a factual error and either enforcing the contract would be unconscionable or the non-mistaken party knew of the error.

A party that seeks to void a contract due to misrepresentation must show five things:

1.   The defendant made a misrepresentation.

2.   The misrepresentation was either fraudulent or material.

3.   The misrepresentation induced the plaintiff to enter into the contract.

4.   The plaintiff's reliance on the misrepresentation was justified.

5.   The plaintiff suffered damage as a result.

A *misrepresentation* is an assertion by either words or conduct that is not supported by the facts. A misrepresentation is *fraudulent* if it is both knowingly false and intended to mislead. The maker intends to induce a party to enter into the contract by making a statement they know is not true while intending the party to rely on it. For example, if a used car salesman knows the car has bad head gaskets that need replacing but tells the prospective buyer "this car is in excellent condition" so that she will buy it, he has fraudulently misrepresented the condition of the car. If he was unaware that the head gaskets were bad and made the same statement, he would be merely misrepresenting the condition of the car, but his misrepresentation would not be fraudulent.

A misrepresentation is *material* if either it is something a reasonable person would attach importance to in making his or her choice of action or the person making the misrepresentation knew it was likely to induce the other party to enter into the agreement.

A party is justified in relying on the misrepresentation unless it is only incidentally important to the contract or unless a reasonable person would not be expected to take the misrepresentation seriously.

A party loses the power to void or rescind a contract for misrepresentation if, after the party knows of a misrepresentation, the party manifests to the other party an intention to affirm the contract anyway or fails to demonstrate an intent to rescind the contract within a reasonable time.

Note: False representations may be the basis for rescinding a contract if those representations are either fraudulent or material. However, in tort law, a misrepresentation does not result in liability for fraudulent misrepresentation unless it is *both* fraudulent and material.

Undue Influence

A contract made as a result of undue influence can also be rescinded. To prove undue influence, a party must prove (1) a relationship between the parties of trust and domination and (2) improper

persuasion by the stronger party. The lawyer and client relationship

or a medical advisor and patient may, as a matter of law, give rise to

the presumption that undue influence has been exercised.

HYPOTHETICAL CASE

Sally is on vacation in Arizona and is browsing around a tourist shop when she spies what she thinks is an antique Navajo blanket. She asks the store owner if it is an antique Navajo blanket, and the owner says, "I think it is, but I haven't had a real expert examine it yet." The store owner knows it was purchased from someone who has a reputation for making great-looking fakes, but she says nothing about that. Sally, who knows a bit about Native American rugs, examines the rug more closely and asks how much the owner wants for the rug. "Well, since I can't swear it is an antique, although it has all the indications of being one, I'll sell it to you for $2,000." Sally thinks that's a pretty good price for what she believes is a genuine antique and buys it. When she has an antique Native American rug dealer examine it, he tells her it is a fake and that he knows who made it and where she probably bought it.

Does Sally have any cause of action(s) against the store owner who sold her the rug? Explain your answer.

Chapter 14: Contract Capacity

Introduction

What does "capacity" mean when talking about contracts? *Capacity* is the ability of a party to enter into a legally binding contract. To have the capacity to enter into a legally binding contract, a person must be of legal age and have the mental ability to understand the obligations required of the agreement.

Age

To be able to understand the ramifications of entering into a contract, most states believe a person needs to be at least 18 years old. Anyone under the age of 18 is a minor, and the law says minors do not have the legal capacity to enter into contracts. Because minors lack the capacity to enter into a contract, their contracts are voidable.

Voidable Contracts

A *voidable contract* is one that exists but may be canceled. By contrast, a *void contract* is one that the law treats as never having existed. This distinction is important because a party to a voidable contract may choose to waive the right to rescind it and decide to abide by it instead. If a contract is void, there is no way it can be made enforceable.

A contract in which one party lacks capacity is voidable and may be canceled by the party who lacks capacity. Thus, a minor who lacks capacity may choose between enforcing the contract or disaffirming it. The other party, however, has no choice and must abide by the contract if the minor decides to affirm it. If a minor decides to disaffirm a contract, it must be disaffirmed within a reasonable amount of time or the minor will be held to it.

Minors may disaffirm a contract by notifying the other party that they refuse to be bound by it. They may also seek a court order that rescinds the contract. A minor who disaffirms a contract must return the consideration received to the extent he or she is able or must compensate the other party for the property that cannot be returned. Restoring the other party to the position it was in before the contract took place is called *restitution,* and minors must make restitution once they disaffirm a contract. They cannot keep the benefit of the bargain while simultaneously disaffirming their portion of it. For example, a 17-year-old cannot sign a contract to buy a car and then disaffirm the contract by asserting they are a minor and not pay for it and keep the car.

Most states will not allow a minor to disaffirm contracts made for necessities. *Necessities* are such things as food, clothing, housing, and medical care.

Mental Capacity

For a party suffering a mental impairment, such as dementia or some condition that makes them permanently unable to comprehend the requirements of a contract, any contract they sign will likely be considered *void ab initio* or invalid from the time it was written and/or signed.

However, just as minors must make restitution when they disaffirm or void a contract, so must those who are mentally infirm.

Intoxication

If a person is so intoxicated he or she cannot understand the nature or consequences of the transaction, the contract entered into is voidable. This is usually quite a difficult legal argument to make successfully. In contract disputes involving intoxicated persons, the law does not distinguish between voluntary and involuntary intoxication. During contract disputes in which the intoxicated party attempts to prove that the contract should be declared voidable, they must prove that they were intoxicated to the point that they were unaware of the legal consequences of entering into the contract. It is rare that such disputes are settled in favor of the intoxicated person because it is very difficult to conclusively establish the degree of intoxication that would result in this loss of awareness.

Just as with minors, contracts to obtain necessary services, such as medical care, cannot be disaffirmed due to intoxication. Disaffirmation can only be completed by providing restitution for the contracted service or by returning the item or items obtained.

HYPOTHETICAL CASE

Sam is 17 years old but has been working for two years and saving every dime so he can buy his own car. He finally has $4,000 and goes to a local car dealer. He decides to buy an older-model Jeep for $3,800. When the contract is prepared, the dealer looks at him and says, "You are eighteen, aren't you?" Sam says he is, and the contract is concluded. Sam enjoys driving the car for six months, and then the transmission blows. He's quoted a cost of $2,000 to fix the transmission. When he complains to a friend that he doesn't have the money to fix his car, the friend tells him, "You're really only seventeen, so the dealer shouldn't have sold the car to you since you can't legally make contracts. Just take it back and tell the dealer you want your money back." Sam decides he'll do just that.

Will Sam be successful in voiding the contract, returning the Jeep, and getting his $3,800 back? Explain why or why not.

Chapter 15: Written Contracts

Introduction

Although there are some instances in which the law insists that a contract be in writing to be enforceable, it should be obvious that a written contract is the best way to prevent misunderstandings and protect one's interests. Certainly, if enforcement of an agreement is required, a written contract avoids a "he said, she said" dispute and shows definitive proof of the parties' obligations. Some contracts are considered so important that the law requires them to be in writing to be enforceable. The doctrine that specifies which contracts must be in writing to be enforced is called the *Statute of Frauds*.

Statute of Frauds

An old English law, the Statute of Frauds provides the basis for which contracts must be in writing to be enforced. It also requires that they be signed by the defendant to be enforced. Under the Statute of Frauds, a contract must be in writing if it fits one of these six criteria:

1. *It is for an interest in land.* Agreements for an interest in land include mortgages, life estates, and leases.

2. *It is to pay the debt of another.* When one person agrees to pay the debt of another as a favor, it is called a *collateral promise,* which must be in writing to be enforced.

3. *It will take more than one year to perform.* For such agreements, the date is calculated from the day the parties make the agreement. If a contract *could* be performed within one year but actually isn't, that does not invalidate the contract.

4. *The executor of an estate makes the contract.* If the executor of an estate (who makes sure the decedent's debts are paid) promises to pay a decedent's debt out of his or her own funds, it must be in writing to be enforceable.

5. *The goods cost more than $500 or whatever the amount is defined by state law.* The UCC requires a written contract for the sale of goods worth $500 or more.

6. *It is made in consideration of marriage.* For example, a prenuptial contract is a contract made in consideration of marriage in which each party agrees to a pre-determined

division of property and assets if the marriage should end in divorce.

Although the Statute of Frauds requires these six types of contracts to be in writing, if a party renders full performance of its part of the bargain concerning an interest in land, the law will not allow that party to disaffirm it merely because the agreement was not written. Sometimes even when a buyer paid part of the purchase price and either took possession of the land or made improvements to it, the buyer will not be able to void the contract just because it isn't in writing.

Even though the Statute of Frauds requires that these types of contracts be in writing to be enforced, they are considered voidable and not *void ab initio.*

Another exception to the requirement that an agreement be in writing to be enforced is in situations where promissory estoppel may be applied. Promissory estoppel is used when one party makes a promise that reasonably causes the other party to rely on it, and the other party does act in reliance on it to their detriment.

Elements of a Valid Written Contract

A written contract must contain four things:

1. The name of each party to the contract

2. The signature of the defendant

3. The subject matter of the agreement

4. All the essential terms and conditions of the agreement

An agreement must always be signed by the party against whom enforcement is sought. The term *signature* is interpreted loosely. A stamped signature, a logo, or even an "X" have been acceptable as signatures to the court. Each state determines what is acceptable as a signature in that jurisdiction. Today, most states accept electronic and digital signatures for most documents.

The Uniform Commercial Code (UCC)

The key difference between the UCC and the Common Law rule is that the UCC does not require all of the terms of the contract to be in writing. The two things that remain essential, however, are the signature of the defendant and the quantity of the goods being sold.

There is a *merchant's exception* to the UCC's written requirement. For routine business between merchants, a letter from one merchant to the other confirming an order, which is definite enough to bind the sender, will be an enforceable contract unless the receiving merchant objects to it within ten days. Any objection should explicitly state the terms or conditions being objected to.

Electronic Signatures

Under federal and many state laws, an electronic signature can be used to execute contracts. Electronic signatures may be a symbol, sound, retinal scan, or other unique identifier. Electronic signatures are not acceptable for insurance contracts, wills, or medical release forms.

Parol Evidence

The parol evidence rule prevents a party to a written contract from contradicting or adding terms to a contract by seeking the admission of evidence that is outside of the contract. Parol evidence is anything that is outside of the written agreement that was said or done before the agreement was signed. The purpose of the parol evidence rule is to prevent the introduction of outside evidence to alter the meaning of the written document. Therefore, most contracts contain this clause that specifies that all the terms and conditions to the agreement are contained within it and no other agreements are binding. Rarely, if a court determines that a contract is incomplete or ambiguous, it will allow parol evidence to fill in the missing information.

For example, Sally and Sam enter into a contract in which Sam agrees to paint Sally's house blue for $4,000. Nothing in the contract specifies that Sally is to pay for the paint. When Sam finishes painting the house, Sally gives him a check for $4,000. He says, "Thanks, but you also owe me another $1,000 for the cost of the paint." If Sam sues Sally for the additional $1,000 and tries to introduce testimony that they had an oral agreement that she would also pay him for the cost of the paint he used, the parol evidence rule will prevent from being admitted the testimony that she also agreed to pay for the paint.

HYPOTHETICAL CASE

Sally and Sam negotiate Sam's purchase of Sally's motorcycle. When he agrees to buy it for $1,500, she says, "Great, I'll even throw in the helmet for free." Sally grabs a piece of paper and writes up the following: "Sally agrees to sell Sam her Honda motorcycle for $1,500, payable within seven days." Sam signs the contract and dates it. He returns in three days with $1,500, and Sally gives him the motorcycle and signs off on the title. Sam says, "Hey, where's the helmet?" Sally responds, "Oh, I gave it to my cousin since he lost his." Sam is really upset since he doesn't have a helmet and didn't buy one because he thought he was getting Sally's.

If Sam sues Sally for breach of contract to get the helmet (or its value), is he likely to prevail? Explain why or why not.

Chapter 16: Third-Party Contracts

Introduction

Typically, a contract can only be enforced by the parties who sign it and are parties to it. Sometimes, however, a person or business wants to enter into a contract that is for the benefit of someone else. Under certain circumstances, these contracts may be enforced by the party who is to benefit from them, even though the beneficiary is not the party that signed the contract and is not the one providing the consideration for the contract.

Third-Party Beneficiary Contracts

Third-party beneficiary contracts are contracts that are made to benefit someone other than the party to the contract.

Third-Party Beneficiaries

A third-party beneficiary is someone who is not a party to the contract but who is intended to benefit from it. For example, if Sam pays Sally's Lawn Service to mow his grandmother's lawn so his grandmother won't have to do it, he is making his grandmother the beneficiary of the contract he is entering into with Sally's Lawn Service.

A third-party beneficiary may seek to enforce a contract (to which it is not a party) if it can prove one of three things:

1. It was an intended beneficiary of the contract.
2. Enforcing the contract will satisfy a duty of the promisor to the third-party beneficiary.
3. The promisee intended to make a gift to the beneficiary.

So, as the intended beneficiary of this contract, Sam's grandmother could sue for the breach of this contract if Sally's Lawn Service fails to perform as required under the contract.

The most common example of a third-party beneficiary contract is a life insurance policy. In a life insurance policy, the owner/holder of the policy is the individual who purchases the policy and is usually the insured life. The insurance company is the other party to the contract, and the third-party beneficiary is the named beneficiary who will receive the policy benefits (money) when the insured policy holder dies.

Third party contracts are important because an intended third-party beneficiary of a contract may enforce the contract in court just as if they were a party to the contract. For example, the beneficiary of a life insurance policy may sue in civil court in his own name to enforce the policy after the death of the insured if the insurance carrier refuses to pay the benefits.

A person who is not an intended beneficiary but who still benefits from the contract is an incidental beneficiary, also known as a donee beneficiary. The distinction between an intentional beneficiary and an incidental beneficiary is important because an intentional beneficiary may enforce a third-party beneficiary contract whereas an incidental beneficiary may not. An incidental or donee beneficiary may not enforce the contract because it was not made for their benefit. For example, if the city contracts with ABC Construction Co. to repave Main Street and the local parking garage receives a huge increase in business because people can't park on Main Street during the construction, the parking garage is an incidental beneficiary because it is benefiting from the construction project though the project was not undertaken with the goal of benefiting it. If the construction work is done improperly and the parking garage sues the construction company to have it re-do the road (and further increase its revenue), the construction company will argue that the parking garage does not have the legal right to sue because it is merely an incidental beneficiary, and the contract was not made with the intent of benefiting them. Of course, to avoid this situation completely, the parties to the contract can make it clear in their agreement that "there are no third-party beneficiaries to this contract."

To determine if a third-party beneficiary may enforce a contract to which it was not a party, the court will examine whether the contracting parties were aware that the third party would benefit and whether one of the contracting parties wanted to make a gift to the third party or satisfy an obligation owed.

An intended beneficiary is either a donee or creditor beneficiary and acquires rights to enforce the original contract depending on which category of beneficiary they are. A donee beneficiary is a party receiving a gift (like Sam's grandmother in our earlier hypothetical where Sam contracted a service to mow her lawn). However, if Sam's grandmother had loaned him money to buy his books for school and instead of paying his grandmother back she had him hire the lawn service instead, that would be satisfying the debt he owed her. In that instance, she would be a creditor beneficiary.

Assignment and Delegation

Either party to a contract may transfer its rights under the contract. This is called an assignment of rights. Along with rights, a party to a contract also has duties, since this exchange of obligations is part of what makes up the consideration of a contract.

If a party transfers its duties (obligations) under a contract, it is called a delegation of duties. If a party assigns its rights under a contract, it usually delegates its duties at the same time, thus transferring all rights and duties to a third party.

Assigning business contracts and delegating duties is an extremely important mechanism in transferring business assets. Acquisitions and mergers of businesses are accomplished through this type of contract mechanism.

Assignment of Rights

Any contractual right may be assigned unless one of these three conditions apply:

1. It would substantially change the obligor's rights or duties under the contract. A substantial change to the contract itself is one that makes a significant difference in the obligor's duties.

2. It is forbidden by law or public policy.

3. It is prohibited by the contract itself.

If a party to a contract wants to make sure any or all of the obligations under the contract cannot be assigned, it may insert a clause into the contract that specifically prohibits assigning rights or delegating duties. These clauses are typically enforced. A common example of this is a provision in a lease that prevents it from being assigned.

An assignment may be written or oral, but if the statute of frauds is applicable, it must be done in writing.

Once the assignment is made, and the obligor is notified of the assignment, the assignee may enforce the contract against the obligor. An assignment of rights for consideration generally includes an implied warranty that the claim is valid. The obligor is also entitled to raise all the defenses against the assignee that he or she could have raised against the assignor.

Delegation of Duties

An obligor (the party under obligation) may delegate duties unless three conditions apply:

1. Delegation would violate public policy.

2. The contract prohibits delegation.

3. The obligee (the party to whom the obligation or duty is owed) has a substantial interest in personal performance by the obligor.

Typically, it is considered a violation of public policy to delegate duties in any contract entered into with a government unit or its agencies. A contract may itself state that it forbids delegation. Sometimes, even without a nondelegation clause, the court may disallow delegation if the work is of the kind that requires personal performance, for example, contracts for personal or professional services such as tennis lessons, legal representation, or surgery. Obviously, such people are being hired for their individual expertise, and it would be unfair and unreasonable to allow them to retain the money received while transferring the obligation under the contract to someone with potentially inferior skills.

Assignors who are paid for making an assignment are held to make certain implied guaranties about the assignment.

Also, for an assignment to be valid, the assignor (the party doing the assignment) must notify all parties of the assignment.

Novation

A novation is a three-way agreement in which the obligor transfers all rights and duties to a third party. A novation has the effect of releasing the obligor from liability. Novation is often used in franchise agreements, in which one of the three parties to a franchise agreement is being replaced with a new party. For example, Sam owns a McDonald's franchise and has a contract with McDonald's Corporation that requires him to buy his hamburger patties from Big Beef Farms. Therefore, he enters into contracts with Big Beef Farms to purchase hamburger patties from them. If Sam sells his McDonald's franchise to Sally, all the contracts of Sam's McDonald's franchise will be entered into "new" with Sally. She takes Sam's place as the franchisee and is now obligated under the contracts with McDonald's Corporation and with the contracts with Big Beef Farms.

HYPOTHETICAL CASE

Sam's grandmother is quite elderly but still lives by herself in the same house she has lived in for 40 years. She is in no shape to do yard work, however, and since Sam is too busy to mow her lawn for her, he contracts with Sally's Lawn Service to mow her 100 x 150–foot yard once a week from June through September. He pays Sally's Lawn Service $400 in advance for this year's contract. Unfortunately, Sam's grandmother dies the second week of June. As a result, Sam tells Sally's that, as the executor of his grandmother's estate, he is reassigning the lawn mowing contract to his brother Fred, so Sally's should mow his brother's 200 x 200–foot lawn for the remainder of the contract term.

Will Sally's have to mow Fred's yard for the rest of the summer? Why or why not?

Chapter 17: Insurance Contracts

Introduction

What is insurance? *Insurance* is designed to protect individuals and companies from the uncertainty of events of chance. It is a method of transferring the risk of loss from the individual or business to the insurance company.

There are four types of insurance coverage:

1. Marine and inland

2. Life

3. Fire and casualty

4. Health

A policy for insurance is a contract. Insurance policies are different from other contracts, and separate laws apply to them.

Contents of Insurance Policies

Typically, an insurance policy has nine elements:

1. A description of parties insured

2. The term of policy (its duration)

3. How much each type of coverage costs

4. Endorsements (attached to the policy, modifying or changing the original policy in some way)

5. Legal description of what is insured

6. Description of the insurance coverage

7. Definitions of the terms used

8. Policy exclusions (specific things the policy does not cover)

9. The policy of coverage

Although state legislature often requires certain language to be included in an insurance policy, there are often ambiguities about the scope of the coverage that result in litigation when insurance companies refuse to pay a claim that an insured believes was included in the policy.

Who Is an Insured?

An insured is the person or company whose loss or death triggers the insurer's duty to pay the proceeds of the policy. It is almost always the person or company who enters into a contract with the insurer who receives the proceeds in the event of a loss.

Note: In most instances, public policy prohibits paying life insurance benefits to someone who takes an insurance policy out on someone else's life. This is because this situation has the effect of discouraging the beneficiary from protecting the insured's life. However, if the person taking out the policy can show they have a vested interest in protecting the insured's life and making sure they stay alive, such as the insured being their spouse or the CEO of their company, then courts may determine that such an insurance policy is legitimate and necessary to compensate someone for the loss of income generated by the spouse or business leader.

Specific Designations

The most common insurance policies cover a person's life or property. It is usually possible to make additions to insurance coverage after the policy is in effect through an endorsement on the policy. An *endorsement* is a written document that is attached to an insurance policy and modifies the policy by changing the coverage provided under the policy. An endorsement can add coverage for parties, or it can add coverage for acts or property not covered under the original policy.

Omnibus Clause and Coverage

Insurance liability policies designate at least one insured by name and other insureds by description, usually as classes of people who have some relationship to the named insured. The clause usually defines "insured" as the actual person, spouse, or members of the household. Typically, all included individuals have a specified relationship to the named insured. Each person within each described class is an insured for purposes of the policy's coverage. For example, an omnibus clause may cover "all employees" of an insured's business.

The Loss Payable Clause

This clause refers to the measure of reimbursement a person is entitled to receive when multiple parties share an interest in property. Sometimes the person who owns a life insurance policy is not the person insured. This situation usually arises when a person buys a policy to ensure that the debt owed on real property will be paid if one of the purchasers dies before it is paid off. Therefore, the rights of ownership belong to the purchasers, not the insured.

Insurance Policies as Adhesion Contracts

Adhesion contracts are formed when one party has superior bargaining power that it uses to impose its desired terms on the other party. This results in a "take it or leave it" option for the insured. An exclusion of coverage contained in an adhesion contract of insurance must be expressed in words that are plain and clear. An adhesion contract will be strictly construed against the insurer.

Doctrine of Reasonable Expectations

When an insurance contract is ambiguous and subject to two interpretations, and one interpretation is absurd while the other is reasonable, the court will apply the reasonable one.

The reasonable expectations doctrine does not apply unless the contract language is ambiguous. An ambiguous clause is one that is capable of more than one meaning.

Forming an Insurance Contract

The initial insurance contract requires the submission of an application, issuance of binder, investigation by the insurer, and delivery of the policy.

Most insurance agents are considered employees, and most brokers are considered independent contractors. A broker has access to a number of insurers and is actually an agent of the insured.

Duty of the Agent or Broker to the Insured

The insurance agent has a duty to obtain the insurance that the potential insured requests. The agent does not have the duty to offer advice, but if the agent undertakes to offer advice, he or she is then liable for the advice offered.

An agent has a duty to tell the insured what kind of insurance to get if the agent is a specialist in the area, such a duty is imposed by statute, or a special relationship exists between the agent and the potential insured.

Duty of the Agent to the Insurance Company

The duty of the agent to the company is the same as in agency law, meaning the agent must act with due care and act only within the authority of what the principal or the company has authorized. The agent has a duty to act within the authority granted to it and to abide by the company's rules. The agent can be sued by the insurer if the agent orally binds the company to a contract to which it has not

agreed or if the agent misrepresents a material fact to the insured.

An agent binds the insurance company if two conditions hold:

1. The agent has either express (actual) or implied (apparent) authority.
2. The facts of the case indicate the agent had authority. The court will look to see if the agent's actions were undertaken with the permission or acquiescence of the insurer (even if the agent acted in excess of their actual authority).

Beneficiaries of Life Insurance Policies

A beneficiary in a life insurance policy is the person who, although not a party to the contract, is entitled to receive the proceeds of the insurance. The two types of recognized life insurance relationships are family and business relationships.

Beneficiary's Rights

Most insurance policies explicitly reserve to the insured the power to change the beneficiary without the designated beneficiary's knowledge or consent. The insured is reserved the power to receive the cash value of the policy, take out loans against the policy, or assign the policy, all without the beneficiary's consent. The beneficiary does not have a vested right and only has an expectancy of receiving proceeds under the insurance policy.

Naming and Designating the Beneficiary

The person who takes out the insurance policy has the right to name and change the beneficiary so long as the beneficiary has an insurable interest in the insured.

Changing the Beneficiary

The insurance policy states how the beneficiary may be changed and when the change becomes effective. Most courts require that the person substantially comply with these provisions rather than comply exactly as the provision specifies.

Creditor or Beneficiary

Most state laws exempt insurance policies from creditor claims. However, the courts will examine five elements:

1. Whether the cash value of proceeds are being claimed as exempt

2. The kind of policy involved

3. The relationship of debtor to policy

4. If debtor is owner or has right to change in beneficiary

5. The relationship of beneficiary to insured

Creditor as Beneficiary

Courts will usually infer that the insured intended to designate the creditor as a beneficiary only to the extent of the debt, although some courts will allow the creditor to keep all the proceeds.

Covered Risks

Homeowners insurance policies incorporate into one policy several kinds of property coverage: additional living expenses, comprehensive personal liability coverage, property replacement costs, and coverage on the dwelling and adjacent structures.

Auto insurance policies cover many types of liability, such as medical payments, uninsured motorist, property damage, and general liability.

Umbrella policies provide liability insurance in excess of that provided by the homeowners and auto policies. This insurance applies only when catastrophic events happen, and the insured usually must demonstrate having the maximum coverage with their primary policy before being allowed to purchase umbrella coverage.

Commercial liability coverage provides general insurance coverage to an insured regardless of the nature of the insured's business.

Limitations of Coverage

An insurance policy may, and often does, include explicit limitations, exclusions, or exceptions. These appear in the policy as affirmative grants of coverage or in specific limitations on those grants of coverage. Exclusions and exceptions are areas singled out in the policy where no insurance coverage will be provided. One of the main legal limitations of insurance policies is that they will compensate an insured for a loss resulting from acts of negligence but not for a loss or injury resulting from intentional torts.

Termination of Coverage

When an insurance contract has been fully performed, the parties' duties are discharged, and the contract terminates. A policy may also terminate on the date of a breach of warranty, a misrepresentation, or the concealment of material information.

Cancellation of Coverage

Insurance coverage can be canceled in four ways:

1. The policy may be rescinded by mutual agreement.

2. An insured fails to pay the premium.

3. The insured may have an explicit right under the policy to cancel it unilaterally.

4. An insurer has the right to cancel the policy unilaterally if not restricted by statute.

Unilateral Cancellation

Usually, the insured can unilaterally cancel the policy at any time, but this right may be abrogated by statute. An insurer always has the right to cancel a policy when there is misrepresentation, concealment or breach of warranty or if the premium is not paid.

Statutory Cancellation Procedures

Most state statutes require an insurer to give notice to the insured before effectuating a cancellation. If notice is not given by the insurer, the cancellation is considered void. This is to give the insured both the opportunity and time to obtain other insurance to replace the canceled policy.

Coverage for Intentional Conduct

An insurer will only pay for a loss that is fortuitous, meaning the loss must be accidental. Insurance policies specifically exclude coverage for intentional acts that result in a covered loss.

Property Insurance

If an insured party intentionally causes damage to their own insured property, the loss will not be covered.

The public policy behind this is that allowing damages to be collected on property deliberately damaged by the insured would encourage insureds to destroy their property to collect the insurance money. Also, when an insured intentionally fails to take steps to preserve property after it is damaged, the insured will not be allowed to recover for any additional loss caused thereby.

Personal Insurance, Life, and Accidental Death

Typically, a death due to suicide within two years of the policy being issued excludes coverage. The rationale behind this rule is to prevent a person from purchasing insurance while having the intent to kill oneself for the enrichment of the beneficiaries. In addition, the law views suicide as being inherently non-accidental.

Determining an Accident

One of the most litigated aspects of insurance policy is determining whether an act is the result of an accident or intentional conduct. This is important because insurance policies do not cover or pay claims resulting from intentional conduct.

An accident is usually considered an unusual event that the insured does not foresee. An example would be an event that happens unexpectedly and without the insured's intent. When determining if the insured's death was accidental, the examiner will determine the following:

- Was the death-producing event an accident? (Was the event unforeseen and unexpected from the viewpoint of the insured?)

- If the event was accidental, did the accident cause the death?

- If there are multiple causes of death:

  - Was the accident not too remote?

  - Was the accident the dominant cause of the loss?

Some accidental death provisions require that the insured's death be within a specified number of days of the death-inducing injury. These clauses are increasingly controversial as the ability of the medical profession to prolong life improves.

If the event causing the claim caused property damage, such as in a fire, the insurance carrier will pay the claim if the fire was the result of an accident but not if it was intentionally set (i.e., arson).

Disability Insurance

Disability insurance covers the loss of a person's capacity to work. Disability insurance pays an insured person an income when that person is unable to work because of an injury or illness. However, depending on the amount of the policy, it may, or may not pay an amount equal to the income earned while the insured was working

Occupational Insurance

Occupational disability insurance provides coverage if the insured is disabled while performing the duties of the particular occupation in which the insured is engaged.

General Disability Insurance

General disability insurance policies require that the insured must, as a result of the disability, be unable to pursue an occupation for profit for which he or she is reasonably suited by education, training, or experience.

Health Insurance

Health insurance covers the cost of medical treatment and care when an insured suffers an injury or illness.

Preexisting Conditions

Prior to the Affordable Health Care Act (Obamacare), insurers would often exclude from coverage any sickness or illness that existed before the effective date of coverage. It became illegal for insurance carriers to continue this practice under this statute.

Medically Necessary Services

Medically necessary services refers to treatment that is not considered by the insurance provider to be a medically accepted care protocol, and therefore it is deemed not medically necessary and is not covered by the insurance provider.

Claim Process

To receive insurance proceeds, the insurer typically must file a claim stating the loss suffered. This process is usually specified in the policy and requires that notice be given to the insurer as soon as possible. However, the insured's noncompliance with the claims processing requirements does not usually allow the insurer an excuse for not performing the duties it has undertaken. The purpose of requiring the insured to give notice of a loss to the insurer is to enable the insurer to investigate the circumstances of the loss before information becomes stale or disappears. It assists in dealing with fraudulent claims and thereby reduces the costs of coverage.

Proof of Loss

The insured must provide proof of their loss with their claim to give the insurer an adequate opportunity to investigate the loss and to prevent fraud against the insurer.

Substantive Requirements

A proof of loss requires a formal statement of the claim, usually sworn with the notarized signature of the insured. The insurance policy specifies what proof of loss is required.

Effect of Noncompliance

Generally, noncompliance with the provision requiring proof of loss will only relieve the insurer from providing liability if there is a lack of substantial compliance by the insured.

False Statements

Most insurance policies will be considered void if the insured willfully concealed or misrepresented a material fact concerning a loss. However, if the insured makes a mistake, most courts will usually construe it as "false swearing," and the policy will not be considered void.

Disposition of Claims

An insurer must process the claim of an insured in a timely manner. In fact, many insurance contracts provide specific language as to what the time limit is. The time limits cannot be unreasonably short or longer than the time allotted under the statute of limitations.

Insured's Duty to Cooperate with the Insurer

The duty of the insured to cooperate with the insurer may be expressly stated or implied through the insurance contract.

The duty to cooperate does not have to be expressly stated for it to be required. However, a non-breaching party is not allowed to suspend acting in faith because the other party did not cooperate. It will be allowed to do so only if the breach of the duty to cooperate is material. In such an instance, the non-breaching party may be allowed to suspend and ultimately discharge its obligations. Obviously, the cooperation of the insured is necessary because it is the only way that the insurer can obtain the information it needs.

Bad Faith and Breach of Covenant of Fair Dealing

Bad faith occurs when an insurer denies a claim that is not "fairly debatable." An example would be if the insurer fails to pay a claim in a manner that would eliminate the insured's hardship where the insurer is aware of the insured's dire circumstance and has no legitimate reason not to pay the claim.

Duty to Defend

The insurance company has a duty to defend the insured in any lawsuit alleging claims covered under its policy if liability were later established and the insurer would be required to pay damages on behalf of the insured. This duty to defend is based on the allegations in a complaint and is not dependent on their truthfulness.

Duty to Pay Proceeds

Under the contract, the insurer will pay the proceeds of a loss if it is within the coverage provided under the policy. If the insurer wrongfully refuses to make such payments, it may be liable for acting in bad faith.

Note: If a person or business is sued for an event covered by insurance and a judgment against the insured is returned by a jury or judge in a lawsuit that exceeds the amount of money available from the insurance policy, the defendant is personally liable to pay the remaining amount owed.

Measuring the Amount of Loss

The goal of property insurance is to indemnify the insured for the loss covered. Indemnity is to reimburse the insured for the loss sustained and no more. The objective is to put the insured in the position in which the insured would have been had the loss not occurred. As such, the insured is not entitled to recover more than the damaged property is worth or more than its decline in value suffered as a result of the damage.

If the insured's loss is partial, they will not be allowed to recover an amount exceeding the policy limits, even if the insured's actual loss is greater. Whatever the limits of policy, the insured will not be allowed to recover more than the insured's interest in the property. In no event can the insured recover more than the value of the property. However, if the insured can show that his damaged boat, for example, cannot be restored to as good a condition as it was in before the accident, some courts will allow the insured to recover the difference between the reasonable value of the boat before the accident and the reasonable market value after repair in addition to the cost of repairs.

Co-insurance

Co-insurance is a loss-sharing agreement between the insured and the insurer wherein the insured bears a portion of the loss based on a percentage of the property's total value not covered by the insurance. The insured is also an insurer along with the underwriter, meaning if the underwritten amount is less than the value of the property, the insured is a co-insurer in the sense that the owner bears a portion of the risk of loss.

Coinsurance requires the insured to pay beyond a deductible before the insurer will provide coverage.

Chapter 18: Remedies

Introduction

What is a remedy? A remedy is a method used to compensate the injured party in a lawsuit.

To obtain a remedy, a party must be able to demonstrate that it has suffered injury, which entitles the party damages. The court's purpose in assessing damages is to help the injured party without unfairly harming the other. In most instances, the idea is not to punish the wrongful party, although sometimes punitive damages are allowed in an effort to prevent others from engaging in particularly reprehensible conduct.

When determining what remedy to apply, the first step the court takes is to identify the interest to be protected. An interest is a legal right in something. A person may have a legal interest in property, a contract, or in personal safety (tort) claim.

The most common remedy for legal violations in both tort and contract causes of action is an award of monetary damages. To recover monetary damages, a plaintiff must prove an injury to person or property. For example, if the defendant isn't paying attention while driving his boat and runs into the plaintiff's boat, which causes $10,000 in damage to the plaintiff's boat, the plaintiff may sue the defendant for negligence and get a $10,000 money judgment, which compensates the plaintiff for the $10,000 it cost her to get her boat fixed.

Remedies in Tort

The type of damages one can claim depends on the cause of action alleged. Lawsuits based on a tort claim may seek five types of damages:

1. Nominal damages

2. Compensatory damages

3. General damages

4. Punitive damages

5. Special damages

Nominal Damages

Nominal damages are those awarded when the plaintiff has not sustained an actual loss or injury. Nominal damages are intended as a statement that the type of conduct the defendant has engaged in should not be permitted. They are used to show the plaintiff is correct, to prove a point, but when no compensation is determined to be deserved.

Compensatory Damages

Compensatory damages are also referred to as actual damages. They are awarded to compensate the plaintiff for what was lost, for the injury or harm suffered by the defendant's conduct and breach of duty.

General Damages

General damages are noneconomic damages, which are not easily demonstrated. These include things such as pain and suffering or the loss of a bodily function (such as the inability to have children or the loss of vision or hearing) or appearance.

For example, if the defendant negligently causes a fire in the chemistry lab and the plaintiff is burned and disfigured for life, the plaintiff may recover $1,000,000 after demonstrating she has developed a phobia of chemistry labs and has a horribly disfigured face.

Punitive Damages

If the defendant's misconduct is found to be intentional, willful, wanton, or malicious, the court may permit an award of punitive damages in addition to compensatory damages.

Punitive damages are uncommon, and some states do not permit them, but if a defendant's conduct is so egregious, the court may use punitive damages to punish the defendant and to discourage others from engaging in the same or similar type of conduct. An example is found in lawsuits filed against cigarette manufacturers. These lawsuits alleged that cigarette manufacturers knew that their product (cigarettes) were addictive and caused cancer and other serious health problems even as they continued selling them and lying about their health risks. When plaintiffs succeeded in proving these companies had intentionally misled the public about the health risks of smoking cigarettes, some courts imposed punitive damages in addition to compensatory damages.

Special Damages

Special damages in tort cases consist of medical expenses, in-home medical care, loss of wages, and the loss or impairment of future earning capacity. Special damages, which are sometimes referred to as economic damages, are measured by out-of-pocket expenses.

For example, if the defendant causes a car accident and the plaintiff is seriously injured, the plaintiff may sue the defendant for negligence and recover $100,000 for medical bills, $20,000 for lost wages, and $1,000,000 for the impairment of his ability to work and earn a living at the job he held.

Remedies in Contract

There are nine courses of damage for those suing for breach of contract:

1. Compensatory damages
2. Consequential damages
3. Liquidated damages
4. Rescission
5. Restitution
6. Reformation
7. Specific performance
8. Reliance
9. Expectation interest

Compensatory Damages

In contract cases, compensatory damages are the sum of money it takes to restore the injured party to the economic position it would be in if the contract had been performed. Compensatory damages reimburse the plaintiff for loss. Compensatory damages flow directly from the contract. They are direct damages.

To receive compensatory damages, the injured party must prove the breach of contract caused the damages and that the damages can be quantified with reasonable certainty. For example, merely saying, "The cost to replace my computer that was destroyed is $1,000," is not sufficient. The court will likely require a purchase receipt showing the plaintiff paid $1,000 for the computer or other evidence as proof of its value.

Consequential Damages

Consequential damages occur after the contract is breached. They are awarded when they can be reasonably anticipated. Consequential damages are those that result from the unique circumstances of the injured party. For example, if Sam's Contracting Co. agreed to remodel an apartment complex by June 1 but fails to finish the job until

October 1, it is reasonably foreseeable that the apartment complex owner will lose three months' rent from tenants as a result of the delay (assuming it can demonstrate it had tenants). So, not only does Sam's breach result in actual damages, it also results in consequential damages consisting of lost revenue for the apartment owner, for which Sam's may be liable.

Liquidated Damages

Liquidated damages are awarded when a contract states in advance how much a party must pay if it breaches the contract. It is common for construction contracts to include a liquidated damages clause that penalizes a contractor for each day after the completion date a project remains unfinished.

The court will usually enforce liquidated damages clauses if two conditions hold true:

1. At the time of creating the contract, it was very difficult to estimate actual damages.

2. The amount of liquidated damages is reasonable. (If the amount of liquidated damages is determined unreasonable, it may be deemed a penalty and will not be enforced.)

Rescission

When rescission is used, the contract is canceled, and both sides are excused from further performance. Any money that has been advanced is returned. To have rescission, both parties to the contract must be placed in the position they occupied before the contract was made. Courts have held that a party may rescind a contract for fraud, incapacity, duress, undue influence, material breach in performance of a promise, or mistake.

According to the UCC, a contract may be rescinded if all the parties to it consent. Any single party to a contract may rescind the contract in the following cases:

1. If the consent of the party rescinding, or of any party jointly contracting with him, was given by mistake, or obtained through duress, menace, fraud, or undue influence, exercised by or with the connivance of the party as to whom he rescinds, or of any other party to the contract jointly interested with such party.

2. If the consideration for the obligation of the rescinding party fails, in whole or in part, through the fault of the party as to whom he rescinds.

3. If the consideration for the obligation of the rescinding party becomes entirely void from any cause.

4. If the consideration for the obligation of the rescinding party, before it is rendered to him, fails in a material respect from any cause.

5. If the contract is unlawful for causes that do not appear in its terms or conditions, and the parties are not equally at fault.

6. If the public interest will be prejudiced by permitting the contract to stand.

Restitution

Restitution is designed to return to the injured party a benefit it has conferred on the other party that would be unjust to leave with that party. It is used when the plaintiff has conferred a benefit on the defendant that requires compensation.

In quasi-contract cases, restitution is used where one side benefits even though the parties never had an enforceable contract. Because it would be unfair to let the party retain the benefit without compensating the other party, the court will require the one who benefited to compensate the party who has provided the benefit.

Restitution is common in fraud, misrepresentation, duress, and mistake cases, and it may be used in conjunction with rescission.

Reformation

If a contract is reformed, its terms are changed to reflect what the parties intended. Reformation occurs when the court "rewrites" a portion of the contract. This remedy is seldom used, but when rewriting the contract can save it, the court may choose to do so.

For example, Sam agrees to sell Sally his 1968 Camaro, but instead of specifying "1968 Camaro" in the contract, he writes "1968 Corvette" by mistake. Sam also has a 1968 Corvette, which is worth a great deal more than his 1968 Camaro, and he refuses to sell her his 1968 Corvette. Sally knows the Corvette is worth a lot more and sues seeking to enforce the contract as written. If the court determines that the parties made a mistake in the contract and that they actually had agreed that Sally was buying his 1968 Camaro, it may "reform" the contract so that it reads 1968 Camaro, as was intended.

Specific Performance

Specific performance is an equitable remedy used when money damages will not help the injured party. In specific performance, the party is ordered to perform the contract as entered into. This remedy is only used in cases involving the sale of land or some other unique asset such as artworks, patents, and trade secrets. Either the seller or buyer may be granted specific performance. Specific performance is not used when the injured party can purchase an identical item with money damages.

Reliance Damages

Money spent on the anticipation that the contract would be performed is considered reliance damages. Reliance occurs when the plaintiff may not be able to demonstrate expectation damages but may still prove that the plaintiff expended money in reliance of the contract being performed.

The reliance interest is intended to put the injured party in the position it would have been in if the parties had never entered into a contract.

Reliance damages are the only type awarded in promissory estoppel cases. In promissory estoppel cases, there has been no bargain (no contract), so there can be no expectation damages for the full benefit of the bargain. For example, Sally promised to pay Sam $1,000 if he painted her garage. Sam was halfway finished painting her garage when it burned down. Sally tells him that she is not obligated to pay him for his work since the garage has been destroyed. Since Sam can show he reasonably relied on Sally's promise to pay him and that it would be unfair for her not to pay him, the court will likely award him reliance damages to compensate him for the amount of work he performed before the garage burned down.

Expectation Interest Damages

An expectation interest is what the injured party reasonably thought it would get from the contract. Expectation interest is intended to put the injured party in the position it would be in if the contract had been performed. Lost profits are considered expectation damages.

Incidental Damages

Incidental damages are the minor costs the injured party suffers when responding to the breach.

Speculative Damages

Speculative damages are not entitled to compensation by the court system since they cannot be proven. They are damages based on what a plaintiff may lose in the future. Thus, they are only a guess or estimate of what the plaintiff might suffer. For example, Sam was an excellent football player and had just tried out for a position on the Green Bay Packers when someone ran over his foot in a parking lot and crushed both his foot and his hopes of playing for this professional football team. He sued the driver of the car and claimed damages for $100,000,000 that he might have made as a professional football player had the defendant not destroyed his chances of playing in the NFL. The court will reject this claim on the basis that Sam did not have a contract to play for any NFL team, so his claim to this amount of damages is only a hope and a dream, not a certainty. If, however, he had just signed a contract to play for a team for this amount and now could not, then his damages would be real, and he would be entitled to compensation.

UCC Rules

The UCC has specific rules for breach of contracts for the sale of goods.

Seller's Remedies

Under the UCC, the seller may be awarded the difference between the original contract price and the price the seller would have been able to obtain in the open market.

For example, if the buyer breaches a contract to purchase corn from the seller at $2.00 a bushel and the seller was then able to get only $1.50 a bushel by selling the corn on the open market, the seller may sue the intended buyer for $0.50 for each bushel the intended buyer was contracted to purchase.

Buyer's Remedies

Under the UCC, the buyer may obtain the difference between the original contract price and the cover (substitute) price of the goods. The buyer is also entitled to consequential damages if the seller could have reasonably foreseen them.

For example, if the seller breaches the contract by failing to deliver tires and the buyer cannot manufacture and deliver the cars it makes as a result, its lost profit would be a foreseeable consequence of the breach, for which the seller would be responsible.

Injunctions

An injunction is a court order that requires a party to refrain from doing something it otherwise would do. The requirements for obtaining an injunction are usually established by statute. For example, an injunction may be issued by the court to stop a city from tearing down a dilapidated building if the property owner demonstrates the statutory requirements necessary to obtain an injunction. Injunctions are often sought in efforts to prevent projects that cause environmental damage—once water is contaminated or a forest destroyed, the harm is irreparable and cannot be undone.

The typical elements necessary to obtain an injunction require a party to show all four of the following:

1. Potential irreparable injury

2. A likelihood the irreparable injury/harm will occur if not enjoined (stopped)

3. No other remedy being available (i.e., monetary compensation will not be sufficient)

4. A need for the court to act to prevent the harm

Reparative injunctions are used to undo or reverse harms that have already occurred. For example, if farmer Sam erected a dam on a river as it flowed through his property, which prevented the river from flowing elsewhere, the court may order him to remove the dam so other farmers can access the river's water.

Mandamus

Mandamus is a court order that directs a public official to perform a nondiscretionary official duty. It cannot be used to order a private party.

For example, if the city clerk doesn't like the new law requiring cities to issue marriage licenses to gay couples and he refuses to issue them, a gay couple seeking to obtain a marriage license from him may obtain a court order compelling him to issue the license. The court will order the clerk to do what his job legally requires.

Mitigation of Damages

Courts will not allow a party who is injured by a breach of contract to recover for damages it could have avoided with a reasonable effort. Parties are expected to mitigate or lessen their damages if possible. That means the injured party must keep damages as low as reasonably possible and must prevent unnecessary loss.

For example, if a tenant breaches a lease and the landlord has another person who wants to rent the apartment, the landlord cannot refuse to re-lease the apartment and then claim the remainder of the unpaid lease as monetary damages. Or, a restaurant owner whose baker fails to deliver bread as scheduled has an obligation to attempt to obtain bread from another baker rather than to close the restaurant and declare a total loss because they couldn't operate without bread.

Reducing or Increasing Damage Awards

Sometimes a party may appeal a case on the basis that the amount of money damages awarded by the judge or jury is too great or too little.

If the appellate court reduces the amount of damages or compensation on appeal, it is called remittitur. If the appellate court increases the amount of damages or compensation on appeal, it is called addititur.

Effect of Third-Party Sources of Compensation

A plaintiff who is injured and receives compensation from a source independent of the defendant may still recover from the defendant for the same loss compensated for by the independent source. This typically refers to insurance payments and provides that although a party has received proceeds from an insurance policy, it is still entitled to recover from the party that was in the wrong.

Attorney Fees

Both tort and contract cases may ask for an award that pays attorney fees. Typically, court rules and statutes allow judges to award these to the successful party, but such awards are usually discretionary. Sometimes a contract may specify that the losing party to a lawsuit is to pay attorney fees.

HYPOTHETICAL CASE

Sam's Construction Company has a contract to build a warehouse for Sally's Car Dealership. The contract specifies $1,000,000 in liquidated damages if the warehouse is not completed by May 1. Due to a late thaw, the ground remained frozen, so construction of the warehouse wasn't completed until May 30.

Will Sam's company have to pay the $1,000,000 in liquidated damages? Why or why not?

Chapter 19: Agency

Introduction

What is agency? *Agency* is a personal, non-assignable obligation to act on behalf of another. It is based on trust and confidence. In agency relationships, the agent is authorized to act on another's behalf in situations involving money, property, specialized knowledge or judgment, and discretion. Agency relationships are often used in commercial transactions, but they may be used for non-commercial purposes as well. Whenever a person or organization seeks to act through the efforts of others, an agency situation may arise. Agents may be individuals or business entities such as corporations or partnerships. Neither written consent nor compensation is necessary to create an agency relationship.

All agents are fiduciaries, meaning all agents have a legal obligation to act in the best interests of their principal. However, not all fiduciaries are agents, meaning not all fiduciaries are acting on behalf of someone else.

In single agency situations, an agent represents one party to the transaction. In dual agency situations, an agent represents both the principal and the third party in the transaction. In dual agency situations, both the principal and third party must understand the conflict and agree to having the same agent represent them.

Parties to an Agency Relationship

There are three parties in any agency relationship: the principal, the agent, and the third party.

Principal

The principal is the person who delegates the authority to the agent.

Agent

The agent is the person who accepts authority and acts on behalf of the principal.

Sometimes a principal hires an intermediary agent who is given the authority to hire others. The persons hired by the agent are *subagents* of the principal, and the principal may be liable for their actions as well as those of the agent. An example of this is when a store owner hires a person to manage the store (agent) and the manager hires salespeople to work in the store (subagents).

Third Party

The third party is the person whom the agent deals with on behalf of the principal—for example, the customer in a retail business situation.

Forms of Agency

There are several types of agency. Each is based on the authority that is delegated and the purpose for which the agency relationship is formed.

Universal Agency

Universal agency is the broadest and most general form of agency. In this form, the agent is delegated every authority legally possible for that type of transaction. It is ongoing in nature, and the agent can bind the principal if authorized to do so. It is used for the acquisition and transfer of assets, expenditure of the principals' funds and to enter into contracts.

General Agency

General agency is narrower in scope than universal agency and has a more specific purpose. It can be ongoing in nature, and the agent may bind the principal if authorized to do so. In this form, the agent is authorized to conduct an ongoing series of transactions for the principal and can obligate him or her to certain types of contractual agreements. It is the type of agency used in real estate transactions.

Special Agency

Special agency is limited in scope and authority to a single act. It is not ongoing, and the agent may bind the principal only if authorized to do so.

Duties and Liability of the Principal

The principal's duties to the agent are to provide information necessary for the agent to do his/her or its job, to be available to the agent as needed, to indemnify the agent in certain circumstances, and to pay the agent compensation if the agency is for hire.

A principal is bound by the acts of their agent if the agent has the authority to obligate them to perform the acts.

If an agent exceeds its authority, the principal must repudiate the unauthorized act as soon as the principal becomes aware of it or risk the possibility that the court will order that the principal is bound by it. If, however, a principal wrongfully revokes the agency, the agent may sue for damages if the revocation results in a breach of contract.

When determining if an agent was acting within the scope of its authority, the court will examine such factors as whether the act was the kind that the agent was employed to perform and whether it was undertaken, at least in part, by a purpose to serve the principal.

The Agent's Duties to Third Parties

An agent has the duty to act honestly, competently, and fairly when dealing with third parties on behalf of the principal. Often, the third party will be a customer, or potential customer, of the principal. When dealing with third parties, the agent must follow all laws and disclose all relevant information and material conditions of which they are aware.

The Agent's Fiduciary Duties to the Principal

An agent acting on behalf of a principal must act in the best interests of the principal, remain loyal and obedient to the principal, and disclose all relevant information to them. They must also keep confidential any information with which they have been entrusted and provide an accurate accounting of all money and resources that they have been provided. In addition, they must exercise reasonable care and due diligence in all their undertakings.

Methods of Creating Agency

An agency relationship may be created by apparent authority, inherent authority, an express agreement, an implied agreement, estoppel, or ratification.

Apparent Authority

Apparent authority exists when the principal manifests consent to a third party in a way that gives the impression that the principal has authorized the agent to act on the principal's behalf. Courts use the doctrine of apparent authority to protect third parties who have been misled into believing an agent has the authority to bind the principal. Apparent authority may be deduced from words, written documents, and/or the conduct of the principal.

Inherent Authority

Inherent authority is authority that arises solely from the designation by the principal of a kind of agent who ordinarily possesses certain powers. If there is authority that is neither actual nor apparent, then it is inherent. An example of inherent authority is when a real estate agent, who has been authorized to sell a house for the principal, places a "For Sale" sign on the property. The agent does not need to seek special permission from the principal to do this since the action is typically understood to be within the authority given to real estate agents.

Express Agreement

In an express agreement, the principal and agent specifically agree to create an agency relationship either orally or in writing. The terms and conditions of the agency relationship are typically specified in detail.

Implied Agreement

It is possible for the court to find an implied agency agreement if the principal and agent appear to have created an agency relationship by words or action.

Agency by Estoppel

If the principal leads a third party to believe a person is the principal's agent through words or conduct, then the courts will not allow the principal to deny the agency relationship.

Under the doctrine of estoppel, the principal may not claim that a person was not his or her agent if the principal knew that others thought the person was acting on his or her behalf and failed to correct the mistaken belief. In such instances, the principal will be prevented (estopped) from denying an agency relationship, and the results of it will be enforced.

Agency by Ratification

If the principal accepts an unauthorized act of an agent after the fact, and accepts the benefits of it, the court will rule that the principal has ratified the agent's act and thereby created an agency relationship.

Legal Consequences of the Agency Relationship

Not only may an agent obligate their principal according to the authority and terms of their agency agreement, under common law, the principal may also be responsible for certain authorized acts of the agent and any subagents.

Liability in Contract

The principal is liable for the contracts entered into by its agent if made with actual, apparent, or inherent agency authority. If an agent has no authority, the principal is not liable to the third party, but the agent is. If the agent disobeys the principal's instructions, he or she will be responsible for any damages that result from the disobedience. For example, if a principal hires an agent to bid up to $1,000 for the principal on a painting at an art auction and the agent wins the auction by bidding $2,000 for the painting, the principal will not be obligated to pay $2,000 for the painting (but the agent may be required to). The principal will have to immediately notify the third party of the unauthorized act of the agent and disavow it to avoid liability.

Any notice that is given to the agent by a third party is considered to be notice given to the principal. As such, if a customer notified a store manager that it will not be accepting another shipment of product because the last shipment did not meet quality control requirements, it is considered as if notice was given to the manager's "principal." If the manager fails to tell his or her boss or company headquarters of this important breach of a contract term, it will not be considered a defense since it is the agent's duty to do so. In addition, the agent also has a duty of confidentiality concerning company secrets, and this duty is deemed to continue even after the agency relationship ends.

An agent cannot secretly represent both the principal and a third party. They can do so only if both the principal and third party are aware the agent is doing so and have agreed to it.

Agents are not liable for any contract they make on behalf of a fully disclosed principal. Principals are fully disclosed if the third party knows of their existence and their identity.

Undisclosed Principal

There are some situations, such as the purchase of land, in which the principal does not want its identity revealed to the third party. In these situations, the acts of the agent bind an undisclosed or a partially disclosed principal, if doing so is usual or necessary in such transactions. Sometimes liability attaches even when the agent's acts were forbidden by the principal.

If the principal is undisclosed, the third party can recover from either the principal or the agent. A principal is undisclosed if the third party did not know of the principal's existence. A contract with an undisclosed principal is binding if the agent informs the third party that there is an undisclosed principal. Real estate purchases are often made by undisclosed principals.

Partially Disclosed Principal

If a principal is partially disclosed, the wronged third party can recover from either the agent or the principal. A principal is partially disclosed if the third party knew of the principal's existence but not the identity. In the case of a partially disclosed principal, the agent and the principal are jointly and severally liable, meaning the injured party can recover from either or both.

Ratification

In some instances, an agent may act outside the scope of his or her authority in contract-negotiating situations on behalf of their principal, exceeding the scope of their authority in agreeing to a condition or term beyond what they have been authorized. They are certainly taking a risk in doing so since their principal may immediately contact the third party and disavow their actions by notifying them that the agent did not have the authority to agree to such terms. But why would an agent do such a thing and apparently violate their duty of loyalty and obedience? Sometimes an agent will act outside the scope of their authority when they are confident they are acting in their principal's best interest and that their principal will ratify their actions.

A principal can ratify, or approve, an agent's actions that were not pre-approved. This subsequent adoption of the activity is referred to as ratification. Sometimes the person was an acknowledged agent who merely exceeded the scope of their agency, and other times the person may not have been an agent at all but held themselves out to be one and obligated the principal contractually as if they were their agent. When this happens, as soon as the purported principal becomes aware of the situation, they must make up their mind whether they want to follow through on the obligations to which their agent has committed them, or whether they want to disavow them. The necessity to disavow as soon as the principal becomes aware is important because once the third party can show reliance and harm as a result of the agent's conduct, it may be too late to avoid legal liability for their actions.

Also, when someone appears to act on the behalf of another in a transaction with a third party, and estoppel cannot apply, the act is deemed ratified if the principal accepts the benefits of the unauthorized transaction, or fails to repudiate it. In such instances, they are bound by the act as if they had originally authorized it. Thus, even if an agent acts without authority, the principal can later decide to be bound by the agent and the agent's acts if four conditions are met:

1. The agent indicates to the third party that the agent is acting for the principal.

2. The principal knows all the material facts of the transaction.

3. The principal accepts the benefits of the entire transaction.

4. The third party does not withdraw from the contract before the principal ratifies it.

There can be no ratification of the agent's acts if the third party withdraws before the ratification takes place.

Liability in Tort

An agent will be held responsible for any damage that results from his own negligence in the performance of his duties. However, typically, if an agent is employed to secure another agent for the principal, the agent will not be held responsible for the other agent's negligence if due care and diligence were used in securing that agent. An agent will be held responsible for the negligence of his own agent if he hired the person to help him with his agency.

Even though a principal may be held responsible for an agent's torts, the agent may also be held responsible for them. It is possible for a lawsuit to name both the principal and agent as defendants and for a judgment to be entered against both of them.

Respondeat Superior

A principal may also be held liable for physical harm caused by the negligent conduct of agents who are acting within the scope of their employment. The doctrine of *respondeat superior,* which is Latin for "let the master answer," is used to impose liability on the principal for the negligent acts of their agent. Under respondeat superior, the principal is liable for the agent's misconduct even though the principal was not at fault. This may be true even if the principal tried to prevent the agent from engaging in the tortious conduct. An example of this is when a bar owner is held responsible for the actions of his employee who was hired to expel rowdy customers from the bar. Even if the bar owner tells the employee not to "hurt people," it is foreseeable that if the employee is instructed to physically remove drunk customers from the bar and he forcibly removes a customer from the establishment and tosses him onto the pavement, a customer might hit his head on the pavement and suffer injury. Therefore, the owner may still be held liable for the negligence of the employee.

Scope of Employment

Principals are liable for the torts of their agent/employees that are committed only while the employee/agent was acting within the scope of their employment. An agent is usually considered to be acting within the scope of their employment if the agent's actions meet several of these six criteria:

1. The activity is one for whom agents are usually responsible.

2. The action took place during hours the agent/employee is generally employed.

3. It is part of the principal's business.

4. The action is similar to one the principal authorized.

5. The principal supplied the tools.

6. It is not an intentional tort.

An act may be determined to be within the scope of employment even if expressly forbidden by the principal if it is of the same general nature as that authorized.

The employer is not liable for the torts committed by agents who are acting outside the scope of their employment unless it can be shown that the principal intended the tortious conduct, the employer was negligent or reckless, or the conduct violated a non-delegable duty of the employer.

Although a principal may be held liable for the torts of an employee acting within the scope of employment, the principal is not liable for the torts of someone working as an independent contractor. When determining whether the agent is an employee or an independent contractor, the court will consider these six questions:

1. What amount of control did the principal exercise over the details of the work?

2. Did the principal supply the tools and the place of work?

3. Did the agent work full time for the principal?

4. Is the agent paid for the time or by the number of jobs performed?

5. Do the principal and the agent think they have an employer–employee relationship?

6. Is the principal in business?

Basically, the more control a principal has over an agent and the work they are performing, the more likely the agent is to be considered an employee of the principal rather than an independent contractor.

Negligent Hiring

Generally, principals are not liable for the physical torts of an independent contractor, but if the principal is shown to have been negligent in the hiring or supervising of the contractor, the principal may be held liable for the contractor's actions. An example is when liability is imposed on stores that failed to check the criminal backgrounds of people they hired as security guards. In some instances, when a security guard with a violent criminal background has assaulted a suspected shoplifter, the store has been found liable to the injured party because the store was determined to have acted negligently by failing to adequately screen the people it hired for security guard positions.

Criminal Liability

A principal may also be held liable for the criminal acts of the agent if the principal authorized the acts or consented to them. In instances where it has been shown that the principal directed the commission of a crime, the principal has been charged as an accessory to the crime, and, in some instances, a corporation may also be found criminally liable for the actions of its agents since it is considered a legal person. Also, corporate officers, acting on behalf of the principal corporation, have been found liable for performing criminal acts on behalf of the corporation.

Agency Authority

Three forms of agency authority are recognized by courts:

1. Master/servant

2. Employer/employee or proprietor/independent contractor agency

3. Principal/agent agency

Every party seeking to enforce or sue based on an agent's acts must demonstrate to the court's satisfaction that the agent was authorized to act on behalf of the principal, master, or employer. To do this, the party may demonstrate that the agency relationship was based on apparent or implied authority or that the acts of the agent were ratified.

Under common law, the terms used were *Master* and *Servant,* and in many old cases those are the terms used regardless of the status of the parties (i.e., whether they are employer and employee). Today, however, it is common for the courts to be specific and refer to work situations and acknowledge the employer as the principal and the employee as the agent. In other situations, it is clearly a contractual situation wherein one party is stated as the principal and the other is designated as the agent acting on the principal's behalf.

Duties and Liability of Agents

Unless otherwise agreed, agents must act solely for the benefit of the principal in all matters connected with their agency. It is also assumed that agents will undertake only actions that are within the bounds of the agency arrangement. An agent is liable to the principal for breach of their duty of loyalty, the misappropriation of assets entrusted to the agent's keeping, and a breach of duty of care in performing their agency duties.

An agent employed to buy or sell property on behalf of another cannot secretly buy the property and sell it to himself. If it is discovered that he has done so, the transaction can be rescinded.

Agent's Fiduciary Duty

Agents must account for all profits made in connection with their agency relationship.

Employees, who are agents of a corporation, cannot use to their advantage proprietary information gained while employed by that corporation if they take a job with a company that competes with their current employer.

If a person undertakes a gratuitous agency relationship, the person must still act with due care or notify the principal that he or she will be unable to fulfill the agency relationship.

Principal's Remedies for Agent's Breach of Duty

Principals can recover from their agent any damages the agent's breach of duty has caused. If an agent breaches the duty of loyalty, the agent must turn over to the principal the profits earned as a result of the wrongdoing. The principal may also rescind the transaction wrongfully entered into by the agent.

Duties of Principals to Agents

Just as agents have a duty of loyalty to their principal, principals have a duty to cooperate with their agents. Principals cannot unreasonably interfere with their agents' ability to accomplish their task, and the principals must perform their part of the agency contract.

Principals must reimburse agents (indemnify them) for any expense or damages the agents incur while carrying out their responsibilities. The duty to indemnify agents includes tort claims brought by a third party if the principal authorized an agent's behavior and the agent did not know a tort was being committed. The principal must also indemnify the agent for any liability incurred from third parties as a result of entering into a contract on the principal's behalf.

Termination of Agency

If an agent violates his or her duty of loyalty, the agency agreement automatically terminates. A significant change in circumstances may also terminate an agency relationship. If the change is significant enough to undermine the purpose of the agency agreement, then the relationship ends automatically. Sometimes, when the agent's responsibilities become illegal due to a change in the law, the agency relationship terminates. The following list includes eight other reasons the agency relationship may be terminated:

1. Completion of the agency objective

2. Lapse of the time specified in the agency agreement

3. Rescission—a mutual agreement of the parties to terminate the relationship

4. Renunciation of authority by the agent

5. Revocation of authority by the principal

6. Destruction or condemnation of the property that is the subject of the agency

7. Death or incapacity of the principal or agent

8. Bankruptcy of the principal

Remedies for Wrongfully Terminating an Agency Relationship

If an agency relationship is wrongfully terminated, the injured party may sue for the reasonable value of the services rendered or any actual damages sustained.

HYPOTHETICAL CASE

Sam manages the local ski hill for the owner, Mr. Widget. Widget tells Sam that because business is not good, he is to do everything possible not to give refunds or other compensation to customers who complain. Sally and her sister buy lift tickets and go skiing. Unfortunately, on the first run down Sally's sister falls and breaks her leg. Sally accompanies her sister to the hospital. Later, she returns to the hill and asks Sam to refund her ticket price since she didn't get to ski at all due to taking care of her sister. When Sam refuses to give her a refund, Sally starts yelling so other people in the ski lodge can hear her. She screams that Sam is a heartless beast and that Widget Slopes is the worst ski hill in the country. Sam tries to grab Sally and force her out of the building, but she pulls away and screams that he's assaulted her. By this time, a small crowd has gathered. Sam decides he must get Sally outside and away from customers fast, so he uses a maneuver from his days in the military and twists both her arms behind her back and drags her outside. Once outside, he throws her to the ground and tells her to get out and never come back. He leaves her on the ground and walks back into the lodge. A couple months later, Sally sues Sam and Widget Slopes for $1,000,000 in damages. Sally claims Sam assaulted and battered her and as a result her shoulders needed surgery, her wrist was broken, and she suffered severe emotional damage due to the humiliation, embarrassment, and degradation he inflicted on her.

Can the doctrine of respondeat superior be used to impute liability against Widget Slopes in this case? Why or why not?

Chapter 20: Landowner Liability

Introduction

What is a landowner's duty of care to the people who enter his or her property?

If a person is injured while on someone else's property, the owner, occupant, or tenant responsible for maintaining the property may be liable.

If a person suffers an injury due to the negligent maintenance of the property—such as spills on the floor, abandoned appliances, falling shelves, or fallen trees—that person may successfully sue the landlord if it can be demonstrated that the landlord has failed to maintain the common areas of an apartment complex, including pathways and common stairways, while the tenant might be responsible for the tenant's individual unit.

Common areas are defined as places open to members of the public, such as corridors, hallways, lobbies, pools, bathrooms, and other areas available to all occupants, owners, tenants, and guests.

Under common law, a landowner has three defined duties of care to people who enter his or her property. These duties are based on the three legal classifications of people who come onto the landowner's property:

1. Trespassers

2. Licensees

3. Business invitees

Trespassers

A trespasser is someone who enters property without the owner's permission. Under common law, such a person does not have to be warned of a dangerous condition on the property unless:

- The condition could cause serious injury or death.

- The condition is dangerous and is unlikely to be noticed.

- The trespasser frequently intrudes on the property and a dangerous condition exists.

If any of these circumstances exist, then the law will impose a duty of care on the landlord.

Attractive Nuisance

If an adult trespasser were injured when entering a dilapidated shed on someone's property because the roof collapsed and injured them, it would be unlikely for the court to find the landowner violated a legal duty of care to them because they were on the premises without permission. However, if the injured party were a child, the landowner might be found liable under the doctrine of attractive nuisance.

Attractive nuisance is a response to trespass used by children used in tort law. The doctrine of attractive nuisance is based on the belief that a property owner who maintains on their property a dangerous condition likely to attract children has a duty to warn or take some action to protect children from the dangers of that attraction. It imposes a duty to be aware of dangerous conditions on one's property that are likely to attract and harm children. This doctrine is an exception to the general rule that no duty is owed to protect trespassers from anything but lethal harm.

Items that may be considered an attractive nuisance are unenclosed pools, machinery, rotting buildings, or building materials. Anything that presents an irresistible lure and hidden danger to young children can be considered an attractive nuisance. Most natural conditions, such as ponds, rivers, or a naturally steep bank, are not considered attractive nuisances. Typically, to be liable for injury, an owner must create or maintain the harmful object.

Licensees

A licensee is a visitor who is explicitly or impliedly invited onto the owner or occupant's property for social purposes. For example, a licensee is someone a landowner allows to hunt on his or her property without paying a fee. If, however, the visitor's presence is partly due to business, it becomes more difficult to determine the visitor's status. For example, someone who trips on your porch steps while coming to sell you a lawn service you don't want may be a *licensee* if you didn't post a sign on your property prohibiting solicitations. But, that person probably isn't a *business invitee* since the purpose was not to benefit you.

Landowners owe a greater duty of care to a licensee than to a trespasser but less than to a business invitee. This is because a licensee enters the property with permission from the landowner but does so for his or her own benefit and not to benefit the landowner.

Therefore, the landowner must repair known dangerous conditions and warn the licensee of hazardous situations, but there is no requirement to warn of all dangerous conditions, nor is there an obligation to keep the property in a reasonably safe condition for them.

For example, if someone allows friends to hunt on their land, they should inspect their property for hazards such as abandoned mines or wells, unsafe structures, or dangerous animals and make every effort to eliminate these hazards. If there are known dangers that cannot be removed, they should point them out to the hunters. Following these precautions will reduce the likelihood that the licensee landowner will be found liable if a hunter is injured on the property.

Business Invitees

A business invitee is someone who is expressly or impliedly invited onto the property for a business purpose that benefits both the visitor and the owner or occupier. The most common example of a business invitee is someone who goes into a store to buy merchandise. Both the customer and the store benefit from the potential customer's presence. The invitee is not necessarily a visitor to a store but might also be someone who pays to hunt or fish or cut a Christmas tree on someone else's property. Since the invitee enters property at the landowner's invitation and for the landowner's benefit, the invitee is owed the highest duty of care. The invitee must be warned of any dangerous condition, and the property must be kept in a reasonably safe condition at all times.

Business invitees who venture outside the area where they are authorized to be, such as a customer who trips over a mop while looking for a bathroom in an area marked *"Employees Only,"* is usually considered an invitee and not a licensee. Similarly, a person who comes into a store or office to visit an employee but not to conduct business is also a licensee. This difference is important because the owner or occupier of property owes a greater duty of care to a business invitee than to a social guest (invitee). For business invitees, the owner or occupier is obligated to regularly inspect the property and make sure it is free of dangerous conditions. However, in the case of licensees, the owner or occupier is required only to fix or warn about known dangers. If, for example, the property owner does not know there is water on the bathroom floor and a guest slips and is injured, the owner may not be liable. However, if business invitees are known to use the bathroom, the property owner has a duty to inspect and make sure the bathroom remains safe.

Although hunters are typically licensees, a hunter who is charged a fee for a hunting trip or to hunt on someone's land (i.e., on a hunting preserve) may be considered a business invitee. If the hunter is a business invitee, then they have a right to assume that the property and conditions on it are safe. Landowners engaged in fee access operations must inspect their property for hidden dangers and make every effort to warn of all known hazards. If known dangers cannot be removed, the landowner must give adequate warning to people on the property so they know where the hazards are located and can avoid them.

HYPOTHETICAL CASE

Susie is the landlord and manager of a six-unit townhouse apartment complex owned by Mega Rentals Inc. Jesse has never been to visit his friend Sam, who lives in the apartment complex. Sam is a tenant in unit #1. As Jesse is walking to Sam's first floor apartment, a laundry rack falls off the balcony of apartment #4, hitting him in the head and causing him a serious brain injury.

Can Susie be held liable for Jesse's injury? Why or why not?

Chapter 21: Landlord Tenant Law

Introduction

What is landlord tenant law? *Landlord tenant law* is a combination of property, negligence, and contract law that is built around the unique relationship between property owners and their tenants. Whenever the owner of a freehold estate in land allows another to have temporary, exclusive possession of their property, the owner has created a landlord–tenant relationship. The person with the freehold (owner) is the landlord, and the person being given temporary possession of the property is the tenant. The tenant is said to have a *leasehold* in the property that they are being allowed to possess. A leasehold may be for a commercial or residential purpose.

Forms of Tenancy

Tenancies, or leaseholds, are nonfreehold estates. The owner of the property leased retains the freehold, and the tenant merely has a possessory interest in the property; they do not have an ownership interest. There are different forms of tenancy that may be for a specific period of time or be at the will of the property owner.

Term of Years

A tenancy with a specified beginning and end date that is stated from the outset and expires without notice, and on which the death of the landlord or tenant has no effect, is a lease for a term of years.

Periodic Tenancy

A tenancy for a fixed period that continues for succeeding periods (i.e., month-to-month) until the landlord or tenant gives notice is a periodic tenancy. A periodic tenancy may arise by express agreement or by implication or operation of law—such as when a lease for a term of years expires. Under common law, half a year's notice is required to terminate a year-to-year tenancy, and a month's notice is necessary to terminate a month-to-month tenancy.

Tenancy at Will

A tenancy that is terminable at the will of either the landlord or the tenant can arise expressly or by operation of law. Most statutes require a period of notice for one party or the other to terminate a tenancy at will. A tenancy at will ends at the death of one of the parties.

Holdover Tenant

A holdover tenant is not a true tenant but is, rather, a tenant who wrongfully stays in possession of the property after their lease has ended. If the tenant remains after the lease expires, he or she effectively becomes a trespasser, and the landlord can sue and seek money for the time the tenant remained wrongfully in possession of the property, as well as damages for trespass. If, however, the tenant only wants to stay one more month and the landlord and tenant do not want to enter into a new lease, they may enter into a periodic tenancy agreement.

Abandoned Tenancy

If a tenant intentionally vacates the property and relinquishes it to the landlord before the lease term expires, then the tenant is deemed to have abandoned the property (and breached the lease agreement). Traditionally, the landlord had no duty to mitigate damages by seeking a new tenant for the premises, but increasingly states are requiring landlords to mitigate their damages by attempting to re-rent the abandoned property. If, however, state law does not impose any duty on the landlord to mitigate their damages, then the landlord may make no effort to re-rent the property and can sue and recover from the tenant damages based on the remaining lease term.

The Lease

A lease is both a conveyance and a contract. It gives the tenant the right to possess and use the landlord's property, and it defines the duties between them. The Statute of Frauds requires that leases for more than one year be in writing to be valid, while leases for less than a year may be based on an oral agreement.

Leases usually contain specific provisions called *covenants* that are promises made by the landlord to do something or refrain from doing something. For example, a covenant may specify who is responsible for maintaining the premises or how the tenant may use the property.

Subleases and Assignments

Sometimes a tenant may wish to vacate the leased premises and turn it over to someone other than the landlord, or the landlord may sell the property to someone else. Generally, when leased property is sold, the new landlord is substituted for the old one, and the lease is not affected. However, when a tenant turns the property over to someone else, it may result in either a sublease or an assignment of the lease.

The way to distinguish between an assignment and a sublease is to consider how much of the tenant's rights are being transferred. Most states hold that an assignment arises when the lessee transfers his entire interest under the lease (right to possession for the duration of the terms). If the lessee transfers anything less than an entire interest, even one day less, it is considered a sublease and not an assignment.

In most instances, a landlord is allowed to refuse, even arbitrarily so, a tenant's request to assign their lease. However, more and more states are passing laws that require landlords to consent to the assignment of commercial leases if doing so is reasonable under the circumstances.

Tenant Duties

Tenants, like landlords, have legally recognized duties that are usually specified in the lease agreement. For example, tenants may have duties to refrain from making excessive noise, to maintain certain aspects of the property such as mowing the lawn and disposing of the trash, or not to allow pets on the property.

Duty to Pay Rent

The first duty a tenant has is a duty to pay the rent agreed to in the lease. If no rent amount is specifically agreed upon, the law imposes a duty requiring the tenant to pay a reasonable rental value.

Duty Not to Disturb Other Tenants

Most leases provide that the tenant will not substantially interfere with the ability of other tenants to enjoy their premises. If no such provision is included in the lease, courts will typically follow the common law rule that requires tenants to refrain from committing a nuisance upon their fellow tenants. Since excessive noise can be a nuisance, a violation of this duty occurs when the residents of one apartment play the stereo so loud it prevents neighboring apartment dwellers from sleeping at night.

Duty Not to Commit Waste and Duty to Repair

Tenants have an obligation to keep the landlord's premises clean and sanitary and to refrain from any conduct that will deface or damage the landlord's property. In some instances, the tenant's failure to make repairs or to prevent decay and dilapidation of the landlord's property is regarded as permissive "waste," and the tenant may be liable for the damage that results. *Waste* is a legal term that describes the action of improperly or unreasonably using property in a way that causes damage to it. Waste may occur from an affirmative act or by a failure to take action.

Duty to Surrender the Landlord's Property

Once the lease term expires, the tenant has a duty to vacate the premises and leave it in habitable and good condition. This means the roof cannot leak; doors and windows cannot be broken; and plumbing, electricity, hot and cold running water, and heat must all be in working order.

Tenant Rights and Remedies

Tenants are entitled to stay in possession of the premises for the duration of their lease so long as they pay the required rent and abide by the other terms of the lease agreement. If, however, the landlord breaches the lease, tenants may sue for damages equal to the difference between the value of property with and without the breach. However, traditionally, tenants have been required to vacate the property if they claimed the conditions made the property uninhabitable.

Damages

Various states compute tenant damages differently. It is important to check the statute that applies when calculating tenant damages. In some states, the court will subtract the fair market value of the property from the rent due under the lease. In other states, the court will order that rent is whatever the fair market value of the property is determined to be. In still others, the rental amount may be reduced from the original amount based on the court's determination of the diminution in value caused by the landlord's conduct.

If the landlord's breach is substantial, however, tenants may have to rely on the theory of constructive eviction. Under this doctrine, they will have to move out but will be relieved of liability for future rent and may be entitled to recover damages for the landlord's breach. Sometimes relying on this theory can be risky, because if the tenant moves out and the court determines that the conditions did not amount to constructive eviction, the tenant will then be considered to have abandoned the property and will be the party considered to be in breach of the lease agreement.

Landlord Duties

Under the lease agreement, the landlord who leases property to a tenant also incurs legal obligations.

Duty to Deliver Possession

The most obvious duty a landlord has to a tenant is to deliver the property being leased. Usually this is not a problem, but if the previous tenant refuses to leave, then obviously the new tenant cannot move in. In this situation, the landlord is typically required to take action to remove the holdover tenant. However, in a minority of states, the landlord is not required to deliver physical possession of the property, and it is up to the new tenant to either evict the holdover tenant or begin charging them rent.

Implied Warranty of Habitability

Traditionally, under common law, a landlord conveyed no warranty of any kind, and no implied promises were recognized when the tenant acquired possession of the leased property. It was truly a take-it-or-leave-it situation for the tenant. However, most states now recognize certain duties on the part of the landlord to the tenant. First among these is the landlord's duty to warrant that the premises leased to the tenant are habitable for the purpose leased. If the property turns out not to be habitable, then the tenant may abandon the property and be absolved from the obligation to pay rent. In some states, the law may also allow the tenant to continue staying in possession of the uninhabitable premise while continuing to pay rent and file a lawsuit for damages. Still other states allow a party to obtain injunctive relief, which requires the landlord to make necessary repairs to bring the property into a habitable state.

Quiet Enjoyment

Common law recognized a tenant's right to enjoy the leased property free from physical interference by the landlord. This is known as the *covenant of quiet enjoyment.* This covenant was deemed breached if the landlord physically caused the tenant's eviction. If such an eviction occurred, the tenant had the right to terminate the lease and stop paying rent, and the courts would not hold the tenant liable.

"Enjoyment" in this context has been interpreted to mean the right to use and benefit from use of the property—rather than the right to derive pleasure from it. If this right is substantially interfered with, a tenant may claim damages or possibly an injunction to stop the interference.

Today, this doctrine has been expanded so that the law now enforces an implied covenant of quiet enjoyment that recognizes instances of *constructive eviction*. Constructive eviction occurs when the landlord's action, or failure to act, renders the leased premises unsuitable for the tenant's purpose as defined in the lease. A tenant's right to sue on this basis may, however, be waived if the tenant remains on the premises and expressly or implicitly accepts the interference.

Duty to Return Security Deposit

In most lease situations, a tenant is required to pay a security deposit. A security deposit is to be used by the landlord to cover the cost of expenses incurred to repair damage to the premises caused by the tenant. In most states, the law requires a landlord to return the security deposit to the tenant within a specific period of time after the tenant moves out. If the landlord fails to do so, they must notify the tenant of any damage that the security deposit will be used to repair. Several state laws impose statutory damages of two or even three times the amount of the security deposit if a landlord wrongfully refuses to return a tenant's security deposit.

Landlord's Tort Liability

Under the common law rule, a landlord's responsibilities to the tenant were so limited that there were few instances in which a landlord could be found liable to the tenant. However, the law has increasingly recognized exceptions to this rule that impose duties on landlords.

Liability for Negligent Repair

Under the negligent repair rule, the landlord does not have duty to repair dangerous conditions that arise after a tenant moves in, but if he or she does so and the repairs are negligently made, the landlord is liable for any personal injury that results from those negligent repairs.

Liability for Common Areas

Under premises liability law, a landlord is recognized to have a duty of reasonable care to maintain the common areas of building. Common areas are such places as hallways, foyers, and pathways used by all tenants and visitors to a building. If these areas are not maintained by the landlord, their failure to do so may result in liability for injuries caused thereby.

Liability for Latent Defects

A landlord has a duty to disclose (but not fix) known and latently concealed defects that exist at beginning of tenancy. If they do so, they have no liability for injuries caused by them.

Liability for Public Use

Where the premises are leased for a public or semi-public purpose, and the landlord knows at time of leasing that a dangerous condition exists, then the landlord can be held liable for any injury sustained by a public patron (not the tenant).

Liability for Premises that Violate Housing Code Standards

Courts often interpret housing code violations as evidence of negligence—or negligence per se.

HYPOTHETICAL CASE

Keri wants to open a store specializing in the sale of snowmobiles and personal watercraft, and she negotiates a lease with Jason whereby she will rent a 13,000-square-foot building he owns on Main Street for this purpose. They enter into a lease in which Keri agrees to pay $10,000 a month rent for three years and Jason will pay all taxes and utilities for the building. After 16 months, Keri has established a good business, but one day when she and her employees show up to conduct business as usual, they discover there is no running water in the building. Keri discovers that Jason has not been paying the water bills and that the utility company has turned off the water.

If you are Keri, what action(s) are your legal options?

Chapter 22: Criminal Law

Introduction

What is a crime? Most people think of a *crime* as an act that breaks the law. A crime is that, but it injures more than just the victim; it is a wrongful act that negatively impacts every member of society. Therefore, criminal law differs from civil law because it seeks to punish an individual for wrongs committed against society instead of seeking to compensate a single individual for the breach of a legal duty owed that individual. Thus, the prosecutor in a criminal case represents the "people" of the jurisdiction in which the crime is committed, and punishment and future deterrence is sought on behalf of all the people.

Classification of Crimes

The law distinguishes crimes and classifies them in several ways.

Mala in se

Common law distinguishes crimes in two ways. The first classification is composed of crimes that are innately bad, such as rape, murder, arson, and theft. These are *mala in se* offenses, which most everyone agrees are intrinsically and intuitively bad.

Mala Prohibita

The other common law classification is for crimes that are not intrinsically bad but are defined by the law as bad. These are *mala prohibita* crimes. Examples of mala prohibita crimes are computer crimes, fraud, and a failure to file income tax returns.

In addition to common law classifications, crimes may be distinguished by their victim. Under this approach, crimes are divided as follows:

- Crimes against persons (e.g., rape, murder, assault)
- Crimes against property (e.g., larceny, computer hacking, arson)
- Crimes against the government (e.g., perjury, contempt, bribery)

Misdemeanors and Felonies

Crimes may be further separated according to their severity. Statutes usually classify crimes as either misdemeanors or felonies. Misdemeanors are less serious crimes that, in most jurisdictions, do not entail a punishment greater than one year in jail (typically 90 days is the maximum) and/or a fine of $500. Drunk driving and shoplifting of items valued at less than $100 are typical misdemeanor offenses. Felonies are more serious crimes. Punishment for these offenses is usually more than a year in prison and/or a fine greater than $500. Murder, rape, and robbery are examples of felonies.

Each state may define its own crimes and penalties as long as they do so within constitutional limits. In addition, the federal government has its own laws defining federal crimes.

The Constitution

The Constitution limits the criminal liability and punishment that the federal and state governments can impose on individuals. If a criminal statute is too vague (meaning people can't understand what conduct is prohibited) or overly broad (meaning it makes innocent conduct criminal), the courts will rule that it violates the due process clause of the Constitution. For example, the Supreme Court has struck down a statute that was so broad it could be used to arrest a person engaged in free speech activities that are protected by the First Amendment.

The Constitution also prohibits the government from enacting *ex post facto* laws. Ex post facto laws are laws that make acts criminal that were not criminal at the time they were committed. For example, if an individual assisted someone in committing suicide by buying him the ingredients he used to poison himself and there was no law prohibiting this at the time the act was undertaken, then the government could not arrest, convict, and punish that person later by passing a law prohibiting the act of assisting a suicide.

Statutes that imposed a greater punishment or made it easier to prove guilt have also been considered ex post facto laws and declared unconstitutional.

The Equal Protection Clause

The Equal Protection Clause of the Fourteenth Amendment also limits the legislature's ability to define crimes. This constitutional amendment was originally intended to secure freedom from slavery to black people, but it is now used to prohibit state legislatures from passing laws that discriminate against anyone on the basis of their race, religion, or country of origin.

Laws that create classifications based on these categories are subject to strict scrutiny by the courts and can only be justified and enforced if there is a compelling state interest.

Proving a Criminal Offense

When determining if a criminal offense has been committed, a prosecutor typically looks for several things:

1. A wrongful act (*actus reus*)
2. A guilty mind (*mens rea*)
3. Concurrence (when a wrongful act is combined with a wrongful state of mind)
4. Causation

The Wrongful Act

The wrongful act at the heart of a crime is usually defined by statute. For example, in a battery the wrongful act is the unjustified, offensive, or harmful touching of another person without their permission. Sometimes the law classifies a failure to act as a wrongful act worthy of criminal punishment. This happens when the law recognizes a legal duty to act—such as registering with Selective Service, registering firearms, or a parent's duty to care for a child. The law also distinguishes between acts that are classified as voluntary, such as punching a person, and acts that are reflexive, such as an epileptic seizure.

The U.S. Supreme Court has ruled that *status crimes,* or making it criminal for a person to have a certain status, are unconstitutional. That is why it is a crime to possess or use controlled substances but not a crime merely to be a "drug addict."

The Guilty Mind (*mens rea*)

Most criminal convictions require that the defendant possess a guilty mind at the time the crime is committed. A guilty mind may be demonstrated by showing that a person had the intent to commit the crime.

Mens rea is often difficult to prove, and the prosecution must often rely on circumstantial evidence to do so. In such instances, the court will instruct jurors that they can assume a defendant intends the natural and probable consequences of his or her deliberate acts.

Common law recognizes three categories of intent:

1. General intent

2. Specific intent

3. Criminal negligence

In general intent crimes, the prosecutor must prove the defendant intended to commit the wrongful act and that he intended the consequences of those deliberate acts. The court will instruct the jury that intent can be inferred from the defendant's conduct.

In specific intent, crimes conviction requires proof of the commission of an *actus reas* (wrongful act) and a specified level of knowledge or an additional intent, such as an intent to commit a felony. For example, a person who possesses a controlled substance with the intent to sell it may be guilty of a specific intent crime.

In criminal negligence crimes, the law creates a crime that results from the creation of an unconscious risk. Criminal negligence crimes usually involve understanding a substantial risk of harm while knowingly disregarding that risk. For example, people who willingly drive intoxicated and who cause an accident that injures or kills someone may be convicted of criminal negligence in addition to other drunk driving offenses.

Concurrence

For a successful conviction of some criminal offenses, the prosecutor must not only prove that the defendant committed a prohibited act, but he or she must also demonstrate that the defendant had a guilty mind at the same time. Thus, there is a concurrence between the criminal act and the criminal intent.

Causation

In any criminal case in which proving causation is an element of the crime, the prosecution must establish it beyond a reasonable doubt. A key to establishing causation is the legal concept of *proximate cause.* Criminal liability can attach only to conduct that is determined to be the proximate or legal cause of the harmful result.

Proximate cause in the criminal context is similar to that used in tort cases. It says that defendants can only be held responsible for the "foreseeable" consequences of their acts. Thus, in a criminal case, just as in the tort realm, it means a defendant cannot be held liable for consequences that follow an intervening, new, or independent causal force.

Burden of Proof—Beyond a Reasonable Doubt

For a prosecutor to successfully convince a judge or jury that a defendant is guilty of the crime charged, he or she must convince them that the defendant has committed each and every element of the crime charged beyond a reasonable doubt. The definition of a reasonable doubt is defined by the jury instructions in the jurisdiction in which the trial is held, but basically it is taken to mean that no other logical explanation can be arrived at other than the defendant is the one who committed the crime.

This burden of proof is higher than that required for a plaintiff to prevail in a civil trial, where all that is needed to prevail is for the plaintiff to prove each element of the cause of action by a preponderance of the evidence. A preponderance of the evidence is "clear and convincing" evidence, not evidence beyond a reasonable doubt.

Strict Liability Crimes

Strict liability crimes are those that impose criminal liability without requiring a guilty act and a guilty mind. To be convicted of a strict liability crime, the prosecutor needs only to prove the defendant committed the prohibited act. It is not necessary to prove the defendant had any criminal intent. These are always statutorily defined crimes. An example of a strict liability criminal offense is the prohibition against selling liquor to minors. If the prosecutor demonstrates that a person sold liquor to a child, it is not necessary to demonstrate that she knew or intended to break the law by doing so. Intent is irrelevant, and only the fact that she sold alcohol to an underage person is relevant or necessary to demonstrate.

Vicarious Liability

Vicarious liability crimes allow individuals or groups to be held criminally responsible for acts committed by another. Under vicarious liability, an employer can be held responsible for the acts committed by their employees. It is this theory of vicarious liability that is used to hold a bar owner criminally liable if one of his or her bartenders serves alcohol to a minor.

Inchoate Crimes

Activities that are undertaken in preparation of committing a crime, conspiring to commit a crime, or soliciting others to assist in the completion of a crime are called *inchoate crimes.*

Defenses to Crimes

The law recognizes several defenses to criminal charges, and creative defense attorneys often attempt to stretch the application of such defenses or to convince the judge or jury to accept entirely new defenses in an effort to raise a reasonable doubt.

Insanity

The insanity defense is used when the defendant admits he performed the criminal act but denies criminal responsibility for that act. For example, he may admit he killed a person but claim it wasn't murder because the person he killed was possessed by Satan and God told him to kill that person.

Different states apply different tests to determine if a defendant was insane at the time the criminal act was committed. One of the oldest tests, and one still used by many states today, is the *McNaughten Rule,* or *McNaughten Test.* The McNaughten Rule holds that a defendant is not guilty if he or she was suffering from a mental disease or defect, and as a result of the mental disease or defect did not know the nature and quality of the act that they were committing. For example, if the defendant thought he was killing Satan instead of a human being, he did not know that what he was doing was wrong.

Irresistible Impulse

In some states, a defendant is not guilty if she knows that an act is wrong and is aware of the nature and quality of the act but cannot refrain from committing it due to an irresistible impulse. A typical use of the irresistible impulse defense is when someone catches her spouse in the act of committing adultery and kills him and/or his lover.

Entrapment

Entrapment occurs when police or other law enforcement officers provide a person, who was otherwise disinclined to commit a crime, with the idea and opportunity to do so. The rationale behind the entrapment defense is that it serves to deter law enforcement personnel from engaging in misconduct by enticing individuals who are not initially inclined to commit crimes into committing them.

Self-defense

Under this doctrine, a person who is not an aggressor is justified in using force upon another if he reasonably believes that such force is necessary to protect himself from the imminent use of unlawful force by the other person. Self-defense recognizes a person's legal right to defend himself and property from others. This doctrine of self-defense allows a person to use reasonable force to defend himself from death or serious bodily harm. The amount of force that may be used depends on the amount of force being repelled. For example, a person is not entitled to use deadly force if the other person merely threatens to punch him. Under the self-defense rule, when the attack has been repelled, the defender does not have the right to continue using force to obtain revenge. Today, most states have statutes that define which situations justify the use of deadly force in self-defense.

Typically, for self-defense to be applicable, a defendant must show four things:

1. The use of force was necessary.

2. The force used was proportional to the threat that was being combated.

3. The belief that harm was imminent was reasonable.

4. The defendant was not the initial aggressor.

Even when being threatened, individuals have, under common law, a duty to retreat if they are not in their home and it is possible to retreat. When individuals are threatened or attacked within their own home, there is no duty to retreat.

Duress or Coercion

Duress or coercion occurs when a person commits a crime only because the person, or an immediate family member, was being threatened with death or serious bodily harm if he or she did not do as commanded. In duress cases, the defendant knew the act was a crime but had no choice but to commit it. The rationale is that the defendant was not acting of his or her own free will when the crime was committed. Usually, duress is not a viable defense in murder cases. Duress is a difficult defense to establish, since there is almost always some reasonable alternative to committing the crime.

Intoxication

Intoxication is a limited defense to some crimes in some states. Most states distinguish between voluntary and involuntary intoxication. A defendant may not be convicted of a crime requiring specific intent if the intoxication was so severe that the person was incapable of forming the requisite intent for conviction.

Although rare, a situation of involuntary intoxication may arise when someone inadvertently ingests incompatible medications or medications and alcohol that make it impossible to convict him or her of one of the elements necessary for conviction of the crime.

Consent

Consent is not usually a defense except in violent sporting events or when it negates an element of the offense. Consent is most often used as a defense in rape cases.

Prosecution of Businesses

Since a corporation is considered a person under the law, it may be charged with committing a crime. A corporation acts through natural persons, and those persons, as the corporation's agents, may be held responsible for the criminal acts of the corporation. Thus, corporate executives may be charged personally with crimes for actions they took on behalf of the corporation.

A corporation may be charged for even minor offenses if the wrongdoing was pervasive and undertaken by a large number of employees. For example, the violation of agency regulations, antitrust violations, financial fraud, criminal negligence, and the intentional violation of environmental laws have all resulted in criminal charges against corporations.

One example of a corporation being criminally prosecuted is that of Pfizer Pharmaceutical Co. In 2007, Nigeria brought criminal charges against Pfizer for the drug company's role in the deaths of hundreds of children who were treated with an unapproved drug during a meningitis epidemic. According to the indictment, Pfizer used the epidemic as an opportunity to conduct biomedical research experiments on Nigerian children by giving them its new and untested antibiotic called Trovan instead of using already available and effective treatments. Nigeria alleged that Pfizer failed to explain to the children's parents that the proposed treatment was experimental and that they could refuse it. The consequences of this unconscionable corporate behavior were even more devastating than the loss of life it initially caused. Because the distrust of Pfizer and other foreign drug companies was so high after this incident, thousands of Nigerian parents refused to have their children immunized against polio. As a result, Nigeria is now one of the last strongholds of polio.

Other, more recent examples in which corporations have been charged criminally involve the following:

- Halliburton Co. paid $18 million in fines to the Labor Department for improperly classifying employees in order to avoid paying them overtime pay.

- Goodyear Tire and Rubber Co. paid $16 million in fines to the Securities and Exchange Commission resulting from charges that company subsidiaries paid bribes to obtain business in Kenya and Angola.

- Bumble Bee Co. paid $6 million to settle charges that it willfully violated worker safety rules, which resulted in the death of an employee who was trapped in an industrial oven at one of the company's plants.

- ConAgra Co. was fined $11.2 million for distributing salmonella-tainted peanut butter.

U.S. Attorney Guidelines for Business Prosecutions

Although states have the power to prosecute businesses criminally, and many do, the federal government is often the entity that charges a business with criminal conduct. The U.S. Office of the Attorney General (OAG) is the agency responsible for federal prosecutions, and it has a guideline it follows when determining whether to bring criminal charges against a corporation and its officers. Following are seven of the factors the OAG considers when determining whether to bring charges against a business:

1. The nature and seriousness of the offense, including the risk of harm to the public

2. The pervasiveness of wrongdoing within the corporation, including the complicity in, or condoning of, the wrongdoing by corporate management

3. The corporation's history of similar conduct, including prior criminal, civil, and regulatory enforcement actions against it

4. The corporation's timely and voluntary disclosure of wrongdoing and its willingness to cooperate in the investigation of its agents

5. The corporation's remedial actions, including any efforts to implement an effective corporate compliance program or to improve an existing one, to replace responsible management, to discipline or terminate wrongdoers, to pay restitution, and to cooperate with the relevant government agencies

6. Collateral consequences, including disproportionate harm to shareholders and employees not proven personally culpable

7. The adequacy of noncriminal remedies, such as civil or regulatory enforcement actions

Sarbanes-Oxley

Sarbanes-Oxley, also known as "Public Company Accounting Reform and Investor Protection Act" and the "Corporate and Auditing Accountability and Responsibility Act," is an especially important statute for accountants to know. It criminalizes certain behaviors as a result of major accounting scandals that resulted in the failure of the huge corporations Enron and WorldCom. Because of the fraudulent accounting practices of some firms, this statute sets new or expanded reporting requirements for all U.S. public company boards, management, and public accounting firms. Although most provisions apply to publicly held corporations, some provisions of the Act apply to privately held companies as well, and it also criminalizes the behavior of privately held companies that do not comply with these requirements—such as the willful destruction of evidence that impedes a Federal investigation.

Specific sections of Sarbanes-Oxley that may result in imprisonment (in addition to fines):

Section 802 imposes criminal penalties of up to 20 years imprisonment for altering, destroying, mutilating, or falsifying records, documents, or tangible objects with the intent to obstruct, impede, or influence a legal investigation, which may or may not have yet been commenced.

Section 807 imposes a criminal penalty of up to 25 years imprisonment for securities fraud.

Section 904 imposes a criminal penalty of up to 10 years imprisonment for willfully violating the reporting and disclosure requirements concerning employee retirement benefit plans.

Section 906 imposes criminal penalties of up to 20 years imprisonment for certifying a misleading or fraudulent financial report, in addition to up to $5 million in fines.

Section 1102 imposes criminal penalties of up to 20 years imprisonment for anyone who corruptly alters, destroys, mutilates, or conceals a record, document or other object with the intent to impair the object's integrity or availability for use in an official proceeding, or who corruptly obstructs, influences, or impedes an official proceeding.

The Racketeer Influenced and Corrupt Organizations Act (RICO)

RICO is a federal law that criminalizes certain acts that were not originally thought of as applying to business. RICO was intended to be applied to those businesses that engaged in ongoing criminal activities, such as organized crime, but law enforcement realized it could be applied to other businesses as well. It has been used to prosecute a wide range of business individuals and organizations such as financier Michael Milken, Hells Angels, Major League Baseball, and anti-abortionists. It also provides a civil cause of action for those injured by violations of certain criminal acts.

Under RICO, a person who is a member of an organization that has committed any two of 35 state or federal crimes within a ten-year period can be charged with racketeering. Under this law, racketeering activity means any of the following:

- Any violation of state statutes against gambling, kidnapping, murder, robbery, arson, obscene mail, dealing in a controlled substance
- Embezzlement of union funds
- Securities fraud

- Money laundering

- Bringing in, aiding, or assisting aliens in illegally entering the country (if the action was for financial gain)

- Acts of terrorism

HYPOTHETICAL CASE

Sam Smith was a new hire at Mega Stoneworks, Inc., where he began operating a stone-stacking machine that organized the large paving stones made by the company. Although the machine he operated was equipped with a safety device and guarding system, it had been disabled at management's instruction about two years earlier to make it quicker to remove stones that occasionally jammed the machine. The company did not have a program to ensure that the safety device was operational, and it provided only cursory safety and hazard awareness training to its employees. The company had no procedures to address safety hazards, and employees were unaware of the dangers their machinery posed. As a result, when the machine Sam was operating became jammed, he jumped down from it and attempted to clear the stone that was stuck. When he removed the stone, the machine lurched forward, and its load of stones came crashing down and crushed Sam to death.

What agency might file criminal charge(s) against Mega Stoneworks, Inc. as a result of Sam's death, and what facts support the charge?

Chapter 23: Criminal Procedure

Introduction

What is criminal procedure? *Criminal procedure* is the administration of criminal justice from the initial investigation of a crime through the arrest of the defendant, their trial, sentence, and release. It is the entire process by which crimes are investigated and defendants are prosecuted. Under the U.S. Constitution, a court cannot impose a criminal penalty against individuals who have not received notice of the charges against them or if they have not received a fair opportunity to present evidence in their defense.

Arrests

Unless police witness a crime happening in front of them, they may arrest a person only if they have probable cause to believe that a crime has been committed and that the person they are arresting is the person who committed the crime. An arrest does not require a warrant if the police officer witnesses the illegal conduct as it occurs or if it occured in a public place with other witnesses who saw it and informed police. Although an arrest must be based on probable cause, this does not mean a police officer is required to observe the act firsthand. Information from reliable sources may be sufficient to draft a written complaint that provides the basis for an arrest warrant. The arrest warrant contains the name of the accused (or a description) and a description of the criminal circumstances alleged. To arrest a person in a protected place (i.e., his own home), a warrant is needed.

Probable Cause

Probable cause is necessary when deciding if there is enough evidence to arrest and charge an individual with the crime or to obtain a search warrant. Probable cause is a reasonable suspicion that a crime has been, or is about to be, committed. It can be based on the suspect's statement or conduct, witnesses' statements, and the experience of the police officer. In some instances, a person's consent may eliminate the probable cause requirement. For example, if a couple agrees to let the police search their house, there is no need to obtain a warrant based on probable cause. However, if a warrant is necessary, it must contain a sworn affidavit or sworn live testimony of an officer that describes with particularity the place to be searched, the crime that is being investigated, and the source of the information given.

No search warrant necessary if any of the following is true:

- There is no expectation of privacy.

- The illegal item is in plain view.

- The evidence has been dropped or abandoned.

- A person with authority has given consent to search.

- Preservation of the evidence is necessary.

- A search dog found the evidence.

- It is a border search.

- It is a stop-and-frisk situation.

- It is a search incident to an arrest.

- It is a motor vehicle search.

- There are exigent circumstances.

There are a great many court cases discussing what *exigent circumstances* are. Most of them agree that such a circumstance exists when any of the following is true:

- Evidence will be destroyed.

- The defendant or someone else is in imminent danger.

- A prisoner has escaped.

Arraignment

A defendant is arraigned shortly after being arrested. At the arraignment, the defendant is informed of the charges against him or her as required by the Sixth Amendment to the Constitution. The defendant enters a plea to the charge(s), and if he or she refuses to enter a plea, the court will enter a plea of "not guilty" on his or her behalf. Possible pleas a defendant may enter are guilty, not guilty, or no contest (*nolo contendere*). A no contest plea is a defendant's way of saying, "I'm not saying I didn't do it, but I'm not saying I did do it. I'm going to let the court read the charge and police report and decide for itself whether I'm guilty." In most instances, since the court will only read the police and prosecutor's information, a no contest plea will result in a finding of guilt, and the defendant will be sentenced accordingly.

No contest pleas are often used when defendants may not be able to tell the court what they did (perhaps because they were too intoxicated and can't remember) and when an admission of guilt or a jury conviction could be used against them in a civil case. Unlike a criminal conviction, a no contest plea typically cannot be admitted as evidence against a defendant in a civil case.

Bail

Contrary to what some people believe, the Constitution does not give a defendant an unqualified right to bail. It merely says a person cannot be deprived of liberty without due process of law and that a person has a right to a speedy trial. If there are good reasons, such as a significant risk the defendant will flee the country, a judge may refuse to set bail.

Right to an Attorney

Although the Constitution does not guarantee a person a right to an attorney in a criminal case, the U.S. Supreme Court has held that an indigent defendant is entitled to a court-appointed attorney at all critical stages of a criminal case when their liberty is at stake. Critical stages are interrogation, line-ups, trial, and sentencing.

Preliminary Examination

In a preliminary examination, which follows the arraignment, the prosecution must show that a crime was committed and that there is probable cause to believe the defendant committed the crime. If these two things are established, the defendant is "bound over" for trial. Most of the time, the defendant waives the preliminary examination because the burden of proof is much less than that needed for the prosecutor to prevail at trial and because he or she does not want the prosecutor to see any of the defense strategy. As a result, a preliminary examination is usually held only when the prosecutor's ability to prove the crime charged appears weak or inappropriate, or when the defendant's legal team thinks it can gain an advantage by flushing out the prosecution's strategy.

Plea Bargains

In a plea bargain, charges against a defendant are dropped, reduced, or replaced in exchange for a guilty plea or cooperation with law enforcement. If the prosecutor does not honor the plea agreement or the court does not follow a sentencing recommendation made by the prosecutor, in most jurisdictions a defendant may withdraw the plea and proceed to trial.

Trial

If no plea bargain is reached, then the case will proceed to trial. The Constitution states that a defendant is entitled to a speedy trial, at which the defendant must be presumed innocent. At trial, the prosecution must prove each and every element of the offense or offenses charged, and guilt must be established by proof "beyond a reasonable doubt." A reasonable doubt is not *any* doubt, but a doubt that is based on reason and common sense after careful and impartial consideration of all the evidence, or lack of evidence, in a case.

During the trial, the prosecutor presents evidence and has the burden of proving that the defendant committed the crime alleged. The defendant's defense team may cross-examine the prosecutor's witnesses, produce their own witnesses, and call the defendant to testify on his own behalf, but the defendant cannot be compelled to do so, and, in fact, all criminal defendants have a constitutional right under the Fifth Amendment not to be compelled to testify at their trial. The jury is not to interpret a defendant's failure to testify as evidence of their guilt. If a jury cannot agree on whether a defendant is guilty or not guilty, it is said to be a hung jury. If a trial results in a hung jury, the judge will declare a *mistrial,* and the case may be retried at prosecutor's discretion.

A defendant has a right to a public trial unless the state can demonstrate a "compelling state interest" (such as national security) that justifies having a private trial.

Although the Constitution guarantees the right to a trial by one's peers in significant cases, there is no right to a jury for trials involving "petty" offenses, traffic cases, military trials, or juvenile trials.

During a trial, the defendant has a right to confront his or her accuser and a right to cross-examine witnesses who testify against him or her. However, if a defendant's behavior in court is disruptive, then he or she may be removed from the courtroom. If the defendant has fled before or during trial, his or her presence may be waived and the trial may be continued without them.

Sentencing

If found guilty, a defendant will be sentenced by the judge or, in some states, by the jury. Most states use sentencing guidelines established by statute to ensure that people are sentenced consistently and fairly for the same crimes. The Eighth Amendment of the Constitution also prohibits "cruel and unusual punishment," although it does not define what this means.

Due Process

An essential part of criminal procedure is ensuring that the defendant has received due process of law. Due process is mentioned in two places in the U.S. Constitution: the Fifth and Fourteenth Amendments. When the court looks to see whether a defendant has received due process of law, it examines how and why the law was passed and enforced. All persons being charged with a crime in the United States are entitled to due process, regardless of whether they are United States citizens.

The law recognizes and regulates two types of due process: substantive due process and procedural due process.

Substantive Due Process

Substantive due process examines whether a law is fair and impartial. Substantive due process cases involve areas in which the "substance" of what the law tries to regulate may be prohibited by the Constitution, such as if a state were to pass a law that singles out a group of people based on constitutionally impermissible criteria. Or, for example, if a state were to makes it a crime to attend a religious school, that law would violate the First Amendment. If someone were arrested and prosecuted for enrolling in a religious school, they could claim this prosecution violated their substantive due process rights under the Fourteenth Amendment.

Procedural Due Process

Procedural due process examines whether the law has been fairly applied. For example, in a procedural due process question, the court determines if a law is too vague or too broad for someone to know what conduct is expected of them. Also, in a substantive due process case, the court may determine if the law was fairly applied to all persons. Even if the procedural requirements are met, it is possible that substantive due process may make the law unconstitutional. For example, the proper process may have been followed in enacting a law allowing warrantless searches of people's homes, and the police may follow the newly enacted process as required, but if the substance of the law itself violates the rights guaranteed in the Constitution, it may be determined to unconstitutionally violate due process rights.

Following are some basic due process guarantees found in the Constitution:

- The right to a fair and public trial conducted in a competent manner
- The right to be present at one's trial
- The right to an impartial jury

- The right to be heard in one's own defense

- The right to have laws written so that a reasonable person can understand what is criminal behavior

- The right to be taxed only for public purposes

- The right to be fairly compensated when the government takes one's property

Writ of Habeas Corpus

The writ of habeas corpus, which translated from Latin means "you have the body," is used to question the legality of a prisoner's detention. The writ is granted when a defendant can show that continuing to keep them in jail or prison would violate a Constitutional right.

Search and Seizure

Under the Constitution, all government searches, seizures, and arrests must be "reasonable," meaning that the government must have probable cause for all searches, seizures, and arrests.

Evidence

Procedural due process requires that evidence of a crime be gathered properly, or it cannot be used against the defendant at trial. Unless evidence is in plain view or has been obtained by consent, a warrant is necessary to search and obtain it. If the defendant and prosecutor disagree whether evidence has been properly obtained and can be used, the judge will determine its admissibility. In making this determination, the judge will review the process by which the evidence was obtained and determine if it was proper and if the evidence itself is relevant and material.

Five types of evidence may be presented at trial:

1. Direct evidence

2. Testimony

3. Circumstantial evidence

4. Demonstrative evidence

5. Scientific evidence

Direct Evidence

Direct evidence is evidence that needs no supporting proof or facts. It speaks for itself. Photographs, documents, audio recordings, and videotapes are all examples of direct evidence.

Testimony

Testimony is evidence offered by the words of a witness under oath. Testimony may be direct observations by a witness or circumstantial observations.

Circumstantial Evidence

Circumstantial evidence, or indirect evidence, is proof of a fact by permitted inference or conclusion. It permits a judge or jury to infer the existence of facts that indirectly lead to the conclusion a party is seeking to prove. Circumstantial evidence can be used in civil or criminal trials. An example of circumstantial evidence is a line-up identification of the driver of a blue Ford Mustang by a witness who saw the driver seconds after a similar vehicle drove away from a bank robbery nearby. Direct evidence, on the other hand, would be testimony of a person in the bank who saw the defendant pointing a gun and robbing the teller. Another example of the use of circumstantial evidence would be to infer from fingerprints found on the knife used to murder someone that the person whose fingerprints are found on the knife is the person who used the knife to murder the deceased. In the absence of an eye witness to the murder, circumstantial evidence may be the only evidence available that links a person to the crime.

Demonstrative Evidence

Demonstrative evidence is evidence created to persuade the jury. Examples of demonstrative evidence are charts, video recreations, illustrations, and diagrams.

Scientific Evidence

Scientific evidence is evidence arrived at by scientific processes such as DNA analysis, fingerprints, blood test results, or handwriting analysis. To be admissible in court, scientific evidence must have a foundation, be proven to be accepted by the scientific community, and be relevant, material, and reliable.

Exclusionary Rule

The exclusionary rule holds that if evidence has been obtained improperly, through an illegal arrest or search, it cannot be admitted at trial. There are, however, exceptions to this rule. If the prosecutor can demonstrate the evidence would have been discovered anyway in a legal way, or that there is an independent source for the evidence, or that law enforcement relied in good faith on a defective warrant, the judge may still allow the evidence to be used.

Interrogations and Confessions

Most people are familiar with the term *Miranda rights* and know that it means that a defendant's incriminatory statements may not be used against them at trial if they were not advised of this possibility. However, this right only applies to a defendant's statements made while in police custody and only if the defendant is being charged with an offense where the penalty is likely to be incarceration. Statements that are made voluntarily when a suspect is not in police custody have no such prohibition and may be used at trial. In addition, there are a number of exceptions to Miranda rights. Miranda rights and a defendant's statements are admissible if made in any of the following situations:

- Made during traffic stops

- Made voluntarily

- Made to undercover law enforcement officers

- Made in response to background or routine questions

- Made during an emergency situation

For a defendant's confession to be admissible at trial, the prosecution must prove it was made voluntarily. In determining this, the court will look to see if the defendant was free to go when it was made, whether Miranda warnings were given, and whether the confession was the result of any coercion. As usual, state law and precedent in each jurisdiction determine this issue.

HYPOTHETICAL CASE

Danny's Donut Shop is suspected of being a front for the importation of illegal drugs and the laundering of drug money. However, the store does seem to have a lot of customers whose only interest is in buying donuts and coffee. One day while staking out the Donut Shop, Officer Perry sees a foreign-looking individual carrying a brown paper sack. The individual looks furtively around and then enters the back door of the store. He comes out the same door, without the sack, about ten minutes later. Officer Perry calls in the license plate of the vehicle the man is driving and learns it is a rental car. The next day, Perry and his partner are again parked in their unmarked car and see the same man enter the back of the store. This time he's carrying a black garbage bag. Shortly after the man leaves, Perry decides to go into the store and see if he can find out what was in the bag. When he enters the donut shop, the woman at the counter yells into the back room, "Danny, it's a cop." Perry sees a young man grab a black garbage bag and throw it in the walk-in freezer. The man then comes out front and asks Perry how many free donuts he wants. Perry says he wants what's in the plastic bag that Danny just threw in the freezer. Danny says he doesn't know what he's talking about, but the counter clerk says, "No problem, officer, I'll get it for you," and she goes and gets the bag. She hands it to Perry, and inside he sees what turns out to be several kilos of cocaine and at least $50,000. Perry immediately arrests Danny for possession of cocaine and money laundering.

What due process violation arguments can be made in Danny's defense? What facts and arguments will the prosecution make to counter them?

Chapter 24: Trusts and Estate Planning

Introduction

What is a trust? A trust is a fiduciary arrangement that allows a third party, called a trustee, to hold a person's financial assets on behalf of a beneficiary or beneficiaries.

What is estate planning? *Estate planning* is the process of preparing for the distribution of one's estate at death by using a will, trust, gifts, power of attorney, and other legal means.

An estate is the total property, real and personal, owned by an individual prior to distribution through a trust or will. It may consist of both real property, which is real estate, and personal property, which includes everything else such as cars, household items, and bank accounts. Estate planning distributes this property to the individual's heirs or others.

The process of estate planning occurs when individuals arrange the transfer of their assets in anticipation of death. An estate plan's purpose is to preserve the maximum amount of wealth possible for the intended beneficiaries, while also providing financial flexibility for the individual prior to their death. A major concern for drafters of estate plans is federal and state tax laws.

It is the law of trusts and estates that governs the management of personal affairs and the disposition of an individual's property in anticipation of incapacity or death. This law is also used to carry out the wishes of philanthropic bequests or gifts through the creation, maintenance, and supervision of charitable trusts.

When a person dies, the legal process that involves validating a person's will, inventorying their property, having the property appraised, paying debts and taxes, and distributing the remainder of the property to people designated in their will or, if there is no will, to persons designated by state statute, is called probate. Oftentimes, the reason people set up a trust and engage in estate planning is to avoid paying estate taxes or to avoid the probate process entirely.

Wills and trusts are common ways in which individuals dispose of their wealth. Trusts, unlike wills, have the benefit of avoiding probate, which is a lengthy and costly legal process. Sometimes, however, it is better to make *inter vivos* gifts (gifts made while the donor is alive) in order to minimize taxes. The federal gift tax law exempts certain levels of lifetime gifts.

When individuals die without a will, state law determines how their property will be distributed. These probate laws vary from state to state, but typically, the distribution is to an individual's spouse and children, or, if there are none, to other family members. A state's probate distribution system usually provides protections for certain beneficiaries, such as the decedent's spouse and minor children. A will, however, gives an individual the power to alter the state's default distribution system and allows them to distribute their assets in the way they desire.

Trusts

During the 1500s, English landowners developed a system of conveying the legal title of their land to third parties while retaining the benefits of ownership. They developed this system because if they were not the legal "owners" of the land—and wealth was primarily measured by the amount of land people owned—the property was immune from creditors, and they were relieved of certain feudal obligations. Today, wealth is held in many forms besides land, such as stocks, bonds, and bank accounts, but the practice of placing property in the hands of third parties for the benefit of another is still used. Today it is called a *trust*.

A trust is a right in either real or personal property, which is held in a fiduciary relationship by one party for the benefit of another. The trustee is the one who holds title to the property placed in the trust, and the beneficiary is the person who receives the benefits of the property placed in the trust and its assets.

The person establishing the trust is called the grantor, settlor, or trustor.

The trustee has legal ownership of the property that has been transferred to him or her (or "it" if the trustee is a bank) by the person establishing the trust. The trustee must manage the assets and and act as the fiduciary of the trust on behalf of the trust's beneficiary.

The trust property is known as the trust *principal*, or *corpus*, and its assets are invested and managed for the benefit of the beneficiaries. Sometimes the grantor may also serve as the trustee and beneficiary. Generally, however, if the grantor is the trustee, the grantor cannot be the only beneficiary.

Trust Variations

As a fiduciary, the trustee must properly manage the entrusted property and make sure that it is used only in the manner, and for the purposes, established by the grantor in the trust document.

Trusts can be either *living,* meaning they are established during the grantor's lifetime, or *testamentary,* meaning they are established in a person's will.

A living trust can be revocable, which means it may be terminated or modified at any time by the grantor for any reason. Living trusts are often used to avoid probate, reduce estate taxes, or set up long-term property management.

A significant advantage of living trusts is that property left through the trust does not have to go through probate court. Probate is the court-imposed process of paying the debts of the estate and distributing the remaining estate property to the people who inherit it.

A trust may also be irrevocable. A testamentary trust, which is established by the deceased in their will, is an irrevocable trust. Grantors may change their wills, including any testamentary trust created by it, at any time before their death. In an irrevocable trust, however, grantors may never change or terminate trust or withdraw assets, even in an emergency.

When establishing a trust, all assets must be formally transferred to the trustee, and trust documents must use this title when indicating ownership. For example, any real estate deeds and financial accounts put into the trust must be retitled to show they are owned by the trust. Financial institutions also require authorization, in the form of the trust document, before they will accept instructions from a trustee.

Testamentary trusts require that the will be probated. This can be a significant disadvantage over a living trust.

Wills

A will provides for the distribution of property owned by an individual at the time of his or her death in the manner specified. A will cannot dispose of assets that are not part of the probate estate—such as joint property, life insurance, retirement plans, and employee death benefits—unless they are payable to the estate.

Wills can be used to achieve a wide range of family and tax objectives. A will that provides for the outright distribution of assets is characterized as a simple will. If the will establishes one or more trusts, it is called a *testamentary trust will*. The purpose of the trust arrangement, as opposed to the outright distribution of assets, is to minimize taxes, ensure that certain property continues to be managed, and to provide creditor protection for the surviving family members.

Other important objectives that may be accomplished by a will are designating a guardian for minor children or providing care for a stepchild, elderly parent, or other individuals upon one's death.

Estate and Gift Tax

One of the oldest and most common forms of taxation is the taxation of property held by an individual at the time of their death. This tax is called an *estate tax,* which is a tax levied on the estate before any of the decedent's property is transferred. An estate tax is charged on the decedent's entire estate, regardless of how it is disbursed.

Another form of death tax is an inheritance tax, which is a tax levied on the individuals receiving property from the estate.

Taxes imposed on death often provide an incentive for some people to transfer their assets before their death. Gift tax laws are designed to prevent complete tax avoidance by people transferring their property prior to death. The federal estate tax is integrated with the federal gift tax so that large estates cannot avoid taxation by a lifetime of giving away assets. Many states also have their own estate taxes.

Living Wills or Patient Advocate Documents

A living will (referred to as patient advocate documents in some states) is a document that states the kind of medical treatment individuals wish to receive, or not receive, when they are incapacitated and cannot speak for themselves. A living will is a document that specifies how a person wants to be treated in certain medical situations. A person may use it to inform family and members of the medical community whether, and what kind of, life-sustaining treatments they wish to be given if they become terminally ill or injured.

In addition to terminal illness or injury situations, most states permit individuals to express preferences as to the use of life-sustaining equipment and/or feeding tubes for medical conditions that leave them permanently unconscious and without detectable brain activity.

Living wills apply in situations in which the decision to use medical treatments may determine whether a person lives or dies. They are not used in situations that do not affect continued life, such as routine medical treatment or non–life-threatening medical conditions. In all states, it is a medical professional who makes the determination of whether someone is in a medical condition in which the living will is applicable.

Power of Attorney

A power of attorney document gives one or more persons the power to act on an individual's behalf in legal and/or financial matters. Although it can be used for many legal purposes, it is often an important part of estate planning. The power of attorney may be limited to a particular transaction, such as selling real estate, or it may be very broad in its application by empowering another to act on their behalf in any legal situation.

A power of attorney may take effect immediately or only upon the occurrence of a future event, such as a person's inability to act for him or herself. The latter is referred to as a *springing* power of attorney.

A power of attorney document may give someone temporary or permanent authority to act on an individual's behalf. Although it may be revoked, most states require written notice of revocation to the person named as having the power of attorney.

The person who is given the power of attorney to act on someone's behalf is referred to as the agent or attorney-in-fact. The agent may take any action permitted in the power of attorney document. Typically, the agent must present the power of attorney document to invoke the power. For example, if you are selling a piece of real estate in a place you do not live and you give a realtor power of attorney to sell it, the bank or mortgagor will require that the power of attorney document be presented before the real estate agent will be recognized as having the authority to sign the title over to someone else. This is also true when selling stocks or opening and closing bank accounts. However, an agent usually does not need to present the power of attorney when signing checks for the grantor.

The use of a power of attorney to designate someone to manage one's personal or business affairs may eliminate the need for the court to appoint a guardian to act for the person. People appointed by the court to act on behalf of incapacitated persons are called guardians or conservators. This is different from designating someone as power of attorney because in the power of attorney situation, people choose for themselves who will act on their behalf if they are incapacitated and they are able to define the authority given, instead of leaving that decision up to the court.

In addition to managing a person's day-to-day financial affairs, the power of attorney may take steps to implement the grantor's estate plan. Although an agent cannot revise a person's will, some jurisdictions permit someone with a power of attorney to create or amend trusts during the grantor's lifetime or to transfer trust assets.

A person with power of attorney may also make gifts on behalf of the grantor, so long as that person follows the guidelines set forth in the power of attorney document.

Since a power of attorney is determined by the law of the state in which a person resides at the time it is signed, it is important to consult the law of that state to determine exactly what is allowed.

HYPOTHETICAL CASE

Jake remarried at the age of 40, and his second wife, Sandy, had two young children at the time he married her. Jake and the children grew very close during the next twelve years, especially since Jake had no children of his own. When Jake was diagnosed with cancer, he decided he needed to do something to make sure Sandy and her children were taken care of if he didn't survive long. If Jake asks you what he should do, how will you advise him, and why?

Chapter 25: Business Organizations

Introduction

There are many ways to set up a new business. Each new business owner must decide which is best for that business. The first thing a new business owner must decide is whether the business will be a for-profit or not-for-profit business. This is important because it affects the way you will organize your business and tax consequences. Being a not-for-profit business does not mean the business cannot pay its employees good salaries or be highly successful. It does mean that the business must meet certain criteria established by the Internal Revenue Service (IRS) and state law to avoid paying taxes on income. Depending on the purpose for which the business is formed, it may or may not be entitled to non-profit status.

Non-Profit Businesses

Public charities must be organized under section 501(c)(3) of the Internal Revenue Code if they are to receive tax free status. Internal Revenue Code section 501(c)(4) is the section that provides for the exemption of two other types of non-profit organizations: (1) social welfare organizations, such as civic leagues or organizations not organized for profit but operated exclusively for the promotion of social welfare, and (2) local associations of employees wherein the membership is limited to the employees of designated person(s) in a particular municipality, and the net earnings of which are devoted exclusively to charitable, educational, or recreational purposes. Also, each state has its own non-profit organizational requirements that non-profit businesses must meet, so a non-profit operating in a state must meet both the state and federal non-profit tax exemption requirements.

Most businesses, however, are organized and run as for-profit, so we will concentrate on these.

Sole Proprietorship

Sole proprietorships are the most common form of business organizations. They are the easiest and most common form of for-profit businesses. A sole proprietorship is an unincorporated business owned by one person. The owner may operate the business alone or may employ others. In the sole proprietorship form of business, the owner has total and unlimited personal liability for all debts incurred by the business.

Sole proprietorships are the easiest and least expensive business form to create and operate. Anyone can start making and selling a product or service as a sole proprietor and report that income on their tax return. The disadvantage of a sole proprietorship is that the owner is personally liable for all debt and all tort and contract lawsuits or judgments of the business, which means that all their personal assets are subject to attachment and foreclosure to pay off the judgment.

Partnerships

A partnership is a form of business in which two or more people operate the business for the common goal of making a profit. Each partner has an equal say in running the business, unless there is an agreement otherwise, and each has total and unlimited personal liability for the debts incurred by the partnership.

There are three classifications of partnerships: general partnerships, limited partnerships, and limited liability partnerships.

General Partnership

A general partnership, or, simply, a partnership, refers to an association of persons operating a business with three features:

1. It may be created by agreement (oral or written), proof of existence, or estoppel.

2. It is formed by two or more persons.

3. The owners are all personally liable for any legal actions and debts the company incurs.

In most states, a written document is not necessary to form a general partnership, but a written agreement is still a good idea, especially to proactively address management issues.

The advantages of general partnerships are that they are easy to form and that the business does not pay taxes. The individual partners report the income (and losses) of the business on their personal income tax returns. The disadvantage of a partnership is that each partner is personally liable for the debts of the partnership, regardless of how or who incurred them. For example, if Sam is one of four partners of the business and he drives the company delivery van through a red light causing an accident that results in a million-dollar lawsuit, all other partners may be forced to pay for all or part of that judgment. Also, financing a partnership may be difficult because the firm cannot sell ownership shares in itself the way a corporation can. Therefore, the capital needs of the partnership must be met by the partners or by borrowing the money. In addition, all partners have an equal say in running the business, unless there is an agreement to the contrary, which can often lead to management paralysis, bickering, and fights that end up dissolving the business.

Transferability

A partner may transfer only the value of his or her partnership interest. Partners cannot transfer their interest in the partnership itself. For example, a parent may give a child the value of the partnership interest (i.e., the right to receive their income from the business) but not the right to be a partner in the business (i.e., not the right to run the business).

Partnership Taxes

A partnership is not a taxable entity, so it does not file a tax return or pay taxes itself. All income and losses of the partnership are passed on to the partners, and they must report the income and losses on their personal income tax returns.

Termination of the Partnership

Typically, a partnership terminates upon the death, disability, or withdrawal of any of the partners. However, most partnerships have written agreements that provide for these events by stating that the share of the departed partner can be purchased by the remaining partners.

Profits

Partnership profits are shared equally amongst the partners unless there is a written agreement that expressly provides for a different manner of sharing the business's profits and losses.

Adding Partners

Unless otherwise provided in the partnership agreement, no one can become a member of the partnership without the consent of all partners.

Limited Partnership

A limited partnership is similar to a general partnership, except that in addition to one or more general partners, there is also a new type of partner called a limited partner. The limited partnership has one or more limited partners. The limited partners are individuals who have no interest, or ability, in managing the business. They only invest money in the business, and they must register their investment amount with the state. As such, they are liable only on debts incurred by the business to the extent of their registered investment, and they have no management authority in the business. Hopefully the business is successful, whereupon the general partners pay the limited partners a return on their investment as defined in the partnership agreement.

In this business organization, the general partners have management control, share the right to use partnership property, share the profits of the firm in predefined proportions, and have joint and several liability for the debts of the partnership.

Limited partners must file documents with the state in which they disclose their limited partner status so that third parties have notice that parties dealing with the partnership, or these individuals, are aware of their limited liability. Unlike the general partners, limited partners do not have inherent agency authority to bind the firm unless they are held out as agents and thereby create an agency by estoppel.

Common limited partnership uses are found in the film industry and real estate development or any project that focuses on a single- or limited-term project. The limited partnership is also attractive to firms wishing to provide shares to many individuals without the additional tax liability of a corporation.

Limited Liability Partnerships

A limited liability partnership (LLP) has elements of both partnerships and corporations.

In an LLP, all partners have limited liability and are not liable for another partner's misconduct or negligence. This is an important difference from that of a limited partnership, wherein the general partners still are susceptible to unlimited liability. In an LLP, *all* partners have a form of limited liability within the partnership. This distinction of granting limited liability to all partners, not just a subset of non-managing "limited partners," makes the LLP more suited for businesses in which all investors wish to take an active role in management. This makes the LLP an especially popular form of organization among professionals who wish to have an active role in managing the business, such as lawyers, accountants, and doctors.

This is because each partner may take an active management role in the business while not becoming personally liable, directly or indirectly, for an obligation solely because of being a partner. Statutes defining the requirements for LLPs differ greatly from state to state, much more so than they do for other partnership forms. Also, more restrictions tend to be involved with setting up this form of partnership, so it is not as easy to establish as the other two forms of partnership businesses.

Profits

As in the other two forms of partnership or Limited Liability Company, the profits and losses of an LLP are allocated among all the partners for tax purposes, and the business does not file a tax return.

Disadvantages of an LLP

LLPs have five disadvantages:

1. There are restrictions on ownership.

2. LLPs retain liability for improper distributions.

3. Partnership interests are not as freely transferable as in other partnership forms.

4. They require a minimum number of owners.

5. Merger opportunities are limited.

Terminating an LLP

An LLP may be terminated by the death or dissociation of a partner. However, a partner who dissociates (quits) may have to pay damages to the remaining partners if this departure caused harm to the partnership.

A partnership may also be ended by dissolution. The rules governing dissolution depend on the type of partnership. If the partners have agreed in advance on how long the partnership will last, it is a *term partnership*. Otherwise, it is a partnership *at will*, which means any partner may leave at any time. The partnership automatically ends when a partner leaves unless there is a written agreement that controls and states some other option.

A term partnership automatically ends when any of four conditions is met:

1. All partners agree to dissolve.

2. The term expires or the partnership goals are achieved.

3. A partner leaves and the remaining partners vote to dissolve.

4. The partnership business becomes illegal, such as the export of goods to an embargoed country.

Corporations

A business corporation is a for-profit, limited liability entity that has a separate legal existence from its members/shareholders (owners). A corporation is owned by multiple people (shareholders) who buy ownership shares (stock) in the company and is overseen by a board of directors, which hires the people who manage the business.

The defining feature of a corporation is that it has a legal existence that is independent from the people who create it, own it, and manage it. If a corporation fails, shareholders will lose only their investment (the amount of money they paid for their stock), and employees will lose their jobs, but neither will be liable for the debts that are owed to the corporation's creditors. Thus, it is said that a corporation has limited liability. Its liability is limited to the assets owned by the corporation. If the corporation's assets are not sufficient to pay the debts of the business, no other party can be forced to pay its debts.

Also, because the corporation is treated as a fictional person, it is required to file a tax return as if it were a real person. This is the only business form that files a tax return in its own name. It can also own property and enter into contracts in its own name separate from that of its managers and shareholders. This independent legal personality has two economic implications. First, it grants creditors priority over the corporate assets upon its liquidation. Second, corporate assets cannot be withdrawn by its shareholders, nor can the assets of the corporation be taken by personal creditors of its shareholders.

Because corporations are granted this independent legal existence, they are recognized by law to have rights and responsibilities like actual people. Corporations can exercise human rights against real individuals, and the government has held them responsible for human rights violations. Corporations can even be convicted of criminal offenses, such as fraud and manslaughter.

Benefits of a Corporation

As stated previously, unlike a partnership or sole proprietorship, shareholders of a corporation have "limited" liability for the corporation's debts and obligations, and they can only be held liable up to the amount of money they invested in the corporation (in the form of stock purchase). The economic rationale for this is that it allows anonymous trading in the shares of the corporation by eliminating the corporation's creditors as a stakeholder in the transaction. Without this limited liability, a creditor would probably not allow any share to be sold to a buyer who did not have at least the same creditworthiness as the seller. Limited liability also allows corporations to raise significantly more money for its projects by combining funds from multiple owners of stock. Since limited liability reduces the amount that a shareholder can lose in a company, it greatly reduces the risk for potential shareholders and increases both their number and the amount they are likely to invest.

Another advantage of the corporate business form is that its assets and structure exist beyond the lifetime of any of its shareholders, bondholders, or employees. This provides stability and allows for the long-term accumulation of capital, which can be used to invest in projects of a larger size and over a longer time period than if the business were easily subject to dissolution and distribution.

Disadvantages of a Corporation

Just as with other business forms, there are certain disadvantages to the corporation as a business organization. Because their existence is entirely controlled by statute, there are many more formalities to their creation, which necessarily results in greater costs and fees. Forming a corporation is more complex and is not something undertaken without paid professional assistance. Also, under some state statutes, the names of corporate officers must be disclosed, which may discourage some people from serving on corporate boards. Also, because a corporation has a distinct legal existence, it must pay taxes on its income, and the tax rate for corporations can be much higher than for individuals or other business forms. In addition, there is the problem of double taxation, which occurs when the corporation pays taxes on its income and then the shareholders must pay taxes if some of that income is distributed to them in the form of dividends.

Corporation Status

Corporations are created by filing the requisite documents with the IRS, which grants them specific tax designations under the Internal Revenue Code. They are also incorporated under the law of a particular state. State laws vary greatly in their incorporation and tax requirements, and it is not uncommon for a business to begin its existence in one state only to become so large that it determines it would be advantageous to dissolve and re-incorporate in another state.

C Corporations

A C corporation is not actually a business structure, rather the tax status of the company as defined by the Federal Internal Revenue Code (IRC). This is also true of S corporations.

A C corporation is the designation for a general for-profit corporation. It is the "default" status for all corporations under the IRC. Like all corporations, C corporations are required to pay taxes on the income they generate.

When a corporation is formed, it is formed as a C corporation, and then its incorporators have the option of claiming S corporation status. All corporations are C corporations unless they decide to take advantage of a provision in both federal and state tax laws to become an S corporation.

S Corporations

S Corporation status is a designation created by Congress to encourage entrepreneurship through special tax breaks. The shareholders in S corporations enjoy the limited liability of a corporation *and* the tax status of a partnership. An S corporation is not a taxable entity, and all its profits and losses are passed through to its shareholders, who pay taxes at their individual rates. Thus, if an S corporation loses money, its investors/owners can deduct the corporation's losses against their other income. This option was designed to help small, closely held businesses that wanted the limited liability protection of a corporation but were not large enough to take advantage of the tax loopholes afforded large corporations were thus left paying the larger corporate tax rate.

The Limitations of an S Corporation

Although an S corporation has many attractive characteristics, its limitations often result in a different corporate election, especially now that many states have made the LLC a more attractive option. Five of the more significant S corporation limitations are as follows:

1. There can be only one class of stock.

2. There can be only 100 shareholders.

3. Shareholders must be U.S. citizens or residents.

4. Shareholders must be individuals, estates, charities, pension funds, or trusts. They cannot be partnerships or other corporations.

5. All shareholders must agree that the company should be an S corporation.

The main difference between a C corporation and an S corporation is the way the corporation is taxed. A C corporation is taxed as an incorporated business, whereas an S corporation is taxed as a partnership or a sole proprietorship.

Typically, S Corporation status will benefit companies where the following apply:

1. Shareholders work more than part time for the corporation.

2. Shareholders have a firm grasp on the business and are familiar with the day-to-day business of the company.

3. The corporation plans to distribute the majority of its profits to shareholders of the company each year.

Close Corporations

The majority of corporations are called closely held, privately held, or close corporations. This means that their ownership interest or stock shares are not available for purchase and are not publicly traded. The requirements for a close corporation differ in each state, but generally it must meet four criteria:

1. It must protect minority shareholders.

2. It must have some transfer restrictions for the sale of stock shares.

3. It can operate without a board of directors or formal bylaws.

4. It may establish its own mechanism for dispute resolution.

Although many close corporations are owned and managed by a small group of people or companies, their size can be as large as the largest public corporations.

Advantages of a Close Corporation

Closely held corporations have some advantages over publicly traded corporations. For example, a small, closely held corporation can make company-changing decisions much more quickly than a publicly traded company that must get buy-in from an elected Board of Directors and managers whose main priority may be stock value.

Disadvantages of a Close Corporation

Publicly traded companies have their own advantages over their closely held counterparts. Most notable is that publicly traded companies often have more working capital, and the ability to raise it, and can delegate debt throughout many more shareholders.

Limited Liability Company

A Limited Liability Company (LLC) is a hybrid business entity that has characteristics of both a corporation and a partnership. State laws governing LLCs vary greatly and should always be consulted. However, in most instances, the LLC is an attractive form of business organization for smaller companies with a single owner (although it can have hundreds) because it often allows greater flexibility in operation.

The primary business characteristic is that the LLC has the limited legal liability of a corporation and the partnership characteristic of passing through income for tax purposes without the limitations of an S corporation.

Most states require an LLC to file a charter and an operating agreement, similar to what is required when forming a corporation.

The charter contains the name and address of the company and other contact information, while the operating agreement specifies the rights and obligations of the owners (members) of the company.

Under an LLC, members (owners) are not personally liable for the debts of the company and risk only their investment. However, they are liable for the consequences of their personal actions.

LLC Advantages

LLCs are more flexible than other business forms, such as an S corporation, because in most states they can have both corporate and partnership members. An LLC can also have different classes of stock, and it is not required to have annual meetings. In addition, LLC members may transfer their interests freely to anyone, but if the operating agreement is silent, members must obtain the unanimous permission of the all members before transferring their ownership rights. Also, although it depends on state law, most states permit the LLC to continue operating even after a member withdraws.

Disadvantages of an LLC

One of the major disadvantages of an LLC is that when it goes public, it loses its tax-free status and is taxed as a corporation, not a partnership. Thus, there is no advantage for publicly traded companies in being an LLC. Because of this and the fact that the law governing LLCs is not that stable and varies greatly among states, most privately held businesses that begin as LLCs will change to corporations when they go public.

Changing Business Form

If a company changes from a corporation to an LLC, the IRS treats the change as a sale of the corporate assets and taxes it accordingly. However, if a business changes from a partnership to an LLC or from an LLC to a corporation, it is not considered a sale, and it will not have negative tax consequences for the business. Thus, there is a tax disadvantage, and therefore disincentive, to transitioning from a corporation to another business form, whereas there is no penalty to transitioning from a partnership or LLC to a corporation.

HYPOTHETICAL CASE

Sally and Sam are expert Web site designers and decide to go into business together. Each of them has $10,000 to contribute to starting up the business. They assume that after five years of hard work, they will be successful enough to hire other employees to do most of the work, and they will merely manage the business. They already have a list of satisfied customers for whom they have done work, and they think they have several large corporations interested in contracting with them. They aren't sure what kind of business organization they should form, however, and ask you for advice. What information are you going to get from them, and how will that affect your advice?

Chapter 26: Personal Property and Bailments

Introduction

What is personal property? Personal property in the common law system is often referred to as chattels or personalty. Personal property is distinguished from real property because it is something that can be moved from one place to another. However, just as with real property, ownership of personal property entails the right to transfer it to another person. The law concerning personal property deals with the rights and relationships among people concerning ownership rights and the ability to transfer possession.

Personal Property

Tangible Property

There are two types of personal property. The first is tangible personal property, which is any type of property that has physical substance and can be moved. Examples of tangible property are furniture, clothing, books, and jewelry.

Intangible Property

The other form of personal property is intangible property. Intangible property is property that has no physical presence and cannot be moved. Examples of intangible property are stocks, bonds, securities, and negotiable instruments. Both types of personal property may be transferred at death by will or disposed of by their owner during life.

Gifts

A gift is a voluntary transfer of property without any requirement of compensation.

Under common law, a gift must meet these conditions:

- The donor (person giving the gift) intends to give a gift.
- The donee (person getting the gift) accepts the gift.
- The item to be given as a gift is delivered to the donee.

Whether something is a gift is important under common law because contracts are enforceable while gifts are not. Thus, under common law, a promise to make a gift in the future is legally unenforceable even if the promise is accompanied by a present transfer of the physical property that is the gift.

The person who makes a gift (donor) must have a present intent to make a gift of the property to the other person (donee). For example, if your friend gives you a cell phone and tells you that it's for your next birthday and you are to keep it until then, your friend has not made a gift—he has no present intent to give it to you and could legally demand the cell phone back on the day before your birthday. However, if your friend gives you a deed to a piece of property and tells you to keep it in your safe-deposit box, he has given you a gift of the property and would be unable to legally reclaim it. This is because the deed represents the property, and it was intentionally delivered to you. A gift must be delivered to the donee. If the gift is of a type that cannot be delivered in the conventional sense, such as real property or a bank account, the delivery can be effectuated by "constructive" delivery. Constructive delivery occurs when a tangible item that gives access to the property, such as a deed or the key to a house, is delivered instead of the item itself.

Bailment

What is bailment? Bailment is "the rightful possession of goods by one who is not the true owner for a limited purpose." (Williston on Contracts, § 1032) Bailment allows someone who is not the owner of property to exercise possession, power, or control over it and to exclude others from interfering with it.

The bailor is the party entrusting the property to someone else's care. The bailee is the party receiving the property from the bailor for use or safe keeping.

For a bailment to exist, there must be a delivery of the personal property that gives the bailee exclusive possession of the property, and the bailee must knowingly accept the bailed property.

There are several different forms of bailment:

- *Bailment for the sole benefit of the bailor.* An example would be asking someone to housesit while you are out of town.
- *Bailment for the sole benefit of the bailee.* An example would be borrowing your neighbor's lawn mower.
- *Bailment that is a mutual benefit to both the bailor and bailee.* An example is paying a valet service to park your car at a restaurant.

Standard of Care Owed in Bailment Situations

When a bailee is entrusted with the care of another's property, the law imposes a duty on the bailee to take good care of the property placed in his possession. The standard of care applied to the bailee differs depending on the object entrusted and the circumstances of the situation. In some situations, it may be slight care, in others ordinary care, or in some cases extreme care. For example, the duty may be slight if the property entrusted is a plant that needs watering, greater if it is a cat that needs feeding, and extreme if it is a $100,000 automobile that needs storage.

To prove that a bailee has failed in his duty of care, the bailor must prove that:

1. The bailor surrendered the goods to the bailee.

2. The goods were undamaged before the bailor surrendered them.

3. The goods were damaged when the bailee returned them.

Use of Goods by Bailee

If there is an express agreement between the bailor and the bailee concerning the bailee's use of the property, then the use is governed by the agreement. If there is no express agreement, then the rules of reasonable use apply. If goods are damaged while bailed, the burden of proof is on the bailee to show he or she did not violate the duty of care. If the bailee converts (keeps the goods for their own use), sells, or damages the goods while they are in his possession, the bailee may be sued for the obvious violation of his duty of care.

Bailee Rights

In some jurisdictions, there are statutes that allow a bailee to acquire title to bailed goods if all statutory conditions are met. An example of this would be a statute that allows an automobile mechanic to obtain title to a car left in his shop for repairs if the owner never comes back to pay and retrieve the vehicle.

Finders of Lost Property

People who find objects that are not theirs may be deemed a *finder* or an involuntary bailee. Most jurisdictions do not consider finders to be involuntary or "gratuitous" bailees because they consider there to be some benefit to the finder from the property they possess. A person who finds an object has no obligation to take it into her possession, but if she does, she becomes a bailee to the true owner of the property with a duty to take appropriate care of it. For example, if you find a stray dog and take it home, you have a duty as the bailee to take good care of the dog for the true owner.

Generally, a finder has title to found property against all but the true owner and prior possessors of it. Typically, if property is found in a public place, the rule is that the finder may keep it if no owner is identified. However, if the property is found on private property, then the owner or occupier of the property is entitled to it.

If a person is acting within the course of his or her employment when a lost object is found, there is a split of opinion in the courts. A majority of courts say the employee may keep the item if the rightful owner is not found. A minority of courts hold that it goes to the employer.

Property is considered abandoned if someone voluntarily left it behind with no intent to retrieve it. In such instances, it is treated the same as if it were lost property.

Treasure trove refers to property that the rightful owner has concealed with the intent to recover it at a later time. This was a rule more commonly used when pirates were known to hide their ill-gotten treasure. Under the British rule, if someone were to find "pirate treasure" or something of value hidden in the earth, it goes to the crown (government), but under the U.S. rule, it goes to the finder.

Taxation of Personal Property

Some governments place a tax on personal property, which is an annual tax on the possession or ownership of personal property within the boundaries of government's jurisdiction. Automobile and boat registration fees are a form of personal property tax. Most household goods are exempt from this tax so long as they are kept or used within the household. Most often, the tax is targeted at expensive personal property such as art or jewelry.

HYPOTHETICAL CASE

Sam went on a business trip to California. He drove his own car on the trip and checked into the Nice Hotel. The hotel has a guarded underground parking lot. Sam gave his car key to the parking attendant but didn't say anything to the attendant about his $5,000 golf clubs that were in the trunk. The next day, when he checked out of the hotel, he discovered that his car had been stolen. Sam wants to hold the hotel liable (and receive compensation) for both his stolen car and the golf clubs.

Under what legal theory may Sam seek to hold the hotel liable? How successful do you think he will be on each claim, and why?

Chapter 27: Employment Law

Introduction

What is employment law? *Employment law* is the law governing the relationship between the employer and employee. It covers the nature and degree of the employer's control over employees and how their work is performed. It also encompasses the right of employees to constitutional and statutory protections and benefits.

Until recent times, there was little legal recognition of employee rights, and the rules concerning the employment situation were entirely up to the employer. However, with the advent of the Industrial Revolution and the institution of large, and sometimes unsafe, working environments, there has been a shift in how the law deals with the employer/employee relationship. Today, most employer/employee aspects are governed by statute and agency regulations. One of the first statutes to address workers' rights was the National Labor Relations Act (NLRA), which was passed in response to several instances of anti-union violence. This law prohibits employers from penalizing workers who form unions, and it requires employers to bargain with unions in good faith.

Today, many businesses feel they are overly burdened with laws and regulations that govern their relationship with employees. This is an area comprising numerous federal and state laws and agency regulations that businesses must be aware of and abide by.

Employer Rights and Obligations

An employer has a right to expect its employees to be punctual and honest and to perform all reasonable and legal work-related requests made of them. In exchange, an employer is expected to provide a safe and healthy workplace, pay its employees and keep records of the wages it pays its employees, and avoid discriminatory practices.

When asked, most employers state that the most difficult aspect of their task in dealing with employees is complying with state and federal laws that govern so many aspects of the employer/employee relationship. This is truly a formidable task, which is why so many companies hire experts whose entire job consists of monitoring and ensuring compliance with state and federal laws and regulations. This job is made even more difficult by the fact that employment-related laws and regulations are continually being created, amended, revised, and repealed.

Federal Statutes Applicable to Employers

Many laws and regulations impact the way employers treat their employees. There are laws that govern employment taxes, administer the rights of workers to take unpaid leave to help an ailing family member, and protect workers who report the illegal conduct of their employer. Although there may be federal laws governing a particular subject, state laws should always be consulted since they may, at times, give employees more rights than the federal law does. Here, we will discuss only a few federal statutes, although there are many more that are important for employers to know and follow.

The Americans with Disabilities Act

ADA—Americans with Disabilities Act prohibits public and private employers, employment agencies, and labor unions from discriminating against qualified individuals with physical or mental disabilities in job hiring, firing, advancement, compensation, training, and other aspects of employment. The ADA covers employers with 15 or more employees.

Age Discrimination in Employment Act

ADEA—Age Discrimination in Employment Act prohibits employers from firing or refusing to hire people aged 40 or older due solely to their age. The ADEA applies to employers with 20 or more employees, including state and local governments.

Consolidated Omnibus Budget Reconciliation Act

COBRA—Consolidated Omnibus Budget Reconciliation Act gives workers and their families who lose their health care benefits the right to continue their group health plan for a limited period after they lose their job or in other specified circumstances.

Federal Labor Standards Act

FLSA—Federal Labor Standards Act establishes a minimum wage, overtime pay, recordkeeping, and youth employment standards that affects employees in the private sector as well as those in federal, state, and local governments. States and local governments are free to pass statutes establishing a higher minimum wage than that established by the FLSA, which some have done, but none may mandate a lower minimum wage.

Family Medical Leave Act

FMLA—Family Medical Leave Act provides up to twelve weeks of job protected leave and benefits to employees seeking time off work for certain family and medical reasons. It applies to all public and private companies with 50 or more employees. This means that if an employee takes time off to care for a sick family member, under this statute their employer may not fire them and must allow them to return to their job after their leave expires.

Health Insurance Portability and Accountability Act

HIPAA—Health Insurance Portability and Accountability Act provides federal protection for the privacy of personal health information. It applies to information created or received by a health care provider, employer, life insurer, school or university, or any other health information clearinghouse. It requires individuals to give their consent before information about their health condition is released to third parties.

Occupational Health and Safety Act

OSHA—Occupational Health and Safety Act, established the Occupational Health and Safety Administration, governs workplace safety and health in both the public and private sectors. Among other things, it is designed to protect workers from hazards such as exposure to toxic chemicals, unsanitary conditions, excessive noise levels, and mechanical equipment dangers.

Title VII of the Civil Rights Act

Title VII of the Civil Rights Act prohibits an employer from discriminating against employees because of their race, color, religion, sex, or national origin. It applies to employers who employ 15 or more employees for more than 19 weeks in the current or preceding calendar year.

Whistleblower Protection Act

WPA—Whistleblower Protection Act protects federal government employees who disclose information of wrongdoing or illegal conduct committed by other government employees from retaliation or being wrongfully fired. Actually, there are many different federal whistle blower protection statutes that are unique to specific federal agencies or departments, such as the Department of Defense or Medicare and Medicaid. Many states have their own version of the Whistleblower Protection Act.

Employment Security

Whereas most employers are concerned with abiding by the numerous state and federal laws that govern their relationship with employees, often the most important concern to an employee is knowing that he or she will continue to have a job so long as they perform their job duties as required. Employees want to be secure that if they meet their quota of producing 300 gizmos per day, they will not be fired because their employer learns they are a married to a person of a different race. Discrimination can take many forms, and not all of it is illegal. For example, blind people cannot perform the duties of an air traffic controller or a school bus driver, so it is not illegal to discriminate against them on that basis. A person's expectation of continued employment, however, typically depends on whether the person is an employee who serves at the will of the employer or if they have an employment contract.

At-Will Employment

Individuals are *at-will employees* if their employer can fire them at any time and for any reason. There is no federal statute that prevents states from allowing employers to adopt at-will employment practices, and almost all states allow such. Despite this, most states also recognize four public policy exceptions to this practice:

1. An employee may not be fired for refusing to perform an illegal act.

2. An employee may not be fired for exercising a statutory right (e.g., filing for worker's compensation).

3. An employee may not be fired for fulfilling a statutory obligation (e.g., responding to a summons for jury duty or attending national guard service).

4. An employee may not be fired for reporting illegal conduct of the employer (whistleblowing).

Employment by Contract

If someone is not an employee who serves at the pleasure of their employer, the person's employment status is typically governed by a written employment contract. The terms of the employment contract will dictate the duration of employment, the compensation and benefits, and the employee/employer expectations. If an employee is a member of a union, the union contract may be the contract that governs employment rights and duties.

In some instances, courts have ruled that an employee is protected from termination by an implied contract of employment. In these instances, the terms in an employment application, employee handbook, employer policies and procedures, or manual or verbal representations by management may be used by the court to find an implied employment contract. Because of this, employers will try to protect themselves from possible claims of an implied employment contract by requiring that employees sign a form acknowledging that there is nothing in the employment application, policy manual, handbook, or other document that constitutes a contract of employment. They use such a form to ensure that employees specifically acknowledge that they are at-will employees who may be terminated at any time for any reason or for no reason at all, with or without advance notice.

Wrongful Discharge

An employer is entitled to dismiss employees pursuant to the terms of their employment contract or, if there is no contract and the person is an employee at will, for any reason at all. In instances where a person's employment is terminated without just cause, however, it may give rise to a lawsuit for a cause of action for wrongful discharge or wrongful termination.

It is considered a violation of public policy in many states to wrongfully discharge an employee, even in some instances where the employee did not have an employment contract. As stated previously, it may be a violation of public policy that results in a claim for "wrongful discharge" if an employer fires an employee for refusing to commit unlawful acts, for exercising a statutory right, for fulfilling a public obligation (such as serving on a jury), or for reporting the wrongdoings or illegal acts of their employer.

Unlawful Discrimination in Employment

In addition to concerns about employment security, many employees fear an employer may illegally discriminate against them. Besides constitutional protections against unreasonable discrimination, there are also federal and state laws that are designed to prevent discriminatory practices by employers. Some of these are discussed in the following sections.

Title VII

Under Title VII of the Civil Rights Act, an employer is prohibited from discriminating against employees because of their race, color, religion, sex, or national origin. However, this prohibition of employment discrimination does not prevent employers from discriminating on the basis of a person's religion, sex, or national origin (but not on race) where religion, sex, or national origin is a bona fide occupational qualification that is reasonable or necessary for performing a particular job. If the employer can demonstrate that discrimination is appropriate, it may be allowed to engage in the conduct under the bona fide occupational qualifications exception. To successfully argue this exception, an employer must prove three things:

1. There is a direct relationship between the person's sex and the ability to perform the duties of the job.

2. The reason for the discrimination relates to the "essence" or "central mission of the employer's business."

3. There is no less-restrictive or reasonable alternative.

It should be noted that although this exception may be used, courts scrutinize it very closely and are willing to apply it in very few cases. An employer or customer's preference for an individual of a specific religion is not a sufficient basis to establish a bona fide occupational qualification under Title VII.

The Equal Employment Opportunity Commission

The Equal Employment Opportunity Commission (EEOC) as well as some state fair employment practices agencies (FEPAs) are tasked with enforcing Title VII provisions. The EEOC and state FEPAs investigate, mediate, and sometimes file lawsuits on behalf of employees who have been unlawfully discriminated against. However, although Title VII allows individuals to file private lawsuits for violations of the Civil Rights Act, they must first file a discrimination complaint with the EEOC within 180 days of learning of the discrimination. If they fail to file a complaint with the EEOC as required, they may lose their right to file a lawsuit.

Pregnancy Discrimination

Title VII also prohibits differential treatment of women who are pregnant, unless not being pregnant is a bona fide occupational qualification. There is also a Pregnancy Discrimination Act that prohibits discrimination due to pregnancy and treats it as a form of sex discrimination. Under this statute, women who are pregnant or affected by childbirth must be treated the same as all other similarly situated employees with respect to their ability or inability to work.

Age Discrimination

The Age Discrimination in Employment Act (ADEA) protects people 40 or older from employment discrimination based on age. Its protections apply to both employees and job applicants. Under this statute, it is unlawful to discriminate against a person because of his or her age concerning any term, condition, or privilege of employment, including hiring, firing, promotion, layoff, compensation, benefits, job assignments, and training. The statute also makes it unlawful to retaliate against a person for opposing employment practices that discriminate based on age or for filing an age discrimination charge, testifying, or participating in any way in an investigation or litigation under the ADEA.

Just as in other employment discrimination cases, proving age discrimination as the reason behind a failure to obtain or retain a position may be extremely difficult. There is no specific test for determining age discrimination, and most cases are very factually dependent.

Disability Discrimination

The Americans with Disabilities Act (ADA) makes it unlawful for employers to discriminate against employees or potential employees who are qualified for a job but have a physical or mental disability. It also outlaws discrimination against individuals with disabilities in state and local government services, public accommodations, transportation, and telecommunications. This law is enforced by the EEOC and state and local civil rights agencies that work with the EEOC. Many states have their own version of this law.

Any employer practice that discriminates against an employee in recruitment, pay, hiring, firing, promotion, job assignments, training, leave, layoffs, benefits, and all other employment-related activities because of a disability are prohibited under this act.

Changes made to the ADA that went into effect in 2009 contained important revisions to the definition of *disability* that rejected the holdings in several Supreme Court decisions and portions of EEOC's ADA regulations. Although it retains the ADA's basic definition of *disability* as an impairment that substantially limits one or more major life activities, a record of such an impairment, or being regarded as having such an impairment, the revised ADA changes the way these statutory terms are to be interpreted in several significant ways. Basically, the ADA now expands the definition of "major life activities" by including two non-exhaustive lists. The first includes many activities (such as walking) that the EEOC has recognized, as well as activities that EEOC has not specifically recognized (such as reading, bending, and communicating). The second list includes major bodily functions (such as functions of the immune system, normal cell growth, and digestive, bowel, bladder, neurological, brain, respiratory, circulatory, endocrine, and reproductive functions).

The 2008–2009 ADA amendment also clarifies that an impairment that is episodic or in remission is a disability if it would substantially limit a major life activity when the condition is active. It also emphasizes that the definition of *disability* should be interpreted broadly. It was also intended to make it easier for those with mental disabilities to have an easier time qualifying under the statute.

Sexual Harassment

Discrimination based on a person's gender has been defined by statute to include sexual harassment, which means unwelcomed sexual advances, requests for sexual favors, or other verbal or physical conduct or communication of a sexual nature. Such conduct is indicated where sex is made a term or condition, either explicitly or implicitly, to obtain employment or employment advancement; where submission to or rejection of the conduct is used as a factor in decisions affecting an individual's employment; or where the conduct or communication has the purpose or effect of substantially interfering with an individual's employment or it creates an intimidating, hostile, or offensive employment environment.

Quid Pro Quo

There are two types of sexual harassment cases. The most common and easily recognized form of sexual harassment is the *quid pro quo* situation. *Quid pro quo* is a Latin phrase that means "this for that," or, more colloquially, "You do something for me, and I'll do something for you." In a quid pro quo sexual harassment case, a person claims that because he or she rejected a sexual advance by a person they worked with, the person's employment situation suffered tangible harm, such as not being promoted, being fired, or being given less profitable job duties. To demonstrate tangible harm in such a situation, employees must be able to show they were demoted or were given extra work or an inappropriate job assignment.

If a quid pro quo situation resulted in tangible harm to the victim employee, an employer may be held vicariously liable for the sexual harassment perpetrated by one of its employees against the other.

Hostile Work Environment

Another form of sexual harassment occurs when an employer creates a hostile work environment for one or more of its employees. A successful hostile work environment claim must demonstrate harassing conduct motivated by gender discrimination that is sufficiently severe as to make the victim's work environment a hostile place. In these claims, no tangible employment harm needs to be shown. It is sufficient if the court finds that a reasonable person would conclude that the environment created by the employer is hostile and abusive under the totality of circumstances. Factors such as the frequency and severity of conduct will be considered, as well as whether the conduct unreasonably interfered with the employee's work. The court may examine the effect of the conduct on the employee's psychological well-being in determining whether the environment was abusive to the point of creating a hostile work environment.

An employer may successfully defend itself in a sexual harassment suit by demonstrating that it acted with reasonable care to prevent and promptly correct any sexual harassment behavior and/or if it can demonstrate that the alleged victim unreasonably failed to take advantage of any corrective or preventive opportunities offered by the employer. Thus, if an employee is aware of the company's policy against sexual harassment and its complaint process for addressing such problems and instead fails to use the process and goes directly to court instead, the court may dismiss the case.

Courts have increasingly recognized same-gender sexual harassment claims when it can be shown that the hostile work environment was motivated by a person's sexual orientation or that tangible employment damage occurred because the victim rejected a homosexual advance.

Privacy Protections

Although many employees believe they should be permitted to use their employer's computer for personal use—surfing the Internet during their lunch break or writing and storing personal e-mail on it—the law does not recognize such a right. The company's computer is recognized to be the employer's property, and therefore the employer is entitled to determine how the employee is to use that property. Most courts do not recognize employees' right to privacy in the workplace when they are using company property or resources. Most employers have a workplace policy that specifies what use of company computers is or is not allowed.

Electronic Monitoring in the Workplace

Most courts also permit employers to use electronic means to monitor the conduct and work performance of their employees. As a result, it is not uncommon for employers to use software programs that record an employee's Internet activity, e-mail transmissions, and even each keystroke they type.

Alcohol and Drug Testing

In most states, private employers are free to use drug-testing programs as a condition of employment or continued employment. However, some state and federal courts have ruled that drug-testing programs for public employees are unconstitutional if they are not based on some kind of individualized suspicion. In these cases, the employee must have engaged in some conduct or exhibited some behavior that warrants suspecting they were impaired by drugs or alcohol while on the job.

Off-Duty Conduct

Typically, most jurisdictions hold that what employees do after work is their own business, as long as their conduct is not illegal or of an immoral nature that portrays their employer in a bad light. However, there are some jobs or employment contracts in which the employer makes the employees' exemplary personal conduct a condition of continued employment. An example of this is a company that hires a professional athlete to endorse its products or act as its spokesperson.

Workers' Compensation

Workers' compensation laws are state laws that provide payment to employees for injuries they incur at, or during, work. If employees' injuries are compensated by workers' compensation, they are not allowed to sue their employer for negligence in causing their injury. The rationale behind workers' compensation laws is that although the compensation the employee receives may be less than what the employee could get through a lawsuit, it is a sum certain, and the employee may receive it a lot quicker. Conversely, an employer who pays into the workers' compensation fund is protected from potentially catastrophic legal judgments from negligence-based employee lawsuits. This tradeoff, it is believed, is in the best interest of both the employee and the employer.

HYPOTHETICAL CASE

Regis works as a receptionist at Gizmo Co., which is one of the country's largest suppliers of widgets. He has worked there ten years for the same boss, but when the old boss retires and the new boss, Mr. Snidely, takes over, instant problems begin. Snidely began by commentating to coworkers that Regis was "a fag" and that no man who wears earrings to work should be allowed to keep a job. Whenever Regis would tell Snidely that someone stopped by to see him, he would say things like, "Oh God, I hope they don't think I hired you." Finally, when Regis was the only person in the department to whom Snidely failed to give a holiday bonus, Regis asked him why he keeps harassing him and why he didn't receive a bonus. Snidely responded, "I don't like queers, and I don't give them bonuses." That was the last straw, so Regis went to Snidely's boss, the Department Supervisor, and complained that Snidely was sexually harassing him. The Supervisor asked Regis whether he had confronted Snidely about it, and Regis said no—he was afraid to say anything to Snidely directly. The Supervisor then told him there was nothing he could do about the situation and that Regis would just have to be a man and deal with it himself. Regis quit and sued Gizmo Co., Snidely, and the Supervisor for sexual harassment.

Discuss the merits of Regis's claim and what facts and law there are to support it, as well as all possible defenses.

HYPOTHETICAL CASE

The Vegetarian Bar and Grill has 51 employees, most of whom are members of the Church of Ahimsa. The Grill posts a job advertisement seeking a day shift manager, and Sam, Sheldon, and Sally all apply. Sam is 32 years old and manages an electronics store. He heard about the job from a fellow Church of Ahimsa member who works as a bartender at the Grill. Sheldon and Sally responded to the online advertisement. Sheldon is 45 years old and has 12 years of experience as a restaurant manager but was recently laid off, while Sally is 42 and has been the night manager at a local restaurant for 16 years.

Sally finds it increasingly difficult to care for her young child while working nights and really wants to find a day job. All three candidates are interviewed by the restaurant owner, and Sam is offered and accepts the position. During the interview, the owner asked each candidate the same questions, one of which was, "What would you do if a deer ran out in front of your car and there were trees on both sides of the road?" Both Sheldon and Sally answer that they would hit the deer rather than risk more serious injury by swerving and hitting the trees. Sam answered, "As a member of the Church of Ahimsa, I cannot injure an animal, so I would swerve and hit the tree." When

Sheldon and Sally learn that Sam got the job and they didn't, and that most all employees are members of the Church of Ahimsa, they both sued. Sheldon sued for age and religious discrimination and Sally sued for age, gender, and religious discrimination. What are the arguments for and against Sheldon and Sally's positions?

Chapter 28: Intellectual Property

Introduction

What is intellectual property? Intellectual property refers to property that has been created by someone's mind, such as inventions, music, literary and artistic works, symbols, names, images, and designs used in commerce. Since intellectual property is treated like other property for legal purposes, it may be sold or transferred by someone in their will. Often, the right to use intellectual property is done through the use of a license agreement, which gives someone the legal ability to use the intellectual property without transferring any ownership interest in it.

Intellectual property is divided into two categories:

1. Industrial property—includes inventions (patents), trademarks, and industrial designs

2. Copyright—includes literary and artistic works such as novels, plays, and films; musical works; and artistic works such as drawings, paintings, photographs, sculptures, and architectural designs

The law protects three types of intellectual property:

1. Patent

2. Copyright

3. Trademark

Patent

Patent is a government grant that permits an inventor the exclusive use of their invention for 20 years.

During the 20-year period, no one else may make, use, or sell the invention without the inventor's permission. In exchange, the inventor is required to disclose information about the invention that anyone can obtain and use when the patent expires. This allows other companies to make cheaper versions of the invention (product) once the patent expires.

It is important to note that a person cannot patent an idea but only the tangible application of an idea. Thus, even if you think of a great invention, if someone else makes it first and patents it, you have no legal claim against the person who put that idea into tangible form and patented it. It is also true that patent protection is not available for scientific principles, mathematical formulas, or laws of nature.

To obtain a United States patent, an invention must meet these criteria:

- *Novel.* A novel product is one that is unique and has not been described in a publication or been used before.

- *Nonobvious.* A product is nonobvious if a person of ordinary skill in the area in which the product is created could not invent it.

- *Useful.* A useful invention does not have to be commercially valuable, but it does have to have some current use.

Provisional Patent Application

If an inventor is reluctant to go through the time and expense necessary to obtain a patent, he or she may file a provisional patent application (PPA). A PPA is a shorter, simpler, and cheaper process that gives inventors the opportunity to show their idea and invention to potential investors without the full expense of a patent application. Provisional patent protection lasts only a year, after which time the inventor must file a regular patent application, or they will lose any patent protection, and the information they have filed becomes publicly available.

International Patent Treaties

Each country has its own patent laws, which are not the same as U.S. patent laws. To provide a form of universal patent protection, the World Intellectual Property Organization (of the United Nations) has drafted patent treaties.

The Paris Convention for the Protection of Industrial Properties requires each member country to grant to citizens of other member countries the same patent rights that their own citizens enjoy. Under this Convention, member countries accept and recognize all patent and trademark applications filed with them from member countries so long as they have followed applicable laws. However, there is no standardized patent law, so laws vary greatly by country. That is why large companies that sell their products in many countries typically register for patent protection in several countries.

Copyright

Copyright is the ownership of the expression of an idea. It is a form of intellectual property protection provided by federal law to the authors of "original works of authorship." Original works of authorship include literary, dramatic, musical, artistic, and certain other intellectual works. Copyright protection is available to both published and unpublished works. It is important to note that copyright law does not protect the underlying idea or method of operation. For example, if a person thinks of a great new song but never records it, no copyright protection may be applied.

Unlike patent, however, the underlying idea of copyrightable material does not have to be novel. Thus, the expression of the same idea by many different people may be protected by copyright if the expressions are different. An example of this is when two different film studios produce a movie on the same subject. Although they may both be about the same subject—a giant human-eating monster from another planet—each movie is different, and each may be copyrighted.

What Copyright Allows

Copyright protection allows the protected party to do the following:

- Reproduce the work by making copies.

- Prepare derivative works based on the work (such as making a movie based on a book).

- Perform the work publicly, in the case of literary, musical, dramatic, and choreographic works, pantomimes, motion pictures, and other audiovisual works.

- Display the copyrighted work publicly, in the case of literary, musical, dramatic,

  and choreographic works, pantomimes, and pictorial, graphic, or sculptural works,

  including the individual images of a motion picture or other audiovisual work.

- In the case of sound recordings, perform the work publicly by means of a digital audio transmission.

What Copyright Does Not Allow

Copyright law does not allow anyone to violate any of the rights provided by the copyright statute to the owner of copyright. The most important of these is basically that the copyrighted material may not be used without permission of the copyright holder. These rights, however, are not unlimited in scope.

NOTE: A copyright violation is not plagiarism. *Plagiarism* is a term for an academic offense, usually defined by professional or academic bodies. *Plagiarism* typically consists of not giving credit to someone whose work is used in an academic setting. It is the act of attempting to pass off someone else's work as one's own. Doing this, however, may also entail copyright violation. A person cannot be jailed or fined by a state or federal court for plagiarizing someone else's work. They may, however, be subject to punishment by a non-legal body with the ability to enforce its findings. It is not uncommon for reporters to be fired for improperly using someone else's work or for students to be expelled from a university or college.

Who Can Claim Copyright?

Copyright protection exists from the time the work is created in fixed form. Once a work is placed in a fixed form, copyright in the work of authorship immediately becomes the property of the author who created the work. Only the author, or those deriving their rights through the author, can rightfully claim copyright. Examples of putting a work in fixed form are typing a story into a computer, recording a song on a device that can reproduce it, taking a digital photograph, or designing architectural drawings on a software program.

Works Made for Hire

In the case of works made for hire, the employer, not the employee, is considered the author and owner of the copyright.

Section 101 of U.S. Copyright law defines a work made for hire as "a work prepared by an employee within the scope of his or her employment; or a work specially ordered as a contribution to a collective work, as a part of a motion picture, as a compilation, as an instructional text, as a test, or if the parties expressly agree in a written instrument signed by them that the work shall be considered a work made for hire."

The authors of a joint work are considered co-owners of the copyright in the work, unless there is an agreement to the contrary.

It is important to note that mere ownership of a book, manuscript, painting, CD, or any other copy of a copyrighted property does not give the possessor ownership of the copyright or any of the rights that come from owning the copyright. The law provides that transfer of ownership of any material object that embodies a copyrighted work does not convey any rights in the copyright. Thus, if you buy a music CD or a book, you do not have the right to copy, reproduce, or distribute the songs or text it contains. Your purchase merely gives you a license to use the recording or the book for personal use.

What Works Are Protected by Copyright?

Copyright protects "original works of authorship" that are fixed in a tangible form of expression. The fixation does not have to be directly perceptible, as long as it can be communicated with the aid of a machine or device (i.e., a computer).

Copyrightable works include the following eight categories:

1. Literary works

2. Musical works, including any accompanying words

3. Dramatic works, including any accompanying music

4. Pantomimes and choreographic works

5. Pictorial, graphic, and sculptural works

6. Motion pictures and other audiovisual works

7. Sound recordings

8. Architectural works

The U.S. Copyright Office views these categories broadly. For example, computer programs and most "compilations" may be registered as "literary works," while maps and architectural plans may be registered as "pictorial, graphic, and sculptural works."

What Is Not Protected by Copyright?

Works that have not been fixed in a tangible form of expression—for example, choreographic works that have not been notated or recorded, or improvisational speeches or performances that have not been written or recorded—are not protected by copyright. Similarly, ideas, titles, names, short phrases and slogans, familiar symbols or designs, mere variations of typographic ornamentation, lettering, coloring, or a mere listing of ingredients are not capable of being copyrighted. However, some of these things may be able to be protected under trademark law. Works consisting entirely of information that is common property and containing no original authorship—such as standard calendars, height and weight charts, and lists or tables taken from public documents or other common sources—also cannot be copyright protected.

Joint or Collective Works

The authors of a joint work are co-owners of the copyright in the work unless there is an agreement to the contrary. Copyright in each separate contribution to a periodical or other collective work is distinct from the copyright in the collective work as a whole. The author who contributes the work as part of the collection retains the copyright to his or her work. For example, a book of photographs of a national park may be copyrighted, and each of the individual photographs in it may be separately copyright protected.

How to Secure Copyright Protection

The way in which copyright protection is secured is frequently misunderstood. No publication or registration or other action in the Copyright Office is required to secure copyright. Common law copyright protection exists from the moment the work is put into fixed form. There are, however, definite advantages to registering a work with the U.S. Copyright Office, one of the most obvious being the ability to enforce one's copyright.

Advantages to Federal Copyright Registration

Federal copyright registration may be made at any time within the life of the copyright, and although it is not a requirement for protection, the U.S. copyright statute provides several inducements and advantages to encourage owners to register their work. Among these advantages are the following:

- Registration establishes a public record of the copyright claim.

- Before an infringement lawsuit may be filed in court, registration is necessary for works of U.S. origin.

- If registration occurs before or within five years of publication, it will establish prima facie evidence in court of the validity of the copyright and of the facts stated in the copyright certificate.

- If registration is made within three months after publication of the work or prior to an infringement of the work, statutory damages and attorney's fees will be available to the copyright owner in court actions. Otherwise, only an award of actual damages and profits is available to the copyright owner.

- Registration allows the owner of the copyright to record the registration with U.S. Customs, and the Customs Department will enforce it.

Copyright Notice

Use of the copyright notice is important because it informs the public that the work is protected by copyright, it also identifies the copyright owner, and it shows the year of first publication.

Furthermore, if a work is infringed and a proper notice of copyright appears on the published copy or copies to which a defendant in a copyright infringement suit had access, then no weight will be given to the defendant's claim of innocent infringement (i.e., he/she didn't know the work was copyrighted).

Copyright notice should contain all the following three elements:

1. The symbol © (the letter C in a circle), or the word "Copyright," or the abbreviation "Copr."

2. The year of first publication of the work. The year date may be omitted when a pictorial, graphic, or sculptural work, with accompanying textual matter, if any, is reproduced in or on greeting cards, postcards, stationery, jewelry, dolls, or toys.

3. The name of the owner of copyright in the work, or an abbreviation by which the name can be recognized, or a

generally known alternative designation of the owner. For example: © 2017 Jane Doe.

Copyright Duration

Works created on or after January 1, 1978, are automatically protected from the moment of their creation, and copyright protection lasts for the author's life plus an additional 70 years after the author's death. In the case of "a joint work prepared by two or more authors who did not work for hire," the copyright protection lasts for 70 years after the last surviving author's death. For works made for hire, and for anonymous and pseudonymous works, the copyright will last 95 years from publication or 120 years from creation, whichever is shorter.

Transfer of Copyright

Copyright is a personal property right, and it is subject to the various state laws and regulations that govern the ownership, inheritance, or transfer of personal property, as well as terms of contracts or conduct of business.

Any part, or all, of the copyright owner's exclusive rights may be transferred, but the transfer of exclusive rights is not valid unless that transfer is in writing and signed by the owner of the rights. Transfer of a right on a nonexclusive basis does not require a written agreement.

Copyright Infringement

Anyone who uses copyrighted material without permission is violating the Copyright Act.

To prove copyright infringement, the copyright holder must prove the work was original, plus:

1. The infringer actually copied the work.

2. The infringer had access to the original work, and the two works are substantially similar.

Fair Use Exception to Copyright Infringement

The *fair use* doctrine permits the use of copyrighted works without permission for news reporting, scholarship, or research (educational purposes). However, a use that decreases revenue (i.e., copying textbooks) by competing with the copyright holder will not be recognized as legitimate under the fair use exception.

The court looks at four factors in determining whether a use meets the fair use exception:

1. The purpose and character of the use, including whether the use is of a commercial nature or is for nonprofit, educational purposes

2. The nature of the copyrighted work

3. The amount and substantiality of the portion used in relation to the copyrighted work as a whole

4. The effect of the use on the potential market for or value of the copyrighted work

Contrary to what some people think, there is no specific number of words, lines, or musical notes that may be used safely without permission. Also, acknowledging the source of the copyrighted material is not a substitute for obtaining permission to use it.

The Digital Millennium Copyright Act

The Digital Millennium Copyright Act (DMCA) amended U.S. copyright law to limit the liability of Internet service providers (ISP) for the information of users they store on a system or network that the service provider controls.

The DMCA also makes it a crime to circumvent anti-piracy measures built into most commercial software and outlaws the manufacture, sale, or distribution of code-cracking devices used to illegally copy software.

The DMCA does permit the cracking of copyright protection devices to conduct encryption research, assess product interoperability, and to test computer security systems. It also provides exemptions from anti-circumvention provisions for nonprofit libraries, archives, and educational institutions, under certain circumstances.

In general, the DMCA limits ISPs from copyright infringement liability for simply transmitting information over the Internet. ISPs, however, are expected to remove material from users' Web sites that they have been informed constitutes copyright infringement.

The DMCA limits the liability of nonprofit institutions of higher education when they serve as online service providers and, under certain circumstances, for copyright infringement by faculty or graduate students.

Copyright Treaties

The International Berne Convention requires member countries to provide automatic copyright protection to any work created in another member country. This protection expires 50 years after the death of the author.

Trademark

A trademark is any word, phrase, symbol, design, sound, smell, color, product configuration, or group of letters or numbers that is adopted and used by a company to identify its products or services and distinguish them from the products and services made, sold, or provided by others. Typically, a trademark is used to identify goods. Examples of trademarks are the Apple Inc. logo, McDonald's golden arches "M," the NBC peacock, and the mascot of athletic teams.

The primary purpose of trademarks is to prevent consumers from becoming confused about the source or origin of a product or service. Trademarks tell consumers who made the product or who provides the service. As consumers become familiar with individual trademarks, and the goods or services they represent, trademarks can acquire a secondary meaning as indicators of quality. They can help consumers decide whether a product or service is a worthy purchase.

A service mark is another type of mark. Service marks are like trademarks, but instead of identifying the source of products, they indicate the source or origin of services. Kinko's photocopying, Blockbuster, and Servicemaster Cleaners are companies that use service marks. For all practical purposes, trademarks and service marks are subject to the same rules of validity, use, protection, and infringement.

Trade names are not trademarks. A trade name is a word, name, term, symbol, or combination of these, used to identify a business and its goodwill. Whereas a trademark identifies the goods or services of a company, a trade name identifies the company itself. However, it is possible for trade names to also function as trademarks. Many companies use all or part of their business name as the trademark for their products. When a trade name is used by a company in this dual fashion, it becomes even more important that it prevent competing companies from using a similar trade name or trademark.

Trademarks and Trademark Protection Does Not Expire

Since trademarks are commercial source indicators, they do not expire. The longer a trademark is used, the more valuable it becomes. Trademarks are acquired through adoption and use, with trademark rights arising automatically. However, a trademark must be diligently protected by its owner because if it is not, and an infringer can successfully show others have been allowed to use it or something confusingly similar without objection, the court may find that the trademark has become part of the public domain and conclude it is no longer subject to protection.

Registering Trademarks

Just as with copyright, there are definite advantages to registering a trademark with the U.S. Trademark Office and obtaining statutory protection. Marks registered with the PTO enjoy legally stronger and geographically broader protection. Registered trademarks are indicated by the ® symbol.

Trademark Infringement and Trademark Dilution

An owner protects its trademark rights through registration, maintenance, watching to make sure no one uses a similar or the same mark, and enforcement. Nothing that closely resembles an owner's mark should be permitted. In no case does a junior user's mark need to be identical for infringement to occur. Infringement requires only likely consumer confusion.

In addition to a cause of action for trademark infringement, a trademark holder may also bring a cause of action for trademark dilution. Trademark dilution occurs when a famous mark is trivialized or made fun of by a third party in a way that devalues the trademark's worth. To be successful in a trademark dilution case, a famous trademark owner must demonstrate actual dilution has occurred, not the mere likelihood of dilution. If the trademark violator willfully intended to harm the reputation of the famous mark or intended to trade on the recognition of the famous mark, then additional damages and remedies may be sought.

Trademark Searches

Trademark searches are critical to avoiding legal problems and keeping and maintaining a company's good reputation. To use "Microsoft" without learning whether that name is already used by others on similar goods is unwise and may result in costly litigation.

Initial trademark searches can be done on the Internet, using one or more search engines. Trademarks should also be checked against state and federal registers. It is also important to look for possible non–trademark users and users in remote markets.

Domain Name Issues

A domain name is a unique name that identifies an Internet site without having to know the true numerical address and identifier (e.g., www.nmu.edu). If a domain name has the potential of confusing the public into thinking the trademark holder is somehow affiliated with another's Web site, the trademark holder may bring an infringement claim against the person or company causing the deception. For example, if your domain name is applegear.com, people might assume it is affiliated with Apple Inc. They may buy something from your Web site thinking the product is made by or endorsed by Apple Inc. when it is not. This would entitle Apple Inc. to bring a trademark infringement lawsuit against you.

Personal names can be used as domain names, and they may be trademarked. This is common for famous athletes and movie stars, and they have filed trademark infringement lawsuits to obtain ownership of domain names that were using their personal domain names.

The use and abuse of domain names became a serious problem as the Internet grew.

It became quite common for people to register domain names that they didn't want but knew others would. These "cybersquatters" would then offer to sell the domain names to the corporations or individuals who wanted them, but at hugely inflated prices. Registering a domain name solely for the purpose of making a lot of money from them, with no intent to use them, is called *cybersquatting*. This became such a problem that Congress passed a federal statute to address it.

The Anti-cybersquatting Protection Act (ACPA)

The Anti-cybersquatting Protection Act (ACPA) provides a federal remedy for cybersquatting. It applies to situations in which a person has a bad faith intent to profit from a domain name, including a personal name, which is a protected trademark.

A person violates the ACPA by registering, trafficking in, or using a domain name that:

1. is identical or confusingly similar to a distinctive mark.

2. is identical, is confusingly similar, or dilutes a famous mark.

The ACPA allows the court to order the cancellation of the domain name or the transfer of it to the owner of the trademark, whether the registration of the domain name occurred before or after the enactment of ACPA. It also provides for damages for the registration of domain names that occur after the enactment of the ACPA.

The ACPA permits a plaintiff to seek statutory damages or actual damages and lost profits.

HYPOTHETICAL CASE

Sam works for Mega Works Inc. as a software engineer. He signed an employment agreement that states that any programs he designs during his employment are the property of Mega Works. Sam designs a program that creates 3-D images from traditional animations. The company markets this program at great profit. While at home on weekends, Sam takes the same technology he used to design the animation translation program and designs a program that creates 3-D pictures from architect renderings. He patents this program in his name and sells it at great profit. Mega Works learns of this and sues Sam, claiming it is entitled to the patent he registered and all profits from his architect program. What facts and law support Mega Works' cause of action, and what facts and law support Sam's defense?

Chapter 29: E-Commerce

Introduction

What is e-commerce? *E-commerce,* or electronic commerce, is the buying and selling of products and services through electronic means such as the Internet or any other electronic means. It encompasses a wide range of business activities such as:

- Automatic clearinghouse transactions

- Credit card and cash transactions

- Electronic banking systems

- Electronic data interchange

- Electronic mail

- Electronic support systems for products and/or customer support activities

- Inventory management systems

- Ordering and material procurement support systems

E-commerce occurs when one or more of the processes required to complete the business transaction is performed electronically or with the assistance of electronic tools. Many e-commerce activities are conducted on private networks, direct link telephone systems, the Internet, or other electronic mediums. E-commerce also includes all activities related to the business transaction, such as shopping, ordering, delivery, payment, and customer support functions.

Privacy Issues

Privacy is a collection of legal rights and issues having a common focus built around an individual's right to be free from observation by others in non-public places without their knowledge or consent. E-commerce has given rise to what has become known as *information privacy* issues.

Although U.S. courts have long recognized a person's right to keep private certain aspects of their personal conduct and what transpires in their own home, they have only recently been asked to determine if a person has a legal right to control personal information about them.

Unlike the courts in most European countries, the U.S. Supreme Court has ruled that an individual's control of personal information is not a fundamental right protected by the Fourteenth Amendment. This means that businesses are free to collect information about their customers from their Web sites, including:

- Internet Protocol (IP) address

- Browser, OS, hardware platform

- Browsing activity

- Time and date of visit

- URL of requested Web site

- URL of site from which request was made

- Responses to any questions or data fields

Also, unlike in Europe, the United States offers no overall federal legislation on information privacy that regulates what business entities can do with the consumer information they collect. Instead, many federal statutes deal with specific aspects of privacy in the context of specific industries or types of information such as health or financial information. The U.S. approach to protecting information privacy is basically to let the market decide what is acceptable, at least for adults. However, although there is no legal requirement that Web sites have a privacy policy for the information they collect from users, most do. If a Web site does have a privacy policy, the Federal Trade Commission (FTC) has oversight of the policy, and it has taken steps to regulate misrepresentations by business Web sites. If a Web site's privacy policy states it does not or will not share user information with third parties, and it does so, the FTC may pursue legal action against them or obtain an informal resolution to the problem.

Children's Online Privacy Protection Act

The Children's Online Privacy Protection Act (COPPA) requires businesses with Web sites that target and solicit information from children under the age of 14 to obtain permission from a parent for the child to participate. This statute defines the characteristics of a Web site that targets children and contains specific requirements for how they can obtain and use information from them.

The Electronic Communications Privacy Act

The Electronic Communications Privacy Act (ECPA) outlaws the unauthorized interception of digital communications. The ECPA requires providers of public Internet communication services to keep the contents of communications (e-mail) confidential. However, it contains no such obligation regarding transactional records.

Gramm Leach Bliley Act—Financial Information Privacy

The Gramm Leach Bliley Act (GLBA), also known as the Financial Services Modernization Act, was intended to ease banking restrictions enacted after the Great Depression. It has recently been blamed for deregulating financial institutions to the point that another depression has been made possible. However, the GLBA also provides consumer privacy protections, which significantly impact the financial services industry and consumers.

The GLBA allows the integration of financial services. It authorizes banks, securities firms, and insurance companies to share personal customer information. Financial institutions must disclose to their customers whom they share customer information with and for what purposes. This is an ongoing obligation with which financial institutions must comply at least once a year. In addition, consumers must be given the opportunity to "opt out" of the disclosure of their personal information by financial institutions.

Relevant Statutes

In addition to the statutes pertaining to privacy issues, several more can impact e-commerce. Some of these are discussed next.

Communications Decency Act, Section 230

Section 230 of the Communications Decency Act (CDA) immunizes Internet service providers (ISP) who are "publishers" from any liability for defamatory statements posted by third parties—even when the ISP purposefully solicits and advertises the postings knowing they are likely defamatory. As such, this statute significantly alters the traditional common law liability of publishers that print media forms must follow. The rationale behind this change is that it would be too difficult for online publishers (meaning any Internet service provider that hosts a Web site) to police the content of all its contributors. While this is undoubtedly true, Section 230 has been criticized because it absolves ISPs from liability even when they knowingly publish defamatory information. As such, ISPs have no motivation to remove defamatory content, even when informed of it. If, however, an ISP is informed that it is hosting copyright or trademark infringing material and it fails to remove it when notified, it may face legal liability.

The Computer Fraud and Abuse Act

The Computer Fraud and Abuse Act (CFAA) contains definitions of criminal fraud and abuse for computer crimes and removes the legal ambiguities and obstacles to prosecuting these crimes. The CFAA establishes felony offenses for the unauthorized access of "protected computers." It defines protected computers rather broadly, so that any computer that makes use of a financial system's site or a government site is a protected computer. This is the statute most often used to prosecute computer hackers.

The CFAA makes it a crime to access any of the following without authorization:

- Information contained in a financial record of a financial institution, or of a card issuer, or contained in a file of a consumer-reporting agency on a consumer, as such terms are defined in the Fair Credit Reporting Act
- Any information from any department or agency of the United States
- Information from any protected computer if the conduct involved an interstate or foreign communication

The CFAA also makes it a crime to knowingly

- Cause the transmission of a program that intentionally causes damage to a protected computer (virus, worm).

- Intentionally access a protected computer without authorization and recklessly cause damage.

- Transmit in interstate or foreign commerce any communication containing any threat to cause damage to a protected computer.

- Use a computer to modify or impair the medical examination, medical diagnosis, medical treatment, or medical care of individuals.

- Use a computer to damage, or cause damage to, a computer, computer system, network, information, data, or program.

Security Issues

One of the most obvious concerns when conducting business, or any other transaction, electronically is determining the identity of the person you are dealing with. In electronic transactions, you cannot "see" who the other party is, so there must be another way to authenticate that others are who they say they are and verify their digital or electronic signature. Also, e-commerce requires a trustworthy computer system that provides confidentiality for information, contains access restrictions, and maintains information integrity by preventing its corruption or destruction while guaranteeing system availability. To do this, an e-commerce business must design a trustworthy computer system that provides for the following:

- Authentication

- Access control

- Integrity

- Audit

- Availability

- Secure login (i.e., PIN number or password)

- Digital signatures (i.e., an electronic signature produced through cryptography)

Other E-Commerce Concerns

In addition to the numerous statutes that impact e-commerce, a business that conducts transactions over the Internet also needs to be aware of and address a host of other issues.

Jurisdiction

Unlike brick-and-mortar businesses, a business that operates on the Internet has no physical location that a person can identify. This is a problem because the law has always based its jurisdictional requirements on where the parties are physically located. Thus, when a transaction occurs in "cyberspace," there is no location with obvious jurisdiction where litigation can be initiated. As a result, wise e-commerce businesses will specify on their Web site where jurisdiction resides for any dispute resolution cases.

Intellectual Property

The advent of the Internet has had a huge impact on the area of intellectual property law. The anonymity it provides people who post and copy intellectual property has greatly increased the problem of intellectual property theft and infringement. It has never been easier to share music, photographs, and literary works. This had led to a huge increase in lawsuits for copyright violation and the creation or modification of laws dealing with it. Unfortunately, many Web site designers still don't realize that they cannot post someone else's intellectual property without the owner's explicit permission. Some are under the false impression that so long as they identify the source of the copied text, graphic, or photograph, they are not violating any law. The requirements for use of intellectual property are discussed in detail in that chapter, but suffice it to say here that any e-commerce site should contain only legally obtained and authorized intellectual property.

Tax Laws

As soon as states realized that a significant amount of merchandise was being sold over the Internet, they began efforts to obtain the sales tax revenue from those transactions. This meant they had to deal with several problems. Specifically, both customers and e-businesses wanted to avoid paying taxes and claimed the states had no jurisdiction over sales conducted on the Internet. It required a great deal of costly investment and monitoring ability on behalf of the e-business and the state to keep track of the residency of customers for all transactions made online. Some businesses claimed the imposition of keeping track of and paying state sales tax would having a chilling effect on e-commerce, while brick-and-mortar businesses said they were at a significant competitive disadvantage by having to pay taxes that e-businesses were able to avoid.

Today, most states require that people buying a product on the Internet pay sales tax on it. So far, the federal government has not instituted any federal tax for Internet sales or transactions, but it is a reoccurring topic in Congress. Many large e-commerce sites do charge and collect sales tax based on where the customer geographically resides, and many states have passed laws that require their residents to voluntarily report their Internet purchases and pay taxes on them if it was not charged at the time of purchase. Still, it remains common for e-commerce sites to refrain from charging sales tax on the products they sell.

E-Commerce Checklist

Any individual or business creating a commercial Web site should address the following areas:

- Jurisdiction
- Site security and the safety of any financial and user data
- Copyright, trademark, and patent
- State law governing electronic transactions
- Federal laws governing electronic transactions and data exchange/use

- Taxes

- Dispute settlement procedure

- Disclaimers

- Site use policies and procedures

- Privacy policy

- License and site access

- User account requirements

- Risk of loss

- Product descriptions

- Company's physical address

HYPOTHETICAL CASE

Granada has a great idea for an online business she plans to call "Granada's Great Gizmos." She has already sold more than 100 of her gizmos and anticipates she will sell thousands after offering them for sale on the Internet. Currently, she and her younger brother buy the necessary parts and put the gizmos together in her basement, but she knows she'll have to hire more people and probably rent a manufacturing facility somewhere. She's already contracted with a Web design company to create her Web site, but she asks you for advice on what else she should do and what she should include on the Web site beyond the obvious product description, as well as price and order information for gizmos. What questions are you going to ask Granada, and what advice are you going to give her?

Chapter 30: Negotiable Instruments

Introduction

What is a negotiable instrument? A *negotiable instrument* is a form of commercial paper that provides an unconditional written promise to pay a specific sum of money. Checks, promissory notes, and certificates of deposit are all examples of negotiable instruments. Negotiable instruments are used as a substitute for money. They greatly facilitate business transactions.

Negotiable and Nonnegotiable Commercial Paper

There are two kinds of commercial paper: negotiable and nonnegotiable. Article 3 of the Uniform Commercial Code governs negotiable instruments, while principles and rules of contract law govern nonnegotiable instruments. Although negotiable instruments are not themselves a contract, they are often issued to fulfill a contract. For example, if Sam signs a contract to buy a car from Sally for $5,000 and gives her a promissory note for $5,000 when he takes possession of the car, the note is used to fulfill his obligation to pay under the contract, but it is not the contract for the purchase of the car.

Notes and Drafts

There are two types of negotiable instruments: notes and drafts. The difference between them is that a note is a promise to pay, while a draft is an order requiring someone else to pay.

The transfer of a negotiable instrument, by delivery or endorsement and delivery, gives the new holder the right to enforce payment in his or her own name.

Promissory Notes

A promissory note is a promise to pay money. It is used in virtually every loan transaction regardless of the amount borrowed. A promissory note may be due at a definite date in the future, or the maker may have to pay the note whenever asked (on demand).

If a note is made by a bank, it is called a certificate of deposit (CD). Whenever investors loan money to the bank, the bank gives them a note promising to repay the amount loaned at a specified date in the future. The bank is the maker of the note, and the investor is the payee of the note.

Drafts

A draft is an order that directs someone else to pay money to a person (the holder of the draft). A check is the most commonly used form of a draft. A check is an order telling a bank to pay money to the payee. The drawer (person writing the check) orders the drawee (bank) to pay money to the payee (person to whom the check is written). An example is when you write a check to the student bookstore for the purchase of your textbooks. You are the drawer, the bookstore is the payee, and the bank at which you have the checking account is the drawee.

Note the distinction in the terminology used between notes and drafts. The person who writes a draft (signs the check) is the drawer, while the person who signs a promissory note is the maker. Sometimes the generic term *issuer* is used to describe either a maker or a drawer.

Negotiability

For commercial paper to work as a substitute for money, it must be easily transferable in the marketplace. This means it must be negotiable. For an instrument to be negotiable, it must meet six criteria that are set forth in the Uniform Commercial Code:

1. The promise or order to pay must be in writing.

2. The instrument must be signed by the maker or drawer.

3. The instrument must contain an unconditional promise or order to pay.

4. The instrument must state a specific sum of money to be paid.

5. The instrument must be payable on demand or at a definite time.

6. The instrument must be payable to the bearer or to order.

It is essential that a negotiable instrument contain language that indicates it is payable to the person who possesses it. Typical language is, "Payable to the order of..." If an instrument does not meet this requirement, it is not a negotiable instrument and will not be treated as such, even if it has all the other features of negotiability. The only exception is a check that is payable on demand and drawn on a bank.

Nonnegotiable Commercial Paper

The possessor of nonnegotiable commercial paper has the same rights as the person who made the original contract. The transferee's rights are dependent on the rights of the original party to the contract, which means that if the original party somehow loses its right to be paid, so does the party to whom the right has been transferred (the transferee). This reduces the value of nonnegotiable commercial paper, because the transferee cannot be absolutely certain they will be paid.

Negotiable Commercial Paper

The possessor of negotiable commercial paper has more rights than the person who entered into the original contract. The possessor's rights with a negotiable commercial paper are unconditional. Generally, they are not dependent on the rights of the original party to the contract. This means as long as the transferee is a holder in due course, he or she is entitled to be paid the full amount of the note regardless of the relationship between the parties.

For example, if Sally buys a used boat from Sam's Marina for $20,000 and signs a promissory note with Sam for $20,000 of the purchase price (thereby promising to pay him the money later), her obligation to pay Sam is contingent on the validity of the underlying contract between them. So, if the boat is not as warranted, Sally might not be liable for the full amount of the note. However, if Sam wants money immediately, he may sell Sally's promissory note (meaning the right to collect the money from it) to Mega Finance Company. The price the finance company is willing to pay for the note will depend on whether the note is negotiable or nonnegotiable. If the note is nonnegotiable, the finance company gets the same rights that Sam had. Thus, if a court were to determine that the boat was not warranted, and therefore only worth $10,000, then that is all the finance company can get from Sally, even though the note is for $20,000.

If the note is a negotiable commercial paper, then the finance company is entitled to receive the full $20,000 amount of the note regardless of any claims Sally might have against Sam's Marina. If Sam keeps the note, however, even if it is negotiable, Sally will be able to subtract from what she owes him any amount resulting from his breach of contract because, as the original party to the contract, he is not a holder in due course. As such, the finance company that becomes a holder in due course of a negotiable instrument is in a better position to collect on the note than is the original contracting party.

Holder in Due Course

A holder in due course is anyone in possession of a negotiable instrument that is payable to, or indorsed to, them. The reason for this is they gave something of value for it, and they hold it in good faith.

Holder

For example, if you borrow $100 from your friend Sarah and sign a promissory note for the loan that states, "I promise to pay to the order of Sarah $100," and you sign your name and give the note to Sarah, she is a holder in due course because she is in possession of the instrument, and it is payable to her. If Sarah hands the note to her roommate Seth, Seth does not become a holder in due course, because the note is not payable to him. However, if before giving it to Seth, Sarah writes on the back of the note, "Pay to the order of Seth," he does become a holder in due course if he has given something of value for it. However, if Sarah writes, "Pay to the order of Seth," on the back of the note but does not give the note to Seth, Seth will not be a holder in due course.

Value

In addition to "holding" the negotiable instrument, a party must have given something of value for it to be considered a holder in due course. Someone who receives a negotiable instrument as a gift has not given anything of value for it and is not a holder in due course.

Value means that the holder has done something in exchange for receiving the negotiable instrument. For example, if Sarah's roommate, Seth, had paid the $200 heating bill that the two of them owed for the apartment, then he has already done something of value in exchange for receiving the $100 note.

Good Faith—Subjective and Objective Tests

Finally, a person who is a holder in due course must have acquired the instrument in good faith. To determine if the holder qualifies, the holder must satisfy both the subjective and objective tests. The subjective test requires that the holder believe that the transaction was honest. The objective test requires that the transaction appear to be commercially reasonable.

Defenses against a Holder in Due Course

If a note or draft is transferred to a person who acquires it in good faith, without notice of any defenses to payment, and the person becomes a holder in due course, that person can enforce the instrument without being subject to defenses that the maker of the instrument would be able to assert against the original payee, except for certain "real" defenses, which are rarely applicable.

A real defense is one an issuer may use even against a holder in due course. If the holder is not in due course, the issuer may use both real defenses and personal defenses. Thus, both real and personal defenses may be used against an ordinary holder of commercial paper, but only real defenses can be used against a holder in due course.

Real Defenses

The following are examples of "real defenses" that the courts will accept:

Bankruptcy—If a person lists a promissory note among the debts when filing bankruptcy, the debt will be discharged, even as to the holder in due course.

Forgery—If a payee's name is forged on a note and the note is then sold, the payee is not liable to the holder in due course.

Alteration—If the amount to be paid on a negotiable instrument is wrongfully altered, the holder in due course can collect only the original (legitimate) amount. If the note is incomplete, the holder in due course can collect the full amount stated, even if the instrument was incorrectly filled in. For example, if Sarah writes a promissory note to Seth for $200, but Seth adds another 0 to the end so it appears to be a note for $2,000 and then sells it to a holder in due course, the holder will only be able to recover $200. However, if Sarah gives Seth a signed promissory note with no amount owed filled in and Seth writes in $2,000, then a holder in due course could recover $2,000 from Sarah. In the case where the amount was changed, Sarah was not at fault, but in the case where Sarah turned over a blank note that she allowed Seth to fill in, she was at fault, so she will have to pay.

Mental incapacity—As in other contract cases, mental incapacity is deemed to invalidate the underlying transaction. Since such a transaction is void, any negotiable instrument created as a result of the mental incapacity is void and unenforceable.

Illegality—Just as contracts with mentally incapacitated individuals are void, so are contracts resulting from illegal acts. Thus, a negotiable instrument that is the product of an illegal transaction will be unenforceable even by a holder in due course.

Minority—Since a person under legal age has the right to invalidate a contract, he or she is also given the right to avoid paying on a negotiable instrument, even to a holder in due course.

Fraud in the execution—When the issuer has been fooled into signing a negotiable instrument without knowing what it is, and with no way of finding out, the court will likely find that it was the result of fraud in the execution of the instrument, and even a holder in due course will not be allowed to recover on the instrument.

Personal Defenses

The following personal defenses are valid against an ordinary holder but not a holder in due course:

Breach of contract—If the underlying contract that is the basis for the note is breached (i.e., the odometer of the car purchased has been illegally altered to show lower than the actual miles on the vehicle), then the payee can legitimately refuse to pay anyone other than a holder in due course.

Failure of consideration—If a negotiable instrument lacks consideration, a mere holder is not entitled to payment, but a holder in due course is. For example, Sam writes a $500 check to Sally as a gift, but then they have a fight, so he calls the bank and instructs it to stop payment on the check. Since Sally received the check as a gift and gave nothing of value for it, she is a mere holder and has no right to payment. However, if Sally cashes the check before Sam stops payment, he will still have to pay the bank, since the bank has given something of value for it (paid Sally $500), so it is a holder in due course and is entitled to its money.

Prior payment—If a party pays off a note but does not retrieve it or mark it paid in full, it risks being obligated to pay the amount stated if it is sold to a holder in due course. For example, if Sam buys a car from Seth and gives him a promissory note for it but fails to get the note back or write "paid in full" on it after he pays it off, he may have to pay the amount again if Seth sells the note for value to Sally, who becomes a holder in due course.

Unauthorized completion—If Sam writes a check to Seth to reimburse him for paying Sam's portion of the electric bill, but he fails to fill in the $200 amount owed and Seth writes in $1,000 and cashes the check, Sam will have to pay the bank $1,000, since it paid Seth $1,000 and is a holder in due course.

Non-delivery—If Sally writes a note that reads "payable to bearer," but she loses it before she gives it to Seth, and Sam finds it and sells it to a finance company for value, Sally will have to pay the finance company, even though she never gave it to the company or intended for the finance company to own the note. However, Sally would not have to pay Sam if he kept the note, since he would be a mere holder and she did not deliver the note to him.

Fraud in the inducement—If a promissory note is given on the basis of fraud, then the payee does not have to pay the holder. But if the holder sells the note for value to a holder in due course, then the payee is obligated to make payment even if the underlying contract was fraudulent. For example, if Sally writes a note for $1,000 and gives it to Sam in exchange for a motorcycle he has already sold to someone else, Sally will not have to pay Sam. However, if Sam sells the note to a finance company for value, Sally will have to pay the finance company

because it is a holder in due course.

Outstanding Claims or Other Defects of Negotiable Instruments

Sometimes a holder is aware that an instrument has an outstanding

claim against it or some other defect. The most common problems

that arise are discussed in the following sections.

The Instrument Is Overdue

A check is overdue 90 days after the date it was written. Other

demand instruments are overdue one day after a request for payment

has been made, or a reasonable time after it has been issued. If an

instrument is not paid by the date it is due, the recipient is on notice

that it may have a defect. A reasonable person would wonder why no

one has attempted to collect the money owed.

The Instrument Is Dishonored

A dishonored instrument is one that the party has refused to pay. If

someone knows that payment has been refused, then the person

cannot be a holder in due course. For example, if a bank stamps

"insufficient funds" on the back of a check presented for payment, the check has been dishonored, and no one who obtains it afterward can be a holder in due course.

The Instrument Is Forged, Altered, or Incomplete

If a holder knows that an instrument has been altered or forged, it cannot be a holder in due course. For example, if Seth writes a check to Sarah for $100 but leaves the line for writing out the amount blank and Sarah adds another zero and fills in "one thousand" on the line for writing out the amount while John looks on, if she endorses the check over to John, he is not a holder in due course because he knows she altered the check. However, if John takes the altered check indorsed to him and sells it to the finance company, the finance company becomes a holder in due course because it did not know the check was altered.

The Holder Is Aware of Claims or Defenses

A holder in due course cannot be someone who has notice that someone else has a claim to the instrument or that there is a dispute between the original parties to the instrument. For example, Seth agrees to buy a used car from Sarah and signs a $5,000 note that he gives to her to sell when he no longer owns the car. If Sarah tries to sell the note to her uncle who knows she obtained the note fraudulently, he will not be considered a holder in due course if he buys the note, since he is aware of the fraud.

The Shelter Rule

Typically, if a holder is not a holder in due course, he cannot recover if the person primarily or secondarily responsible can set up a defense to the claim that money is owed. A holder who is not a holder in due course is subject to the same defenses as if the person possessed a nonnegotiable instrument. The only exception to this is a holder who is not a holder in due course but who derived title from a holder in due course. In this instance, the shelter rule is applicable.

Under the shelter rule, the person who transfers an instrument passes on all their rights. When a holder in due course transfers an instrument, the recipient acquires all the same ownership rights— even if the recipient is not a holder in due course.

For example, Consumer Products rebate center sent Sally a check for $200 as a rebate for her purchase of a large-screen TV. Sally claimed she never got the check, so Consumer Products stopped payment on the check it originally sent her and sent her another one. However, Sally took the first check, which she actually had received, and signed it over to Fred, her car mechanic, for work he did fixing her car. At this point, Fred is a holder in due course and is entitled to payment from Consumer Products. However, instead of Fred attempting to cash the check himself, he sells it to the finance company, which knows that the check has been dishonored but buys it anyway. Under the Shelter Rule, the finance company acquired Fred's rights as a holder in due course and is entitled to payment.

The point of the shelter rule is not to benefit the likes of the finance company, but instead, to protect those in the position of Fred. The law is based on the idea that it would not do Fred any good to be a holder in due course if he could not sell the instrument to anyone. There is one exception to this rule, however: if a holder in due course transfers the instrument to a prior holder who was a party to the fraud involving that instrument (i.e., Sally), that prior holder does not acquire the rights of a holder in due course.

HYPOTHETICAL CASE

Sandy wants to buy the house Jake is selling, but her credit isn't good enough to get a mortgage, so Jake agrees to sell it to her on a land contract. She signs a promissory note to him for the $75,000 purchase price. Jake promptly sells the note and indorses it to the Acme Finance Co. for $70,000. Six months later, Sandy finds out that there is a lien on the property for $4,000 in back taxes that Jake failed to pay. Since Jake never disclosed this material fact to her, Sandy wants to rescind the contract. If she is successful, will she be liable to Acme Finance Co. for $75,000? Why or why not?

Chapter 31: Liability for Negotiable Instruments

Introduction

A person or company who purchases a negotiable instrument in the ordinary course of business can expect that it will be paid when presented to the maker without worrying about becoming involved in a dispute between the maker and the person to whom the instrument was first issued.

Sometimes, however, the issuer of an instrument believes it has been defrauded or otherwise dealt with unfairly by the payee and may refuse to pay the holder in due course, which results in a lawsuit to recover on the instrument.

Although a negotiable instrument is a promise to pay a sum of money, it is not a contract. A contract requires offer, acceptance, and consideration, which a negotiable instrument does not have. Also, unlike a contract, the right to payment of a negotiable instrument is tied to possession of the document itself. The rights of the holder in due course (payee) are actually better than those provided by a contract. This is because the right to payment is not dependent on the validity of the underlying contract that gave rise to the debt. It is also possible for the holder in due course to have better title than the party from whom the holder obtains the instrument. This can happen if the transferee becomes a party to the contract and is able to enforce the contract in the holder's own name.

Not everyone who signs a negotiable instrument is an issuer, and not everyone who presents an instrument for payment is a holder. There is, however, legal liability for people who sign a negotiable instrument, just as there is liability for non-holders who receive payment. The liability pertaining to someone who has signed an instrument is referred to as *signature liability*, and the liability of someone who receives payment is called *warranty liability*. These and other forms of liability for negotiable instruments are discussed in the paragraphs that follow.

Signature Liability

Everyone who signs a negotiable instrument is potentially liable for it, but the degree of liability depends on the person's capacity when it was signed. For example, the liability of the maker of a note is different from the liability of someone who indorses the note.

The Maker's Liability

The maker (issuer) is primarily liable for the note since the maker is the one who has promised to pay and must pay unless the maker has a valid defense. Thus, no one is primarily liable for a check written on a bank account until the bank accepts it.

The Drawer's Liability

The drawer is the person who writes the check, and he or she has secondary liability. The drawer is not liable until he or she receives notice that the bank has dishonored the check. If the bank pays the check with the drawer's funds, the drawer will become secondarily liable only if the bank dishonors the check. For example, Sam writes Sally a $5,000 check to pay for the car he just bought from her, and Sally asks him if his check is good. He replies, "You don't think I'd write a bad check, do you?" Sally has no recourse against him if it is bad because he didn't commit to her that it was good (she may have a separate breach of contract cause of action). But if she attempts to cash the check and the bank teller informs her that Sam's account has insufficient funds to cover the check, then Sam is liable to Sally for the $5,000 as the drawer of the check, which the bank refused to pay.

The Drawee's Liability

The drawee is the bank on which the check is drawn. It is incorrect to assume that just because the drawer of the check is secondarily liable, the drawee bank is primarily liable. Unfortunately, when the drawer signs the check, it enters a no-man's land. The bank is not liable to the holder and has no liability for damages to the holder for refusing to pay the check. It is possible that the bank will be liable to the drawer for violating their checking account agreement, but this agreement does not apply to the holder of the check. As such, the bank can either pay the check or dishonor it. If the bank dishonors it, the holder must pursue remedies against the drawer. This is because under the UCC, a bank is not liable for a check until it accepts the check for payment. If it refuses to accept it when the account has sufficient funds, the holder has no claim against the bank because there is no privity of contract between the parties. The holder has a claim only against the issuer of the check. The issuer may then have a claim against his bank.

The Indorser's Liability

The indorser is anyone other than the issuer who signs the negotiable instrument. Indorsers are secondarily liable for the instrument. As such, the indorser must pay if the issuer or drawee does not. There are four exceptions to this:

1. The bank issues a certified check.

2. The check is presented for payment more than 30 days after it is indorsed.

3. The check is dishonored and the indorser is not notified of this within 30 days.

4. The indorser writes "without recourse" next to his or her signature.

The Accommodation Party's Liability

The accommodation party is the party who adds his or her signature to a negotiable instrument for the purpose of being liable on it. Usually, the accommodation party does not receive any direct benefit from the negotiable instrument but agrees to be liable solely to accommodate the other party. For example, when Sam attempts to buy a truck from Fred's Used Cars, Fred will not accept a promissory note from him unless he has someone else, who agrees to pay if Sam does not, also sign it (a co-signer). Sam gets his father to agree to sign as a "co-signer" on the note. Sam is the accommodated party, and Sam's father is the accommodation party.

An accommodation party has the same liability to the holder as the person for whom he signed. Therefore, if Sam fails to pay on the promissory note, the holder can make a claim directly against Sam's father without first demanding that payment from Sam. If Sam's father is forced to pay the note, however, he may try to recover the money from Sam.

Warranty Liability

As mentioned previously, if someone forges a person's name to a negotiable instrument, the forger will be responsible for it, not the person whose name was forged. The drawee bank is liable if it pays a check on which the drawee's name is forged, and in other cases of wrongdoing, the person who first acquires an instrument from a wrongdoer is ultimately liable to anyone who pays value for it.

Transfer Warranties

A person who transfers an instrument promises that it is valid and warrants the following:

- He or she is a holder of the instrument.

- The instrument has not been altered.

- All signatures are authentic and authorized.

- As far as the person knows, the issuer is solvent.

- No defense can be asserted against him or her.

Presentment Warranties

Presentment warranties protect those who demand payment for an instrument from the maker, drawee, or anyone else liable on it.

When individuals present a check for payment, they warrant that they are a holder, the check has not been altered, and that they have no reason to believe the drawer's signature has been forged.

The presentment warranty for a promissory note is different than it is for a check. A person who presents a promissory note for payment only makes one warranty—that he or she is the holder of the instrument. If someone presents a note with a forged signature, the person is violating the presentment warranty because a forged signature prevents subsequent owners from being holders.

Other Liability Rules

Several other rules impose liability on parties who wrongfully create, pay, or redeem negotiable instruments, discussed in the following sections.

Negligence

This rule holds a person liable for negligently creating or paying an unauthorized negotiable instrument to an innocent third party. All the elements of a negligence cause of action must be demonstrated.

Imposter Rule

Even though someone issues a negotiable instrument to an imposter, any indorsement in the name of the payee is valid so long as the person (or bank) who pays the instrument does not know of the fraud. For example, someone knocks on your door claiming to be selling extended car warranties from Longterm Warranty Co., and you sign up and give the salesman a $200 check made payable to Longterm Warranty Co. If there is no Longterm Warranty Co. and the salesperson forges an indorsement in the name of the company and cashes the check, the bank will not be liable for cashing it. The law considers that those who actually dealt with the imposter are in a better position to determine if a fraud was being perpetrated than is the bank.

Fictitious Payee Rule

If an instrument is issued to a non-existent person, then the indorsement in the name of the payee is valid so long as the person (or bank) who pays it does not know of the fraud. For example, if, when paying the company's bills, Sally writes out monthly checks to "Sue Smith" and then cashes them herself, the company can hold her, but not the bank, liable for cashing them.

Employee Indorsement Rule

If an employee who is responsible for issuing instruments forges a check or other negotiable instrument, any indorsement in the name of the payee, or similar name, is valid so long as the person (or bank) who pays the instrument does not know of the fraud. For example, Sally is employed as the treasurer for NewAge Corporation, and once a month, in addition to paying the company's bills, she writes herself a check for $1,000 and forges the name of the company vice president on it, since his signature is required for any check larger than $500. If she successfully cashes these checks, the bank will not be liable since she had the general authority to sign company checks and it was not aware of her forgery. If, however, Sally worked as a company janitor and was not authorized to sign checks, the bank would be liable for the cashed check. This is because when a person has the authority to sign checks, the bank bears no liability for failing to determine the validity of the additional signature. But when the party cashing them does not have the legal authority to cash checks for the company at all, the bank is considered to be violating its basic duty of care.

Discharge

An instrument is discharged when liability for it terminates. Almost any change in an instrument that harms an indorser or accommodation party has the consequence of discharging their obligation. This is true unless the party consented to the change.

The UCC identifies five ways in which an instrument is discharged:

1. By making proper payment.

2. By agreement. The parties to the instrument can agree to discharge it even if the instrument is not paid.

3. By cancellation. This is accomplished by the intentional and voluntary surrender, destruction, or disfigurement of the instrument.

4. By certification. When a bank certifies or accepts a check, the drawer and all indorsers of it are discharged, and only the bank is liable.

5. By alteration. If the terms of the instrument are intentionally changed, it is discharged.

Liability by Banks and Bank Customers

Perhaps the most common negotiable instrument is a bank check. Because they are so relied on for both business and personal transactions, there are many rules dealing with their use. The most common rules are discussed below.

Checking Accounts

Whenever you deposit money into a checking account, the bank owes you money. It becomes a debtor to you. The bank also serves as your agent since you have authorized it to represent you in certain legal capacities.

A bank has a duty to pay a check if it is authorized by the customer to do so and if the customer conforms to the terms of the bank's checking account agreement. If a bank violates this duty and wrongfully dishonors an authorized check, it is liable to the customer for all actual and consequential damages.

Electronic Banking and Electronic Fund Transfers

The Electronic Fund Transfer Act (EFTA) was passed to protect consumers in their dealings with banks. It defines a *consumer* as anyone who is a natural person, thus corporations and businesses are excluded and are not considered consumers. It establishes time frames under which a person's account must be credited with a deposit and when those funds may be withdrawn.

Employers are not allowed to require that employees receive their paychecks by electronic transfer to a *specific* bank—but they are allowed to require that employees receive them electronically at some bank.

Death of a Customer

When a customer dies, the bank may continue to pay checks on their account for ten days after it learns of their death, unless it receives a stop payment order from someone claiming an interest in the account (such as someone who may inherit the money in the account under the decedent's will). Typically, however, banks freeze checking accounts as soon as they learn of the account holder's death.

Incompetent Customers

As soon as a bank is notified that a court has ruled that a customer is incompetent, it is to freeze their account and will be held liable if it pays the customer's checks.

Forgery

If a bank pays a forged check, either the bank or the customer will lose money. The UCC rule is that the bank should bear this risk more than the customer. Therefore, if a bank pays a check on which the issuer's name is forged, the bank must re-credit the customer's account.

Alteration

With only one exception, if a bank pays a check that has been altered, the customer is liable only for the original amount of the check, and the bank is liable for the balance. The exception is if the alteration is obvious; then the bank will be held liable for the full amount of the check because it should have known better than to cash it.

Completion

If a check is incomplete and someone other than the original issuer fills it in, the bank is not liable unless it was on notice that the completion was unauthorized.

Stale Checks

A bank does not have to pay checks that are presented more than six months after their date. If it does pay a check after more than six months, it is not liable.

Post-Dated Checks

A check that is presented for payment before its date is a post-dated check. For example, if Sally writes a check to Sam for the bicycle she is buying from him and dates it the following Friday because that is her payday, but he tries to cash it immediately, he is attempting to cash a post-dated check.

A bank is not liable for paying a post-dated check unless the customer has notified the bank in advance that a post-dated check is coming. So, if Sally tells Sam, "Don't cash this check until next Friday when my paycheck will be deposited," and he tells her, "Hey, I already gave you the bike, so I can cash the check," she should call her bank and warn that a post-dated check made payable to Sam is coming and not to cash it.

Stop Payment Orders

Checks that were authorized when issued may still be nullified by the customer. Generally, if a bank pays a check when a customer has given it a stop payment order, it will be liable for any loss the customer suffers.

An oral stop payment order is valid only for fourteen days, while a written order expires after six months. Thus, if a customer does not renew the stop payment order (usually at a cost charged by the bank), a person may be successful in cashing the check when the stop payment order expires.

A stop payment order is valid only if it describes the check with reasonable certainty and the bank receives the stop payment order before it pays the check.

Customer's Right to Withdraw Funds

The Expedited Funds Availability Act (EFAA) specifies the maximum time a bank can hold funds deposited by check before allowing a customer to withdraw them. Under this statute, a customer must wait longer to withdraw cash from funds deposited by check than they must wait to write checks on them. This is because banks are at greater risk of loss when customers withdraw cash than they are when they write a check.

Customer's Liability for Unauthorized Transactions

If a thief steals your ATM card or debit card, it is important to report it to the bank immediately. This is because if the theft is reported to the bank within two days, you will only be responsible for the first $50 fraudulently charged on the account. If the theft is reported after two days, but within 60 days of receiving a bank statement that shows the unauthorized withdrawal, you will be responsible for a maximum of $500. After 60 days, you will be liable for the full amount of any fraudulent charges made.

Sometimes a fraudulent transfer of funds takes place without the use of a stolen card. In that situation, consumers are not liable at all so long as they report the loss within 60 days of receiving a bank statement that shows the loss. If, however, more than 60 days pass and the consumer has not reported the fraudulent transaction, they will be liable for the entire amount.

Customer's Duty to Examine Bank Statements

Customers have a duty to read over their bank statements and look for forged or altered checks. A failure to report a forgery or alteration more than a year after its appearance on the statement eliminates any liability the bank may have. If a customer fails to notify the bank of a forgery or alteration within 30 days of receiving a statement, the bank will be relieved from liability for cashing any subsequent checks by the same forger.

HYPOTHETICAL CASE

Sam treats Sally to dinner for her birthday and uses his MasterCard to pay for it. Unbeknownst to him, the waiter copies the information on his credit card when he takes it back to ring up the transaction. A few days later, the waiter uses the information from the credit card to order over $1,000 worth of merchandise from various Internet sites that he has sent to a fictitious name but real address. Sam doesn't realize anything is amiss until he gets his MasterCard statement three weeks later. He immediately calls the number on his MasterCard and reports the transactions he did not make. Which, if any, of the fraudulent charges will Sam be responsible for paying? Which, if any, of the fraudulent charges will the bank be responsible for paying?

Chapter 32: Secured Transactions

Introduction

What are secured transactions? A *secured transaction* is one in which a creditor takes an interest in a piece of property that is used as collateral for a loan. This means if the loan is not paid, the creditor may bring legal proceeding to obtain possession of the property, which it can then sell in an effort to receive the money it is owed on the loan. The interest the lender has in this property is referred to as a security interest. The most common example of a secured transaction is the typical automobile purchase. The average purchaser of a new car does not have enough money to pay cash for the vehicle and must take out a loan to pay for it. The financial institution that loans the buyer money takes a security interest in the car that is being purchased with the money it is loaning. This is done through a contract called a *security agreement,* and the car is the collateral for the loan. The security interest the lender has is recorded (typically with the Department of Motor Vehicles or Secretary of State) so that if the buyer fails to make the car payments as required, the financial institution will exercise its rights under the security agreement to obtain possession of the car, sell it for what it can, and hold the

purchaser liable for any remaining money owed on the loan once that

sale price is applied.

Article 9 of the UCC

Article 9 of the UCC governs secured transactions in personal

property and applies to any transaction intended to create a security

interest in personal property or fixtures. Specifically, it recognizes

several types of personal property that may be used as collateral:

- Goods—property that is movable
- Inventory—goods held by someone for sale or lease, such as automobiles for sale at a dealership
- Instruments—drafts, checks, promissory notes, and certificates of deposit
- Investment property—typically securities
- Other property—such as bank accounts, intellectual property, documents of title, and chattel paper

Article 9 of the UCC uses other terms with which most people are

unfamiliar and are defined here:

Authentication—Authentication occurs when a person signs a document by using a method that identifies them and indicates they are adopting the record as their own.

Collateral—Collateral is the property that is the subject of the security interest. For example, the automobile company that finances your car purchase will keep a security interest in the vehicle, which is the collateral. Farm equipment, restaurant equipment, and other business equipment often require loans, which the bank will use as collateral when purchased.

Debtor—The debtor is the person who has an original ownership interest in the collateral. One example is the person who buys the car with the loan from the automobile dealership or bank.

Financing statement—The financing statement is a written document that notifies the public that the secured party has a security interest in the collateral.

Fixtures—Fixtures are goods that are attached to real estate. For example, a ceiling fan is a good when the company makes and sells it, but once it is installed in a house, it becomes a fixture. Flag poles imbedded in the ground and sheds are also considered fixtures.

Perfection—Perfection is a series of legal steps the secured party takes to protect its rights in the collateral against all others outside of the debtor.

Record—The record is the information about the secured transaction that is written on paper or stored in electronic form.

Security agreement—The security agreement is the contract by which the debtor gives a security interest in the collateral to the secured party. It protects the secured party's rights in the collateral.

Security interest—A security interest is the interest in personal property or fixtures that "secures" the performance of the debtor's obligation. The automobile dealership's security interest in the car it sells a person is what gives it the legal right to repossess the car and sell it if the borrower does not make the required payments.

Secured party—The secured party is the person or company that holds the security interest. The automobile dealership that sells you a car and finances it for you is the secured party.

Attaching a Security Interest

Attachment of the security interest is an essential part of every secured transaction. Under article 9 of the UCC, attachment means the secured party has performed three necessary steps to create an enforceable security interest:

1. The parties have made a security agreement, and either the debtor has authenticated a security agreement describing the collateral, or the secured party has obtained possession of the collateral.

2. The secured party has given something of value to obtain the security agreement.

3. The debtor has rights in the collateral.

Obviously, if there is no agreement, there can be no security interest. In most instances, the agreement must be in writing and signed by the debtor. It may be electronically recorded and authenticated by the debtor. The collateral must be identified in the agreement.

There are a few situations in which the security agreement does not have to be in writing. One occurs when the parties have an oral security agreement and the secured party has possession of the collateral. This often occurs during stock purchases, wherein the purchaser leaves the stock certificates in the possession of the secured party.

Perfection

When the security interest has attached to the collateral, the secured party is protected against the debtor. For example, when the security interest in the automobile being purchased is perfected, the dealership may take possession of the automobile if the purchaser fails to make the required payments. There are three ways a security interest may be perfected:

1. Perfection by filing
2. Perfection by possession
3. Perfection of consumer goods

In some instances, a secured party may choose which method to use, but in others only one method will work.

Perfection by Filing

The most commonly used method is perfection by filing. This is done by filing a financing statement with the appropriate state agency (for example, automobile security interests are usually filed with the Department of Motor Vehicles). The financing statement lists the names of all parties to the agreement, describes the collateral, and gives enough information about the security interest to enable any interested person to learn about it. If the financing statement does not contain enough information to put people on notice of the security interest, or if a party fails to file it with the right agency, its interests may be challenged and fail.

A financing statement is usually deemed sufficient if it includes the name of the debtor, the name of the secured party, and an indication of the collateral. The location where financing statements must be filed vary from state to state, so it is essential to check the law of the applicable state.

Perfection by Possession

For most types of collateral, it is permissible to perfect it by possession in addition to filing. For example, if the collateral is a diamond ring, the jewelry store that loaned the money to buy it may perfect its security interest by holding the ring until the loan is paid off. When the secured party retains the collateral, however, it has a duty to use reasonable care in preserving and protecting the collateral in its possession.

Perfection of Consumer Goods

The UCC contains special provisions for security interests in most common consumer goods, which are those used primarily for personal, family, or household purposes. This is because it is impractical and unworkable for merchants to file a financing statement for every piece of furniture or electronic equipment for which a consumer owes money. To deal with this, the UCC recognizes a purchase money security interest (PMSI), which is taken by the party who sells the consumer good (collateral) or the party who advances money so the debtor can buy the collateral. A PMSI in consumer goods perfects automatically and requires no filing.

A PMSI is applicable only when the money loaned is used to purchase a consumer good that is used as collateral. It cannot, for instance, be used in situations where the money loaned is used to purchase a business's inventory.

Buyer Protections

A buyer in the ordinary course of business (BIOC) is someone who buys goods in good faith from a seller who routinely deals in such goods. For example, Sam's Fish Market buys 50 whitefish from Marquette Fisheries. Sam's Market is a BIOC. He is buying in good faith, and Marquette Fisheries routinely deals in whitefish. This status is important because a BIOC is generally not affected by security interests in goods. However, if a buyer is aware that the seller has violated another party's rights in the goods, then the buyer would not be acting in good faith, and the rule would not apply. Typically, however, a BIOC takes the goods free of a security interest created by the seller, even though the security interest may be perfected.

Once a security interest is perfected, it remains in effect regardless of whether the collateral is sold or transferred. For example, Sally borrows $100,000 from Mega Finance Co. to keep her lawn service company in business, and the finance company takes a security interest in the 20 industrial lawn mowers that her company owns. A few months later, she needs still more cash, so she sells five of the lawn mowers to Jack's Lawn Service Co. Unfortunately, even that isn't enough, and six months later, she files for bankruptcy. Will Mega

Finance Co. be able to obtain the five lawn mowers Sally sold to Jack's? Yes, it will. The security interest Mega had in the lawn mowers continued even after Jack's purchased them, and the finance company may take possession once Sally defaults on her loan payments.

Priorities Among Creditors

Sometimes, two creditors have a security interest in the same collateral. What happens then? Quite often, the debtor doesn't have enough assets to pay everyone, so all the creditors compete to be first to be paid. The UCC has rules specifying how this situation should be handled.

The first rule is that a party with a perfected security interest takes priority over a party with an unperfected security interest. The whole point of perfecting a security interest is to ensure that it gets priority over everyone else's loan.

The second rule is that if neither secured party has a perfected security interest, the first interest to attach will be given priority.

The third, and final, rule is that between perfected security interests, the first party that filed or perfected the security interest will be the first to be paid.

Debtor Default

If the debtor fails to perform its obligations or has defaulted, the security agreement may terminate. Usually, the parties will define what constitutes a default in their security agreement. Most always, one instance of default is a failure of the debtor to make the payments required. Whatever is defined as a default, when it occurs, the secured party has two options: (1) it may take possession of the collateral, or (2) it may file suit against the debtor for the money owed.

If the debtor defaults, the secured party may take possession of the collateral without any court order (this is true for goods, not real property), provided it can do so without any breach of the peace. Once the secured party obtains the collateral, it may dispose of it or retain it as full satisfaction of the debt. Until the secured party disposes of the collateral, the debtor has the right to redeem it by paying the full amount owed on the debt. If they pay the debt, they may retrieve the collateral.

If the secured party sells the collateral, it applies the proceeds first to its expenses in repossessing and selling the collateral and second to the debt. Often, there is a deficiency, meaning the proceeds from the sale are not sufficient to pay off the entire debt. If this happens, the debtor remains liable for the deficiency, and the creditor will sue to collect it.

If the debtor pays off the debt, the secured party must complete a termination statement, which is a document stating that it no longer claims a security interest in the collateral.

HYPOTHETICAL CASE

Adam owns a small hotel and decides he needs to update all of its furnishings. He goes to Ted's Furniture Store and buys $100,000 worth of new furniture. Ted's Furniture finances the purchase and retains a security interest in the furniture. Adam begins making the required $2,000 per month payments on the loan and remains current until a fire destroys half of his hotel rooms (and their new furniture). After Adam misses three payments in a row, Ted's Furniture declares him in default.

What action is Ted's Furniture likely to take, and why? Is there additional information that, if demonstrated, might produce different results? If so, explain.

Chapter 33: Real Property

Introduction

Property laws are important and have helped determine history. For example, contrast the English verses the French property inheritance systems.

In England, primogeniture required that land held by a person who died without a will to go in its entirety to their eldest son. Widows were not considered heirs of their husbands. A widow was entitled only to her "dower" rights of one-third of her husband's personal property and the use of one-third of his real property during her lifetime, after her death the property went to the husband's legal heirs (i.e. the eldest son).

However, France used what was called gavelkind. In gavelkind property was divided equally between all of the deceased property owner's sons. So if a property owner had four sons, his property was divided into four equal parcels. And if those sons had four sons their property would be divided into four equal parcels and so on and so on during each generation.

The difference between these two property inheritance systems meant that in primogeniture England there remained large land holdings and estates whose owners were very wealthy whereas in France, gavelkind resulted in numerous small estates that were not large enough to support or feed their owners. Some historians place part of the blame for the French revolution on the fact that gavelkind resulted in so many poor peasants and lots of noblemen with a title no property.

There are four types of property and we will discuss the first in this chapter.

1. Real Property (e.g. real estate)

2. Tangible Property (e.g. car)

3. Intangible Property (e.g. bank accounts)

4. Intellectual Property (e.g. copyright, patent)

Real Property consists of:

1. Land

2. Buildings

3. Subsurface (mineral) rights

4. Air Rights

5. Plant Life

6. Fixtures – A fixture is something that is securely or permanently attached to a building or real property and cannot be easily removed. E.g. a ceiling fan or flag pole.

Note: It is important to exempt fixtures when an owner sells real property if they want to keep them since the buyer is legally entitled to the fixtures with the purchase unless the parties specify otherwise in the purchase contract.

Estates

An estate is an interest in land which is, or which may become, possessory, meaning a person may get possession of it.

Ownership of estates is measured in terms of duration such as a term of years of for a person's life or perhaps until a condition is met or expires.

There are several different "estates" the law recognizes and each affects the legal rights of the people who own it. The type of ownership determines whether the owner may transfer their ownership interest without the permission of other owners and it determines if they can leave the property in their will for heirs to inherit.

Fee Simple Absolute

The most common and complete form of property ownership is fee simple absolute. If property is granted in fee simple absolute it entitles the owner to the property for any legal purpose, without condition and to sell it or transfer leave it in their will, to whomever they choose.

Fee Simple Defeasible

Fee simple defeasible is a more limited form of property ownership. Here, property ownership is subject to a condition. If the condition is not met, ownership of the property reverts back to the previous owner (grantor) or his/heirs if that person is no longer alive.

An example of a condition placed in a fee simple defeasible deed would be "I deed this property to the city of Marquette so long as it is used as a public park and if it ever ceases to be used as a public park it shall revert back to me or my heirs".

Life Estate

A life estate grants ownership of real property that lasts the life of a named person. Upon that person's death the property goes to heirs of the grantor or another person named in the deed.

Tenancy in Common

Tenancy in common occurs when two or more people own the property at the same time and each has an equal interest in the entire property. Each may sell or transfer their interest without written permission (signing of the deed) of the other co-owners.

Joint Tenants

Joint tenants are also concurrent owners but no owner may sell their interest in the property without permission (signed agreement in the deed) of all the other co-owners of the property. Also, no owner may will their interest in the property to someone named in their will and upon the death of a joint property owner, his/her portion of the property goes to the other joint tenant(s). i.e. If four people own a parcel of property together as joint tenants and all but one of them dies, the last surviving owner becomes the sole owner of the entire parcel. To do so, the survivor will have to record the death certificates of the other co-owners with the register of deeds office to demonstrate that he/she is the only living owner of the property and has thereby assumed all property ownership interest.

Tenants by the Entirety

Tenants by the entirety is a form of property ownership used by married coup[le]

It is essentially a special form of joint tenancy for married people where prop[erty]

automatically goes to the surviving spouse if one of them dies. No will or pro[bate]

is necessary. Just as in joint tenancy, the deceased owner's death certificate m[ust]

be recorded before sole ownership will be recognized. If a married couple is

divorced then the property ownership will revert to a tenancy in common.

Community Property

Community property is a form of property ownership that recognizes and

automatic ownership interest (usually 50%) of a spouse in the real property of[the]

other once the are married even if their name is not on the deed. This form of

property ownership is not recognized in Michigan but marriage may still give [a]

person an equitable interest in his/her spouse's property.

Non-possessory Interests

Leaseholds

Leaseholds are a non-possessory interest. They allow a party to inhabit or use

property for a defined term of years but they do not obtain any ownership inte[rest]

in it or right to possess it beyond what is stated in the lease.

Easements

An easement is the right to enter onto another's property and use it without taking away the property owner's rights. For example, an easement may grant permission to cross your property so your neighbor may get to her property. Without the easement she may be landlocked and would be required to obtain permission or trespass on a neighbor's property to reach her property. Easements are important because once granted they "run with the land." This means they are recorded with the register of deeds office and cannot usually be revoked. Therefore, all subsequent property owners also have use of the easement since it goes with the property.

Easements are usually the result of a grant such as giving rights to someone for a particular purpose (like crossing your property to access a lake) but an easement may be the result of a reservation. This occurs when the owner conveys property but reserves the right to enter it for a particular purpose. i.e. They may sell property but reserve an easement for the purpose of crossing it to access the lake.

License

A license is a temporary right to use someone else's property. Licenses do not go with the land although they may be recorded with the register of deeds office and may be transferred. They are usually for a specific and finite purpose such as erecting and maintaining a cell phone tower or cutting timber.

An example of a license clause would be "I grant Paul Bunyan Lumber Co. permission to come onto my property located at 2050 Pine Rd for the purpose harvesting timber from September 1 through November 30th."

Ways to Purchase Real Property

There are two ways to purchase real property.

Mortgage

A mortgage is a loan where the lender takes a security interest in the property exchange for the money loaned to purchase the property. If the loan is not rep as required, the lender will foreclose on the loan and obtain its collateral – the property, and sell it to recover the balance owned on its loan. Any remaining money from the sale is equity owed the property owner and must be given to them.

Land Contract

A land contract is almost like purchasing property on lay-away. It is an agreement to transfer ownership of property to the buyer after the purchase price has been paid in full. Until that time the buyer has no equity in the property and is more like a renter since they do not own the property. Therefore, if a land contract purchaser fails to make the last payment due on the purchase, the seller may foreclose on the property, kick them out and keep all the money paid on the property. The seller may then re- sell the property to another buyer.

It is still important to record a land contract just like a mortgage. This is because it ensure that the land contract holder will get legal notice of any actions taken that affect the property.

Deeds

A deed is the document that is used to transfer ownership of real property. Recording the deed with the register of deeds in the county in which the property resides is critical because it is evidence of who owns the property and it ensures the property rights of the owner and ensures they will receive notice of any legal action affecting their rights in the property. A person or corporation is not considered the legal owner of a piece of property until the deed is recorded in the register of deeds office.

The sale/transfer and recording of real property may be done in one of two wa

Warranty Deed

A warranty deed is a guarantee by the seller to the buyer that he/she/it has cle

title to the property and the legal right and ability to sell or transfer title to the

property. Warranty deeds are typically backed up by title insurance, which is

policy of insurance that will cover the cost of any legal action necessary to ob

good title to the property if it turns out there is, in fact, a problem with it.

Quit claim deed

In a quit claim deed the seller promises nothing. The buyer gets whatever inte

in the property the seller has. So if the seller doesn't even own the property, th

buyer will get the interest the seller has – nothing. Why, you may ask, would

anyone ever accept a quit claim deed if it does not guarantee the seller even ov

the property? Quit claim deeds are very useful in instances where the parties a

certain that the grantor owns the property and that there is no problem such as

taxes owed with the property. Often, they are used when transferring property

between family members. Quit claim deeds are also used when relinquishing

property interests due to divorce, deaths in a family or to eliminate potential o

perceived legal problems identified by title companies.

The Statute of Frauds

The statute of frauds is a statute that requires that all contracts for the sale of real property be in writing to be enforceable.

Title Search

A title search is usually conducted before a lender will give a mortgage for the purchase of real property. Title insurance companies conduct the title search before issuing a title insurance policy. A title search is conducted by having someone look through all the register of deed documents relating to the property being sold beginning from the very first document ever recorded to the very last. The object of the title search is to identify any problems with the title to the property such as liens or judgments against the property, problems with ownership (such as a failure to record a death certificate), non-payment of property taxes or any other issue that would prevent the lender from issuing a warranty deed. It also reveals all easements and licenses affecting use of the property.

Adverse Possession

The doctrine of adverse possession allows people who have continuously use property that legally belongs to another to obtain legal title to it.

To be successful in a claim of adverse possession, a plaintiff must prove:

1. They were in sole physical possession of the property.

2. Their possession has been open & notorious.

3. Their claim is adverse to the real owner. (i.e. they have acted as if the property is theirs.)

4. They have had continuous possession of the property for the required statutory period. (usually 15 or 20 years)

Note: A person cannot adversely possess property owned by the government - it federal, state or local government.

Quiet Title Action

A quiet title lawsuit is a legal action brought to establish a party's title to real property against all other persons. It is undertaken when there is a question as who the rightful owner of a piece of property needs to be determined.

Nuisance

A property nuisance occurs when a property owner uses their property in a way that is unreasonable, illegal or in a way that causes an injury to those nearby or violates their legal rights.

Private Nuisance

A private nuisance is using one's property in a way that disrupts or adversely affects the use of an immediate neighbor's property or perhaps a few neighbors but not the public at large.

An example of a private nuisance would be pointing your drain spouts onto your neighbor's property so that it creates a pond in their yard.

Public Nuisance

A public nuisance is a use that affects a large number of people and involves the general health, safety, or welfare of the public. It invokes the police power (of the state) to stop it.

An example of a public nuisance is pouring used oil into an inland lake used by the public. Everyone who swims in the lake will be harmed by the pollution caused by the oil and perhaps the public beach will have to be closed.

Attractive Nuisance

An attractive nuisance is any item located on real property that attracts children and is likely to, and does, cause injury to them. A landowner may be held liable for the injuries such an object on their property causes even to trespassing children if it can be foreseen that they would be attracted and injured by it.

Eminent domain

Eminent domain is the power of the government to take private property for public use granted by the 5th Amendment. This power can be used by the federal state or local government.

Eminent domain requires that the property owner be compensated fairly for the "taking." Usually this means the fair market value of the property.

The state may delegate eminent domain power to certain public and private companies. Typically, these are utility companies which use the power to run telephone, power, water, or gas lines.

If a business is operating from the condemned real estate, the owner is ordinarily entitled to compensation for the loss or disruption of the business resulting from the condemnation.

In a minority of jurisdictions, the owner may also be entitled to compensation for loss of "goodwill", the value of the business in excess of fair market value due to such factors as its location, reputation, or good customer relations.

"Public use" may be broadly defined to include anything involving the public's "safety, health, interest, or convenience".

Some governments are criticized for using eminent domain for the benefit of developers or commercial interests and not the public. This is because governments increasingly justify taking property for business developments on the basis that anything that increases the value of a given tract of land is a sufficient public use.

Zoning Laws

Zoning laws are laws that regulate building and land use. They govern where homes and businesses can be located, the size of the lot required, how big the building can be, how many parking spaces are required for a business, the size of signs etc.

All states now have "enabling" statutes that allow local governments to regulate land use.

The burden is on the property owner to know what the zoning law allows.

Water Use

Groundwater

The legal rules governing the use of groundwater are mixed.

(1) English rule: Under the English rule a property owner with water on t[...]
property has absolute ownership of the water on it and may draw as m[...]
water as they want. They do not have to consider the water rights or n[...]
of their neighbors.

(2) American rule: Under the American rule, a property owner must u[...]
water reasonably. Wasteful use that hurts his/her neighbors is
inappropriate and legal action may be taken to stop it.

(3) Statutory and administrative regulations may also determine who [...]
how much water a property owner can use.

Surface water

There is a split of authority concerning the use of surface water.

(1) Western states follow the first in time principle called "prior

  appropriation" – under this rule those who capture water may put it

  to reasonable use.

(2) Eastern states follow what are called riparian rights where

landowners along a source of water get to draw and use the water subject

to the rights of other riparians (landowners along the water source).

THE
CONSTITUTION
of the United States

NATIONAL CONSTITUTION CENTER

We the People of the United States, in Order to form a more perfect Union, establish Justice, insure domestic Tranquility, provide for the common defence, promote the general Welfare, and secure the Blessings of Liberty to ourselves and our Posterity, do ordain and establish this Constitution for the United States of America.

Article. I.

SECTION. 1.

All legislative Powers herein granted shall be vested in a Congress of the United States, which shall consist of a Senate and House of Representatives.

SECTION. 2.

The House of Representatives shall be composed of Members chosen every second Year by the People of the several States, and the Electors in each State shall have the Qualifications requisite for Electors of the most numerous Branch of the State Legislature.

No Person shall be a Representative who shall not have attained to the Age of twenty five Years, and been seven Years a Citizen of the United States, and who shall not, when elected, be an Inhabitant of that State in which he shall be chosen.

[Representatives and direct Taxes shall be apportioned among the several States which may be included within this Union, according to their respective Numbers, which shall be determined by adding to the whole Number of free Persons, including those bound to Service for a Term of Years, and excluding Indians not taxed, three fifths of all other Persons.]* The actual Enumeration shall be made

within three Years after the first Meeting of the Congress of the United States, and within every subsequent Term of ten Years, in such Manner as they shall by Law direct. The Number of Representatives shall not exceed one for every thirty Thousand, but each State shall have at Least one Representative; and until such enumeration shall be made, the State of New Hampshire shall be entitled to chuse three, Massachusetts eight, Rhode-Island and Providence Plantations one, Connecticut five, New-York six, New Jersey four, Pennsylvania eight, Delaware one, Maryland six, Virginia ten, North Carolina five, South Carolina five, and Georgia three.

When vacancies happen in the Representation from any State, the Executive Authority thereof shall issue Writs of Election to fill such Vacancies.

The House of Representatives shall chuse their Speaker and other Officers; and shall have the sole Power of Impeachment.

SECTION. 3.

The Senate of the United States shall be composed of two Senators from each State, [chosen by the Legislature thereof,]* for six Years; and each Senator shall have one Vote.

Immediately after they shall be assembled in Consequence of the first Election, they shall be divided as equally as may be into three Classes. The Seats of the Senators of the first Class shall be vacated at the Expiration of the second Year, of the second Class at the Expiration of the fourth Year, and of the third Class at the Expiration of the sixth Year, so that one third may be chosen every second Year; [and if Vacancies happen by Resignation, or otherwise, during the Recess of the Legislature of any State, the Executive thereof may make temporary Appointments until the next Meeting of the Legislature, which shall then fill such Vacancies.]*

No Person shall be a Senator who shall not have attained to the Age of thirty Years, and been nine Years a Citizen of the United States, and who shall not, when elected, be an Inhabitant of that State for which he shall be chosen.

The Vice President of the United States shall be President of the Senate, but shall have no Vote, unless they be equally divided.

The Senate shall chuse their other Officers, and also a President pro tempore, in the Absence of the Vice President, or when he shall exercise the Office of President of the United States.

The Senate shall have the sole Power to try all Impeachments. When sitting for that Purpose, they shall be on Oath or Affirmation. When the President of the United States is tried, the Chief Justice shall preside: And no Person shall be convicted without the Concurrence of two thirds of the Members present.

Judgment in Cases of Impeachment shall not extend further than to removal from Office, and disqualification to hold and enjoy any Office of honor, Trust or Profit under the United States: but the Party convicted shall nevertheless be liable and subject to Indictment, Trial, Judgment and Punishment, according to Law.

SECTION. 4.

The Times, Places and Manner of holding Elections for Senators and Representatives, shall be prescribed in each State by the Legislature thereof; but the Congress may at any time by Law make or alter such Regulations, except as to the Places of chusing Senators.

The Congress shall assemble at least once in every Year, and such Meeting shall be [on the first Monday in December,]* unless they shall by Law appoint a different Day.

SECTION. 5.

Each House shall be the Judge of the Elections, Returns and Qualifications of its own Members, and a Majority of each shall constitute a Quorum to do Business; but a smaller Number may adjourn from day to day, and may be authorized to compel the Attendance of absent Members, in such Manner, and under such Penalties as each House may provide.

Each House may determine the Rules of its Proceedings, punish its Members for disorderly Behaviour, and, with the Concurrence of two thirds, expel a Member.

Each House shall keep a Journal of its Proceedings, and from time to time publish the same, excepting such Parts as may in their Judgment require Secrecy; and the Yeas and Nays of the Members of either House on any question shall, at the Desire of one fifth of those Present, be entered on the Journal.

Neither House, during the Session of Congress, shall, without the Consent of the other, adjourn for more than three days, nor to any other Place than that in which the two Houses shall be sitting.

SECTION. 6.

The Senators and Representatives shall receive a Compensation for their Services, to be ascertained by Law, and paid out of the Treasury of the United States. They shall in all Cases, except Treason, Felony and Breach of the Peace, be privileged from Arrest during their Attendance at the Session of their respective Houses, and in going to and returning from the same; and for any Speech or Debate in either House, they shall not be questioned in any other Place.

No Senator or Representative shall, during the Time for which he was elected, be appointed to any civil Office under the Authority of the United States, which shall have been created, or the Emoluments whereof shall have been encreased during such time; and no Person holding any Office under the United States, shall be a Member of either House during his Continuance in Office.

SECTION. 7.

All Bills for raising Revenue shall originate in the House of Representatives; but the Senate may propose or concur with Amendments as on other Bills.

Every Bill which shall have passed the House of Representatives and the Senate, shall, before it become a Law, be presented to the President of the United States; If he approve he shall sign it, but if not he shall return it, with his Objections to that House in which it shall have originated, who shall enter the Objections at large on their Journal, and proceed to reconsider it. If after such Reconsideration two thirds of that House shall agree to pass the Bill, it shall be sent, together with the Objections, to the other House, by which it shall likewise be reconsidered, and if approved by two thirds of that House, it shall become a Law. But in all such Cases the Votes of both Houses shall be determined by Yeas and Nays, and the Names of the Persons voting for and against the Bill shall be entered on the Journal of each House respectively, If any Bill shall not be returned by the President within ten Days (Sundays excepted) after it shall have been presented to him, the Same shall be a Law, in like Manner as if he had signed it, unless the Congress by their Adjournment prevent its Return, in which Case it shall not be a Law.

Every Order, Resolution, or Vote to which the Concurrence of the Senate and House of Representatives may be necessary (except on a question of Adjournment) shall be presented to the President of the United States; and before the Same shall take Effect, shall be approved by him, or being disapproved by him, shall be repassed by two thirds of the Senate and House of Representatives, according to the Rules and Limitations prescribed in the Case of a Bill.

SECTION. 8.

The Congress shall have Power To lay and collect Taxes, Duties, Imposts and Excises, to pay the Debts and provide for the common Defence and general Welfare of the United States; but all Duties, Imposts and Excises shall be uniform throughout the United States;

To borrow Money on the credit of the United States;

To regulate Commerce with foreign Nations, and among the several States, and with the Indian Tribes;

To establish an uniform Rule of Naturalization, and uniform Laws on the subject of Bankruptcies throughout the United States;

To coin Money, regulate the Value thereof, and of foreign Coin, and fix the Standard of Weights and Measures;

To provide for the Punishment of counterfeiting the Securities and current Coin of the United States;

To establish Post Offices and post Roads;

To promote the Progress of Science and useful Arts, by securing for limited Times to Authors and Inventors the exclusive Right to their respective Writings and Discoveries;

To constitute Tribunals inferior to the supreme Court;

To define and punish Piracies and Felonies committed on the high Seas, and Offenses against the Law of Nations;

To declare War, grant Letters of Marque and Reprisal, and make Rules concerning Captures on Land and Water;

To raise and support Armies, but no Appropriation of Money to that Use shall be for a longer Term than two Years;

To provide and maintain a Navy;

To make Rules for the Government and Regulation of the land and naval Forces;

To provide for calling forth the Militia to execute the Laws of the Union, suppress Insurrections and repel Invasions;

To provide for organizing, arming, and disciplining, the Militia, and for governing such Part of them as may be employed in the Service of the United States, reserving to the States respectively, the Appointment of the Officers, and the Authority of training the Militia according to the discipline prescribed by Congress;

To exercise exclusive Legislation in all Cases whatsoever, over such District (not exceeding ten Miles square) as may, by Cession of particular States, and the Acceptance of Congress, become the Seat of the Government of the United States, and to exercise like Authority over all Places purchased by the Consent of the Legislature of the State in which the Same shall be, for the Erection of Forts, Magazines, Arsenals, dock-Yards and other needful Buildings; -And

To make all Laws which shall be necessary and proper for carrying into Execution the foregoing Powers, and all other Powers vested by this Constitution in the Government of the United States, or in any Department or Officer thereof.

SECTION. 9.

The Migration or Importation of such Persons as any of the States now existing shall think proper to admit, shall not be prohibited by the Congress prior to the Year one thousand eight hundred and eight, but a Tax or duty may be imposed on such Importation, not exceeding ten dollars for each Person.

The Privilege of the Writ of Habeas Corpus shall not be suspended, unless when in Cases of Rebellion or Invasion the public Safety may require it.

No Bill of Attainder or ex post facto Law shall be passed.

[No Capitation, or other direct, Tax shall be laid, unless in Proportion to the Census or Enumeration herein before directed to be taken.]*

No Tax or Duty shall be laid on Articles exported from any State.

No Preference shall be given by any Regulation of Commerce or Revenue to the Ports of one State over those of another: nor shall Vessels bound to, or from, one State, be obliged to enter, clear, or pay Duties in another.

No Money shall be drawn from the Treasury, but in Consequence of Appropriations made by Law; and a regular Statement and Account of the Receipts and Expenditures of all public Money shall be published from time to time.

No Title of Nobility shall be granted by the United States: And no Person holding any Office of Profit or Trust under them, shall, without the Consent of the Congress, accept of any present, Emolument, Office, or Title, of any kind whatever, from any King, Prince, or foreign State.

SECTION. 10.

No State shall enter into any Treaty, Alliance, or Confederation; grant Letters of Marque and Reprisal; coin Money; emit Bills of Credit; make any Thing but gold and silver Coin a Tender in Payment of Debts; pass any Bill of Attainder, ex post facto Law, or Law impairing the Obligation of Contracts, or grant any Title of Nobility.

No State shall, without the Consent of the Congress, lay any Imposts or Duties on Imports or Exports, except what may be absolutely necessary for executing it's inspection Laws: and the net Produce of all Duties and Imposts, laid by any State on Imports or Exports, shall be for the Use of the Treasury of the United States; and all such Laws shall be subject to the Revision and Controul of the Congress.

No State shall, without the Consent of Congress, lay any Duty of Tonnage, keep Troops, or Ships of War in time of Peace, enter into any Agreement or Compact with another State, or with a foreign Power, or engage in War, unless actually invaded, or in such imminent Danger as will not admit of delay.

Article. II.

SECTION. 1.

The executive Power shall be vested in a President of the United States of America. He shall hold his Office during the Term of four Years, and, together with the Vice President, chosen for the same Term, be elected, as follows:

Each State shall appoint, in such Manner as the Legislature thereof may direct, a Number of Electors, equal to the whole Number of Senators and Representatives to which the State may be entitled in the Congress: but no Senator or Representative, or Person holding an Office of Trust or Profit under the United States, shall be appointed an Elector.

[The Electors shall meet in their respective States, and vote by Ballot for two Persons, of whom one at least shall not be an Inhabitant of the same State with themselves. And they shall make a List of all the Persons voted for, and of the Number of Votes for each; which List they shall sign and certify, and transmit sealed to the Seat of the Government of the United States, directed to the President of the Senate. The President of the Senate shall, in the Presence of the Senate and House of Representatives, open all the Certificates, and the Votes shall then be counted. The Person having the greatest Number of Votes shall be the President, if such Number be a Majority of the whole Number of Electors appointed; and if there be more than one who have such Majority, and have an equal Number of Votes, then the House of Representatives shall immediately chuse by Ballot one of them for President; and if no Person have a Majority, then from the five highest on the List the said House shall in like Manner chuse the President. But in chusing the President, the Votes shall be taken by States, the Representation from each State having one Vote; A quorum for this Purpose shall consist of a Member or Members from two thirds of the States, and a Majority of all the States shall be necessary to a Choice. In every Case, after the Choice of the President, the Person having the greatest Number of Votes of the Electors shall be the Vice President. But if there should remain two or more who have equal Votes, the Senate shall chuse from them by Ballot the Vice President.]*

The Congress may determine the Time of chusing the Electors, and the Day on which they shall give their Votes; which Day shall be the same throughout the United States.

No Person except a natural born Citizen, or a Citizen of the United States, at the time of the Adoption of this Constitution, shall be eligible to the Office of President; neither shall any person be eligible to that Office who shall not have attained to the Age of thirty five Years, and been fourteen Years a Resident within the United States.

[In Case of the Removal of the President from Office, or of his Death, Resignation, or Inability to discharge the Powers and Duties of the said Office, the Same shall devolve on the Vice President, and the Congress may by Law provide for the Case of Removal, Death, Resignation or Inability, both of the President and Vice President, declaring what Officer shall then act as President, and such Officer shall act accordingly, until the Disability be removed, or a President shall be elected.]*

The President shall, at stated Times, receive for his Services, a Compensation, which shall neither be increased nor diminished during the Period for which he shall have been elected, and he shall not receive within that Period any other Emolument from the United States, or any of them.

Before he enter on the Execution of his Office, he shall take the following Oath or Affirmation:- "I do solemnly swear (or affirm) that I will faithfully execute the Office of President of the United States, and will to the best of my Ability, preserve, protect and defend the Constitution of the United States."

SECTION. 2.

The President shall be Commander in Chief of the Army and Navy of the United States, and of the Militia of the several States, when called into the actual Service of the United States; he may require the Opinion, in writing, of the principal Officer in each of the executive Departments, upon any Subject relating to the Duties of their respective Offices, and he shall have Power to grant Reprieves and Pardons for Offenses against the United States, except in Cases of Impeachment.

He shall have Power, by and with the Advice and Consent of the Senate, to make Treaties, provided two thirds of the Senators present concur; and he shall nominate, and by and with the Advice and Consent of the Senate, shall appoint Ambassadors, other public Ministers and Consuls, Judges of the supreme Court, and all other Officers of the United States, whose Appointments are not herein otherwise provided for, and which shall be established by Law: but the Congress may by Law vest the Appointment of such inferior Officers, as they think proper, in the President alone, in the Courts of Law, or in the Heads of Departments.

The President shall have Power to fill up all Vacancies that may happen during the Recess of the Senate, by granting Commissions which shall expire at the End of their next Session.

SECTION. 3.

He shall from time to time give to the Congress Information of the State of the Union, and recommend to their Consideration such Measures as he shall judge necessary and expedient; he may, on extraordinary Occasions, convene both Houses, or either of them, and in Case of Disagreement between them, with Respect to the Time of Adjournment, he may adjourn them to such Time as he shall think proper; he shall receive Ambassadors and other public Ministers; he shall take Care that the Laws be faithfully executed, and shall Commission all the Officers of the United States.

SECTION. 4.

The President, Vice President and all civil Officers of the United States, shall be removed from Office on Impeachment for, and Conviction of, Treason, Bribery, or other high Crimes and Misdemeanors.

Article. III.

SECTION. 1.

The judicial Power of the United States, shall be vested in one supreme Court, and in such inferior Courts as the Congress may from time to time ordain and establish. The Judges, both of the supreme and inferior Courts, shall hold their Offices during good Behaviour, and shall at stated Times, receive for their Services, a Compensation, which shall not be diminished during their Continuance in Office.

SECTION. 2.

The judicial Power shall extend to all Cases, in Law and Equity, arising under this Constitution, the Laws of the United States, and Treaties made, or which shall be made, under their Authority; - to all Cases affecting Ambassadors, other public Ministers and Consuls; - to all Cases of admiralty and maritime Jurisdiction; - to Controversies to which the United States shall be a Party; - to Controversies between two or more States; - [between a State and Citizens of another State;-]* between Citizens of different States, - between Citizens of the same State claiming Lands under Grants of different States, [and between a State, or the Citizens thereof;- and foreign States, Citizens or Subjects.]*

In all Cases affecting Ambassadors, other public Ministers and Consuls, and those in which a State shall be Party, the supreme Court shall have original Jurisdiction. In all the other Cases before mentioned, the supreme Court shall have appellate Jurisdiction, both as to Law and Fact, with such Exceptions, and under such Regulations as the Congress shall make.

The Trial of all Crimes, except in Cases of Impeachment; shall be by Jury; and such Trial shall be held in the State where the said Crimes shall have been committed; but when not committed within any State, the Trial shall be at such Place or Places as the Congress may by Law have directed.

SECTION. 3.

Treason against the United States, shall consist only in levying War against them, or in adhering to their Enemies, giving them Aid and Comfort. No Person shall be convicted of Treason unless on the Testimony of two Witnesses to the same overt Act, or on Confession in open Court.

The Congress shall have Power to declare the Punishment of Treason, but no Attainder of Treason shall work Corruption of Blood, or Forfeiture except during the Life of the Person attainted.

Article. IV.

SECTION. 1.

Full Faith and Credit shall be given in each State to the public Acts, Records, and judicial Proceedings of every other State. And the Congress may by general Laws prescribe the Manner in which such Acts, Records and Proceedings shall be proved, and the Effect thereof.

SECTION. 2.

The Citizens of each State shall be entitled to all Privileges and Immunities of Citizens in the several States.
A Person charged in any State with Treason, Felony, or other Crime, who shall flee from Justice, and be found in another State, shall on Demand of the executive Authority of the State from which he fled, be delivered up, to be removed to the State having Jurisdiction of the Crime.

[No Person held to Service or Labour in one State, under the Laws thereof, escaping into another, shall, in Consequence of any Law or Regulation therein, be discharged from such Service or Labour, but shall be delivered up on Claim of the Party to whom such Service or Labour may be due.]*

SECTION. 3.

New States may be admitted by the Congress into this Union; but no new State shall be formed or erected within the Jurisdiction of any other State; nor any State be formed by the Junction of two or more States, or Parts of States, without the Consent of the Legislatures of the States concerned as well as of the Congress.

The Congress shall have Power to dispose of and make all needful Rules and Regulations respecting the Territory or other Property belonging to the United States; and nothing in this Constitution shall be so construed as to Prejudice any Claims of the United States, or of any particular State.

SECTION. 4.

The United States shall guarantee to every State in this Union a Republican Form of Government, and shall protect each of them against Invasion; and on Application of the Legislature, or of the Executive (when the Legislature cannot be convened) against domestic Violence.

Article. V.

The Congress, whenever two thirds of both Houses shall deem it necessary, shall propose Amendments to this Constitution, or, on the Application of the Legislatures of two thirds of the several States, shall call a Convention for proposing Amendments, which in either Case, shall be valid to all Intents and Purposes, as Part of this Constitution, when ratified by the Legislatures of three-fourths of the several States, or by Conventions in three fourths thereof, as the one or the other Mode of Ratification may be proposed by the Congress; Provided that no Amendment which may be made prior to the Year One thousand eight hundred and eight shall in any Manner affect the first and fourth Clauses in the Ninth Section of the first Article; and that no State, without its Consent, shall be deprived of its equal Suffrage in the Senate.

Article. VI.

All Debts contracted and Engagements entered into, before the Adoption of this Constitution, shall be as valid against the United States under this Constitution, as under the Confederation.

This Constitution, and the Laws of the United States which shall be made in Pursuance thereof; and all Treaties made, or which shall be made, under the Authority of the United States, shall be the supreme Law of the Land; and the Judges in every State shall be bound thereby, any Thing in the Constitution or Laws of any State to the Contrary notwithstanding.

The Senators and Representatives before mentioned, and the Members of the several State Legislatures, and all executive and judicial Officers, both of the United States and of the several States, shall be bound by Oath or Affirmation, to support this Constitution; but no religious Test shall ever be required as a Qualification to any Office or public Trust under the United States.

Article. VII.

The Ratification of the Conventions of nine States, shall be sufficient for the Establishment of this Constitution between the States so ratifying the Same.

Done in Convention by the Unanimous Consent of the States present the Seventeenth Day of September in the Year of our Lord one thousand seven hundred and Eighty seven and of the Independence of the United States of America the Twelfth In Witness whereof We have hereunto subscribed our Names,

Go. Washington--Presidt:
and deputy from Virginia

NEW HAMPSHIRE

John Langdon
Nicholas Gilman

MASSACHUSETTS

Nathaniel Gorham
Rufus King

CONNECTICUT

Wm. Saml. Johnson
Roger Sherman

NEW YORK

Alexander Hamilton

NEW JERSEY

Wil: Livingston
David Brearley
Wm. Paterson
Jona: Dayton

PENNSYLVANIA

B Franklin
Thomas Mifflin
Robt Morris
Geo. Clymer
Thos. FitzSimons
Jared Ingersoll
James Wilson
Gouv Morris

DELAWARE

Geo: Read
Gunning Bedford jun
John Dickinson
Richard Bassett
Jaco: Broom

MARYLAND

James McHenry
Dan of St. Thos. Jenifer
Danl Carroll

VIRGINIA

John Blair-
James Madison Jr.

NORTH CAROLINA

Wm. Blount
Richd. Dobbs Spaight
Hu Williamson

SOUTH CAROLINA

J. Rutledge
Charles Cotesworth Pinckney
Charles Pinckney
Pierce Butler

GEORGIA

William Few
Abr Baldwin

Attest William Jackson Secretary

In Convention Monday
September 17th, 1787.
Present
The States of
New Hampshire, Massachusetts, Connecticut, Mr. Hamilton from New York, New Jersey, Pennsylvania, Delaware, Maryland, Virginia, North Carolina, South Carolina and Georgia.

Resolved,
That the preceeding Constitution be laid before the United States in Congress assembled, and that it is the Opinion of this Convention, that it should afterwards be submitted to a Convention of Delegates, chosen in each State by the People thereof, under the Recommendation of its Legislature, for their Assent and Ratification; and that each Convention assenting to, and ratifying the Same, should give Notice thereof to the United States in Congress assembled. Resolved, That it is the Opinion of this Convention, that as soon as the Conventions of nine States shall have ratified this Constitution, the United States in Congress assembled should fix a Day on which Electors should be appointed by the States which shall have ratified the same, and a Day on which the Electors should assemble to vote for the President, and the Time and Place for commencing Proceedings under this Constitution.

That after such Publication the Electors should be appointed, and the Senators and Representatives elected: That the Electors should meet on the Day fixed for the Election of the President, and should transmit their Votes certified, signed, sealed and directed, as the Constitution requires, to the Secretary of the United States in Congress assembled, that the Senators and Representatives should convene at the Time and Place assigned; that the Senators should appoint a President of the Senate, for the sole Purpose of receiving, opening and counting the Votes for President; and, that after he shall be chosen, the Congress, together with the President, should, without Delay, proceed to execute this Constitution.

By the unanimous Order of the Convention

Go. Washington-Presidt:
W. JACKSON Secretary.

* Language in brackets has been changed by amendment.

THE AMENDMENTS TO THE CONSTITUTION OF THE UNITED STATES AS RATIFIED BY THE STATES

Preamble to the Bill of Rights

CONGRESS OF THE UNITED STATES
BEGUN AND HELD AT THE CITY OF NEW-YORK, ON
WEDNESDAY THE FOURTH OF MARCH,
ONE THOUSAND SEVEN HUNDRED AND EIGHTY NINE

THE Conventions of a number of the States, having at the time of their adopting the Constitution, expressed a desire, in order to prevent misconstruction or abuse of its powers, that further declaratory and restrictive clauses should be added: And as extending the ground of public confidence in the Government, will best ensure the beneficent ends of its institution.

RESOLVED by the Senate and House of Representatives of the United States of America, in Congress assembled, two thirds of both Houses concurring, that the following Articles be proposed to the Legislatures of the several States, as amendments to the Constitution of the United States, all, or any of which Articles, when ratified by three fourths of the said Legislatures, to be valid to all intents and purposes, as part of the said Constitution; viz.

ARTICLES in addition to, and Amendment of the Constitution of the United States of America, proposed by Congress, and ratified by the Legislatures of the several States, pursuant to the fifth Article of the original Constitution.

(Note: The first 10 amendments to the Constitution were ratified December 15, 1791, and form what is known as the "Bill of Rights.")

Amendment I.

Congress shall make no law respecting an establishment of religion, or prohibiting the free exercise thereof; or abridging the freedom of speech, or of the press, or the right of the people peaceably to assemble, and to petition the Government for a redress of grievances.

Amendment II.

A well regulated Militia, being necessary to the security of a free State, the right of the people to keep and bear Arms, shall not be infringed.

Amendment III.

No Soldier shall, in time of peace be quartered in any house, without the consent of the Owner, nor in time of war, but in a manner to be prescribed by law.

Amendment IV.

The right of the people to be secure in their persons, houses, papers, and effects, against unreasonable searches and seizures, shall not be violated, and no Warrants shall issue, but upon probable cause, supported by Oath or affirmation, and particularly describing the place to be searched, and the persons or things to be seized.

Amendment V.

No person shall be held to answer for a capital, or otherwise infamous crime, unless on a presentment or indictment of a Grand Jury, except in cases arising in the land or naval forces, or in the Militia, when in actual service in time of War or public danger; nor shall any person be subject for the same offence to be twice put in jeopardy of life or limb; nor shall be compelled in any criminal case to be a witness against himself, nor be deprived of life, liberty, or property, without due process of law; nor shall private property be taken for public use, without just compensation.

Amendment VI.

In all criminal prosecutions, the accused shall enjoy the right to a speedy and public trial, by an impartial jury of the State and district wherein the crime shall have been committed, which district shall have been previously ascertained by law, and to be informed of the nature and cause of the accusation; to be confronted with the witnesses against him; to have compulsory process for obtaining witnesses in his favor, and to have the Assistance of Counsel for his defence.

Amendment VII.

In suits at common law, where the value in controversy shall exceed twenty dollars, the right of trial by jury shall be preserved, and no fact tried by a jury shall be otherwise re-examined in any Court of the United States, than according to the rules of the common law.

Amendment VIII.

Excessive bail shall not be required, nor excessive fines imposed, nor cruel and unusual punishments inflicted.

Amendment IX.

The enumeration in the Constitution, of certain rights, shall not be construed to deny or disparage others retained by the people.

Amendment X.

The powers not delegated to the United States by the Constitution, nor prohibited by it to the States, are reserved to the States respectively, or to the people.

AMENDMENTS 11-27

Amendment XI.

Passed by Congress March 4, 1794. Ratified February 7, 1795.

(Note: A portion of Article III, Section 2 of the Constitution was modified by the 11th Amendment.)

The Judicial power of the United States shall not be construed to extend to any suit in law or equity, commenced or prosecuted against one of the United States by Citizens of another State, or by Citizens or Subjects of any Foreign State.

Amendment XII.

Passed by Congress December 9, 1803. Ratified June 15, 1804.

(Note: A portion of Article II, Section 1 of the Constitution was changed by the 12th Amendment.)

The Electors shall meet in their respective states, and vote by ballot for President and Vice-President, one of whom, at least, shall not be an inhabitant of the same state with themselves; they shall name in their ballots the person voted for as President, and in distinct ballots the person voted for as Vice-President, and they shall make distinct lists of all persons voted for as President, and of all persons voted for as Vice-President, and of the number of votes for each, which lists they shall sign and certify, and transmit sealed to the seat of the government of the United States, directed to the President of the Senate;-the President of the Senate shall, in the presence of the Senate and House of Representatives, open all the certificates and the votes shall then be counted;-The person having the greatest number of votes for President, shall be the President, if such number be a majority of the whole number of Electors appointed; and if no person have such majority, then from the persons having the highest numbers not exceeding three on the list of those voted for as President, the House of Representatives shall choose immediately, by ballot, the President. But in choosing the President, the votes shall be taken by states, the representation from each state having one vote; a quorum for this purpose shall consist of a member or members from two-thirds of the states, and a majority of all the states shall be necessary to a choice. [And if the House of Representatives shall not choose a President whenever the right of choice shall devolve upon them, before the fourth day of March next following, then the Vice-President shall act as President, as in case of the death or other constitutional disability of the President.-]* The person having the greatest number of votes as Vice-President, shall be the Vice-President, if such number be a majority of the whole number of Electors appointed, and if no person have a majority, then from the two highest numbers on the list, the Senate shall choose the Vice-President; a quorum for the purpose shall consist of two-thirds of the whole number of Senators, and a majority of the whole number shall be necessary to a choice. But no person constitutionally ineligible to the office of President shall be eligible to that of Vice-President of the United States.

*Superseded by Section 3 of the 20th Amendment.

Amendment XIII.

Passed by Congress January 31, 1865. Ratified December 6, 1865.

(Note: A portion of Article IV, Section 2 of the Constitution was changed by the 13th Amendment.)

SECTION 1.

Neither slavery nor involuntary servitude, except as a punishment for crime whereof the party shall have been duly convicted, shall exist within the United States, or any place subject to their jurisdiction.

SECTION 2.

Congress shall have power to enforce this article by appropriate legislation.

Amendment XIV.

Passed by Congress June 13, 1866. Ratified July 9, 1868.

(Note: Article I, Section 2 of the Constitution was modified by Section 2 of the 14th Amendment.)

SECTION 1.

All persons born or naturalized in the United States and subject to the jurisdiction thereof, are citizens of the United States and of the State wherein they reside. No State shall make or enforce any law which shall abridge the privileges or immunities of citizens of the United States; nor shall any State deprive any person of life, liberty, or property, without due process of law; nor deny to any person within its jurisdiction the equal protection of the laws.

SECTION 2.

Representatives shall be apportioned among the several States according to their respective numbers, counting the whole number of persons in each State, excluding Indians not taxed. But when the right to vote at any election for the choice of electors for President and Vice President of the United States, Representatives in Congress, the Executive and Judicial officers of a State, or the members of the Legislature thereof, is denied to any of the male inhabitants of such State, [being twenty-one years of age,]* and citizens of the United States, or in any way abridged, except for participation in rebellion, or other crime, the basis of representation therein shall be reduced in the proportion which the number of such male citizens shall bear to the whole number of male citizens twenty-one years of age in such State.

SECTION 3.

No person shall be a Senator or Representative in Congress, or elector of President and Vice President, or hold any office, civil or military, under the United States, or under any State, who, having previously taken an oath, as a member of Congress, or as an officer of the United States, or as a member of any State legislature, or as an executive or judicial officer of any State, to support the Constitution of the United States, shall have engaged in insurrection or rebellion against the same, or given aid or comfort to the enemies thereof. But Congress may by a vote of two-thirds of each House, remove such disability.

SECTION 4.

The validity of the public debt of the United States, authorized by law, including debts incurred for payment of pensions and bounties for services in suppressing insurrection or rebellion, shall not be questioned. But neither the United States nor any State shall assume or pay any debt or obligation incurred in aid of insurrection or rebellion against the United States, or any claim for the loss or emancipation of any slave; but all such debts, obligations and claims shall be held illegal and void.

SECTION 5.

The Congress shall have the power to enforce, by appropriate legislation, the provisions of this article.

*Changed by Section 1 of the 26th Amendment.

Amendment XV.

Passed by Congress February 26, 1869. Ratified February 3, 1870.

SECTION 1.

The right of citizens of the United States to vote shall not be denied or abridged by the United States or by any State on account of race, color, or previous condition of servitude.

SECTION 2.

The Congress shall have the power to enforce this article by appropriate legislation.

Amendment XVI.

Passed by Congress July 2, 1909. Ratified February 3, 1913.

(Note: Article I, Section 9 of the Constitution was modified by the 16th Amendment.)

The Congress shall have power to lay and collect taxes on incomes, from whatever source derived, without apportionment among the several States, and without regard to any census or enumeration.

Amendment XVII.

Passed by Congress May 13, 1912. Ratified April 8, 1913.

(Note: Article I, Section 3 of the Constitution was modified by the 17th Amendment.)

The Senate of the United States shall be composed of two Senators from each State, elected by the people thereof, for six years; and each Senator shall have one vote. The electors in each State shall have the qualifications requisite for electors of the most numerous branch of the State legislatures.

When vacancies happen in the representation of any State in the Senate, the executive authority of such State shall issue writs of election to fill such vacancies: Provided, That the legislature of any State may empower the executive thereof to make temporary appointments until the people fill the vacancies by election as the legislature may direct.

This amendment shall not be so construed as to affect the election or term of any Senator chosen before it becomes valid as part of the Constitution.

Amendment XVIII.

Passed by Congress December 18, 1917. Ratified January 16, 1919. Repealed by the 21st Amendment, December 5, 1933.

SECTION 1.

After one year from the ratification of this article the manufacture, sale, or transportation of intoxicating liquors within, the importation thereof into, or the exportation thereof from the United States and all territory subject to the jurisdiction thereof for beverage purposes is hereby prohibited.

SECTION 2.

The Congress and the several States shall have concurrent power to enforce this article by appropriate legislation.

SECTION 3.

This article shall be inoperative unless it shall have been ratified as an amendment to the Constitution by the legislatures of the several States, as provided in the Constitution, within seven years from the date of the submission hereof to the States by the Congress.

Amendment XIX.

Passed by Congress June 4, 1919. Ratified August 18, 1920.

The right of citizens of the United States to vote shall not be denied or abridged by the United States or by any State on account of sex.

Congress shall have power to enforce this article by appropriate legislation.

Amendment XX

Passed by Congress March 2, 1932. Ratified January 23, 1933.

(Note: Article I, Section 4 of the Constitution was modified by Section 2 of this Amendment. In addition, a portion of the 12th Amendment was superseded by Section 3.)

SECTION 1.

The terms of the President and the Vice President shall end at noon on the 20th day of January, and the terms of Senators and Representatives at noon on the 3d day of January, of the years in which such terms would have ended if this article had not been ratified; and the terms of their successors shall then begin.

SECTION 2.

The Congress shall assemble at least once in every year, and such meeting shall begin at noon on the 3d day of January, unless they shall by law appoint a different day.

SECTION 3.

If, at the time fixed for the beginning of the term of the President, the President elect shall have died, the Vice President elect shall become President. If a President shall not have been chosen before the time fixed for the beginning of his term, or if the President elect shall have failed to qualify, then the Vice President elect shall act as President until a President shall have qualified; and the Congress may by law provide for the case wherein neither a President elect nor a Vice President shall have qualified, declaring who shall then act as President, or the manner in which one who is to act shall be selected, and such person shall act accordingly until a President or Vice President shall have qualified.

SECTION 4.

The Congress may by law provide for the case of the death of any of the persons from whom the House of Representatives may choose a President whenever the right of choice shall have devolved upon them, and for the case of the death of any of the persons from whom the Senate may choose a Vice President whenever the right of choice shall have devolved upon them.

SECTION 5.

Sections 1 and 2 shall take effect on the 15th day of October following the ratification of this article.

SECTION 6.

This article shall be inoperative unless it shall have been ratified as an amendment to the Constitution by the legislatures of three-fourths of the several States within seven years from the date of its submission.

Amendment XXI

Passed by Congress February 20, 1933. Ratified December 5, 1933.

SECTION 1.

The eighteenth article of amendment to the Constitution of the United States is hereby repealed.

SECTION 2.

The transportation or importation into any State, Territory, or possession of the United States for delivery or use therein of intoxicating liquors, in violation of the laws thereof, is hereby prohibited.

SECTION 3.

This article shall be inoperative unless it shall have been ratified as an amendment to the Constitution by conventions in the several States, as provided in the Constitution, within seven years from the date of the submission hereof to the States by the Congress.

Amendment XXII.

Passed by Congress March 21, 1947. Ratified February 27, 1951.

SECTION 1.

No person shall be elected to the office of the President more than twice, and no person who has held the office of President, or acted as President, for more than two years of a term to which some other person was elected President shall be elected to the office of President more than once. But this Article shall not apply to any person holding the office of President when this Article was proposed by Congress, and shall not prevent any person who may be holding the office of President, or acting as President, during the term within which this Article becomes operative from holding the office of President or acting as President during the remainder of such term.

SECTION 2.

This article shall be inoperative unless it shall have been ratified as an amendment to the Constitution by the legislatures of three-fourths of the several States within seven years from the date of its submission to the States by the Congress.

Amendment XXIII.

Passed by Congress June 16, 1960. Ratified March 29, 1961.

SECTION 1.

The District constituting the seat of Government of the United States shall appoint in such manner as Congress may direct:

A number of electors of President and Vice President equal to the whole number of Senators and Representatives in Congress to which the District would be entitled if it were a State, but in no event more than the least populous State; they shall be in addition to those appointed by the States, but they shall be considered, for the purposes of the election of President and Vice President, to be electors appointed by a State; and they shall meet in the District and perform such duties as provided by the twelfth article of amendment.

SECTION 2.

The Congress shall have power to enforce this article by appropriate legislation.

Amendment XXIV.

Passed by Congress August 27, 1962. Ratified January 23, 1964.

SECTION 1.

The right of citizens of the United States to vote in any primary or other election for President or Vice President, for electors for President or Vice President, or for Senator or Representative in Congress, shall not be denied or abridged by the United States or any State by reason of failure to pay poll tax or other tax.

SECTION 2.

The Congress shall have power to enforce this article by appropriate legislation.

Amendment XXV.

Passed by Congress July 6, 1965. Ratified February 10, 1967. *(Note: Article II, Section 1 of the Constitution was modified by the 25th Amendment.)*

SECTION 1.

In case of the removal of the President from office or of his death or resignation, the Vice President shall become President.

SECTION 2.

Whenever there is a vacancy in the office of the Vice President, the President shall nominate a Vice President who shall take office upon confirmation by a majority vote of both Houses of Congress.

SECTION 3.

Whenever the President transmits to the President pro tempore of the Senate and the Speaker of the House of Representatives his written declaration that he is unable to discharge the powers and duties of his office, and until he transmits to them a written declaration to the contrary, such powers and duties shall be discharged by the Vice President as Acting President.

SECTION 4.

Whenever the Vice President and a majority of either the principal officers of the executive departments or of such other body as Congress may by law provide, transmit to the President pro tempore of the Senate and the Speaker of the House of Representatives their written declaration that the President is unable to discharge the powers and duties of his office, the Vice President shall immediately assume the powers and duties of the office as Acting President.

Thereafter, when the President transmits to the President pro tempore of the Senate and the Speaker of the House of Representatives his written declaration that no inability exists, he shall resume the powers and duties of his office unless the Vice President and a majority of either the principal officers of the executive department or of such other body as Congress may by law provide, transmit within four days to the President pro tempore of the Senate and the Speaker of the House of Representatives their written declaration that the President is unable to discharge the powers and duties of his office. Thereupon Congress shall decide the issue, assembling within forty-eight hours for that purpose if not in session. If the Congress, within twenty-one days after receipt of the latter written declaration, or, if Congress is not in session, within twenty-one days after Congress is required to assemble, determines by two-thirds vote of both Houses that the President is unable to discharge the powers and duties of his office, the Vice President shall continue to discharge the same as Acting President; otherwise, the President shall resume the powers and duties of his office.

Amendment XXVI.

Passed by Congress March 23, 1971. Ratified July 1, 1971.

(Note: Amendment 14, Section 2 of the Constitution was modified by Section 1 of the 26th Amendment.)

SECTION 1.

The right of citizens of the United States, who are eighteen years of age or older, to vote shall not be denied or abridged by the United States or by any State on account of age.

SECTION 2.

The Congress shall have power to enforce this article by appropriate legislation.

Amendment XXVII.

Originally proposed Sept. 25, 1789. Ratified May 7, 1992.

No law, varying the compensation for the services of the Senators and Representatives, shall take effect, until an election of representatives shall have intervened.

The NCC is an independent, non-partisan, nonprofit organization that was established in 1988 under the Constitution Heritage Act. The Center's mission is to increase awareness and understanding of the Constitution, the Constitution's history and its relevance to people's daily lives.

National Constitution Center
525 Arch Street
Independence Mall
Philadelphia, PA 19106

(215) 409-6600
www.constitutioncenter.org